iPad at Work

David Sparks

WILEY

Wiley Publishing, Inc.

To Bill and Jean, for showing me the way.

iPad
at Work

iPad at Work

Published by
Wiley Publishing, Inc.
111 River Street
Hoboken, N.J. 07030
www.wiley.com

Published by Wiley Publishing, Inc., Indianapolis, Indiana
Published simultaneously in Canada

ISBN: 978-1-118-10056-1

Manufactured in the United States of America

10 9 8 7 6 5 4 3

For general information on our other products and services or to obtain technical support, please contact our Customer Care Department within the U.S. at (800) 762-2974, outside the U.S. at (317) 572-3993 or fax (317) 572-4002.

Wiley also publishes its books in a variety of electronic formats. Some content that appears in print may not be available in electronic books.

Library of Congress Control Number: 2011932279

Colophon: This book was produced using the ITC Giovanni typeface for the body text, Gotham for the titles, Rotis Semi Serif for the captions and sidebar text, and Rotis Sans Serif for the table text.

Acknowledgments

Sometimes I think I am the luckiest guy in the world. I get to write about things I'm passionate about and I get paid for it. Despite there being just one name on the front of this book, it never could have happened without a lot of help. Thank you Daisy, Samantha, Sarah, Alisa, and Reneé. All of you sacrificed so I could keep moving the cursor.

I would also like to thank Wiley Publishing, particularly Aaron Black. Many thanks also go to my crack editorial team, Galen Gruman and Carol Person, for their assistance throughout this journey. I had additional proofreading help from Tom Cameron, Robert George, Leilani Resurreccion, Robin Mower, and Scott Tullius. Thanks also go to E. John Thawley for my photograph and Dorothy Yamamoto for drawing Figure 21-6.

Particular thanks go to Merlin Mann for his exceptional foreword (and friendship) and Katie Floyd, my partner on the Mac Power Users podcast. Finally, I want to thank all my friends in the Apple community for their generosity and encouragement. The inspiring e-mails, tweets, and kind words are exactly why I wrote this book.

Credits

Acquisitions Editor
Aaron Black

Editorial Director
Robyn Siesky

Business Manager
Amy Knies

Senior Marketing Manager
Sandy Smith

**Vice President and
Executive Group Publisher**
Richard Swadley

**Vice President and
Executive Publisher**
Barry Pruett

Editor
Carol Person, The Zango Group

Technical Editor
Galen Gruman, The Zango Group

Design and Layout
Galen Gruman, The Zango Group

Cover Designer
Michael E. Trent

**Copy Editing, Proofreading,
and Indexing**
The Zango Group

About the Author

David Sparks is a trial attorney in Orange County, California, where he's been eating other lawyers' lunch for years using Apple technologies. David is also the editor of MacSparky.com (where he writes about Apple technology and productivity) and a cohost of the popular Mac Power Users podcast (www.macpowerusers.com). David wrote his first book, *Mac at Work*, in 2011 (Wiley Publishing). David also contributes to *Macworld* magazine.

David is a frequent speaker at the annual Macworld Conference and Expo and a regular faculty member for the American Bar Association's TechShow, the premier legal technology conference, where he speaks on getting the most from technology.

Contents

Chapter 5: **The Cloud** 6

Chapter 6: **E-mail** 8

Chapter 7: **Contacts** 9

Chapter 8: **Calendars** 9

Chapter 16: Notes and Meetings   204

Chapter 17: Brainstorming   216

Chapter 18: Presentations   226

Foreword

David Sparks and I have a lot in common. We both love Macs, piano jazz, and really good animated movies. We both live for hanging out with our kids. We're both suspicious of quick fixes. And, most saliently, at one time or another, we've both found ourselves saddled with the title of "productivity guru."

For those of you who've had the good fortune to avoid ever hearing this gruesome neologism, you need only know that productivity guru has become a title — often as not, self-applied — that ostensibly declares a person to be preternaturally gifted at helping others to become more efficient, effective, organized, and — well — productive. It's certainly a term that gets tossed around a lot in the online self-help racket. But in my experience, it's about as meaningful as a "World's Greatest Grandpa" mug.

The funny part is that even years after my own ardor for the noise and fluff of the online productivity game had irreversibly cooled, it was impossible not to notice this David Sparks character repeatedly popping up with his steady flow of useful, real-world advice. Today, David is rightfully lionized by us legions of tech nerds as one of the legitimate regents of usefulness. This guy is the real deal.

Through his blog (www.macsparky.com), his podcast (www.macpowerusers.com), and his numerous presentations to both lawyers and normal people, David has shared an astonishing breadth of practical, engaging, and entirely sane advice on how we can each learn to improve our work by mastering the tools of our given trade. I really admire the approach David has taken in sharing his experience and expertise. His focus on finding and then mindfully adopting the right tool for the job is refreshingly sane, sustainable, and immediately applicable for anyone who shares David's interest in getting better at doing what they do. David actively listens to his audience for cues to their evolving needs, squares them against the emerging technologies, and then thoughtfully presents it all in the context of a practical, adaptive, and entirely customizable workflow.

And, that's precisely what David has done with his latest effort: the very volume (or binary) you are now about to read, enjoy, and learn many astonishingly useful things from.

As you'll see, David takes the title of his book both seriously and literally. This is not just another pile of words about idly fiddling with the latest electronic gewgaw. *iPad at Work* is about actually putting your iPad to work. Because, in addition to providing cogent and easy-to-follow direction on how to "do stuff" with your shiny new device, David really excels at unpacking the much more salient and useful *why* of the matter. David deeply understands that, like most any piece of consumer technology, an iPad is neither a magic wand nor a fairy godmother. It is, as it should be, just another tool at your disposal. And, as with any tool, repeated use will underscore how the day-to-day usefulness of your iPad is defined less by its awesome range of features and benefits than by your own ardent and mindful willingness to put it to practical use.

It's all on you; Steve Jobs can't help you on this one. But David can. And he does, by getting to the real nut of the challenges facing overwhelmed knowledge workers: Why you might choose this app over that one based on your own specific needs. How to know which tweaks to your workflow can remove unnecessary friction with the least disruption. And, especially, how to navigate a seemingly endless embarrassment of options, preferences, and shiny new baubles to uncover that one combination of pieces that most elegantly addresses your particular needs and challenges.

Most admirably, David shows you how to turn that lickable little rectangle of silicon and glass into a serious and capable workhorse that's so integral to how you think about and complete your work that you'll soon realize you're holding much more than a wonderfully designed little computer. Thanks to David, you will rediscover your iPad as an astonishingly useful partner in the service of completing the work that matters to you. Your work. On your iPad. In your way.

I can't promise that David will transform you into a professional productivity guru. But I'm unquestionably confident that he'll show you how to use your iPad to transform the way you get things done.

—Merlin Mann, 43folders.com

Introduction

I n 2010, Apple changed the world, again. Within minutes of introducing the iPad, Apple showed off three apps: Pages, Numbers, and Keynote. Clearly, Apple thought the iPad was a device to help you get work done. It was right.

The iPad has now been out for a year and a half, and it is a wild success. Competitors are rushing half-baked copies to market as iPads fly off shelves. In a remarkably short span of time, the iPad transformed itself from a strange new technology to a critical tool. This is largely due to the amazing apps that developers created for it. iPads are in board rooms, classrooms, court rooms, and every other room work is getting done. Just like the original personal computer, the iPad is a transformative device and is changing the way we work, forever.

This book is the culmination of my year-and-a-half love affair with my iPad. Since it first arrived, I've been exploring, testing, and even working with my iPad in airports, courtrooms, coffee shops, and, of all places, at my desk.

This book is intended as a resource, not an encyclopedia. You are not going to learn about every iPad app available. (There are more than 100,000, after all) Instead you will discover a selected group of apps that work.

Make no mistake: The iPad is a game-changer. Read this book, tune up your workflows, and be at the vanguard of things to come.

All about Gestures

Throughout this book, I cover how to use the iPad. The iPad is a lot different from your computer. There is no keyboard or mouse. Instead, the iPad just requires your fingers. There are several common gestures used throughout the iPad's iOS operating system and its apps, which I describe here.

Tap: A tap is the most common iPad gesture. It is commonly used to select an item or press a virtual button. To perform a tap, hold your finger over the iPad screen and then quickly touch the screen and lift your finger back up. In other words, tap it.

Double-tap: A double-tap is two quick taps in succession. Some apps in this book use the double-tap gesture like a contextual mouse click (a right-click) on the Mac or PC.

Triple-tap: A triple-tap is just like a double-tap except you tap three times instead of two. A triple-tap is not a standard iOS gesture, so apps that use it can vary widely in what it does.

Tap and hold: The tap-and-hold gesture requires you to press your finger against the screen and hold it there without lifting. Many apps use the tap-and-hold gesture to select an object so you can move it elsewhere on the screen.

Drag: iPad apps often require the drag gesture to move and resize items on the screen. Drags on the iPad are almost always preceded by a tap and hold. To drag an item, slide your finger across the iPad screen. Lift your finger when you are done dragging an item.

Long tap: A long tap is the most difficult (and least-used gesture). A long tap falls somewhere between a tap and a tap and hold. To perform a long tap, press the screen for a moment (about one or two seconds) and then lift your finger. A long tap is typically used to open a contextual menu or popover from text, an image, or other content.

Pinch: Many apps use the pinch gesture to zoom in. To perform a pinch, place your thumb and index finger on the screen at the same time and then pinch them together.

Expand: The opposite gesture of pinch is expand, which is used to zoom out. Put both your index finger and thumb on the screen close to each other, then move them away from each other.

Rotate: Use the rotate gesture to rotate objects on the screen. To do so, place your thumb and index finger on the screen as if starting the pinch gesture but, instead of pinching, rotate your fingers on the screen clockwise or counterclockwise.

Scroll: Scrolling is the most common gesture to move up and down through the contents within a window or pane. To scroll on the iPad, place your finger against the screen and, while keeping your finger against the screen, slide it up and down or right and left as the context requires. Note that some apps require you use two fingers to scroll content within a pane, to differentiate scrolling within the surrounding window.

Flick: A flick is just like scrolling but faster. Place your finger against the screen and quickly slide it up or down or right or left, then lift your finger from the screen at the end of the flick. iPad apps often use the flick gesture to move to a new window or quickly scroll through a row of icons or to the beginning or ending of text.

Of Macs, Menus, and Codes

In addition to the iOS gestures, this book also uses a few special symbols for desktop actions:

⌘: This symbol represents the Mac's Command key.

⊞: This symbol represents the Windows key on a PC.

⇨: This symbol represents the use of a menu option, so File ⇨ Save means to choose the File menu, then choose the Save option, and Type ⇨ Format ⇨ Bold means to choose the Type menu, then choose Format from the menu and then choose Bold from the submenu.

Finally, I use the `code font` to indicate URLs and other text you type in literally, such as in text fields.

All about QR Codes

Throughout this book you will see images in the margin that look sort of like digital mazes. These are called QR (quick response) codes and act as visual links to the Internet and the App Store. To take advantage of QR codes, point your iPhone's or iPad's camera at the QR code while running a QR-scanning app to have your device open the appropriate web page or App Store description. This saves you the trouble of typing website URLs that look like cryptic gibberish. (You'll also see the icons for iOS apps themselves in the margins, so you can quickly tell you're looking at the intended app in the App Store.)

If you search "QR code" in the App Store, you'll find no shortage of QR-code reader apps. My favorite is QR Code City's Scan app. Scan works both on the iPad and iPhone, is free, and gets the job done with minimum interference.

So let's get started with *iPad at Work*!

PART

I

iPad Basics

1

iPad Fundamentals

The iPad changes everything. With its touchscreen and customized operating system, the iPad unceremoniously throws out all the computing paradigms we've accepted over the last 25 years. Instead, we can now get our work done with this small, light piece of technology using nothing more than our fingertips and our wits.

Apple spent a lot of time and effort getting the iPad and its iOS operating system right. Using the iPad is not difficult. Indeed, the iPad removes many stumbling blocks that still exist with traditional keyboard and mouse computers.

Nevertheless, the iPad is different, and there are foundational skills to this operating system that make using your iPad easier for any task. From choosing an iPad to choosing accessories, this chapter gets you up and running.

Choosing an iPad

Choosing an iPad is not as easy as it first may seem. The iPad 2, shown in Figure 1-1, ships in several configurations, including three storage sizes, two variations of 3G networking, and two colors (white and black). This section explains how to make sense of all these options to pick the right iPad for you.

White or black?

The first decision to make when picking your new iPad is color. The iPad ships in white and black models. This decision truly is one of personal preference. I recommend getting your hands on both versions before making your decision. Try visiting your nearest Apple Store or other iPad retailer.

Having spent time with both colors, I prefer the black one. In my experience, the black devices don't show fingerprints as easily and, when watching a movie on the iPad, having a black border around the screen is less distracting than a white one. (If you don't believe me, go to your nearest electronics store and count how many televisions are offered with a white bezel.)

Nevertheless, this is purely a matter of personal preference. Pick the one you like best and move on.

How much storage?

For the past 25 years, the most common data storage technology was the hard disk. Hard disks consist of spinning platters and seeker heads that read data from the spinning disk. Solid-state drives (SSDs) are the new storage technology. They use special memory chips (called flash memory) that hold your data even when the device is turned off. There are several advantages to SSDs, including fewer working parts (making them less prone to damage), less power consumption, and greater speed than traditional hard disks. The iPad uses solid-state storage exclusively.

The iPad 2 ships in 16GB ($500), 32GB ($600), and 64GB ($700) models. So which one do you need? It depends.

FIGURE 1-1

The iPad 2 and its hardware

Light sensor   Camera   Volume rocker   3G radio
                  Multitouch screen   Side switch   Microphone
                                      Sleep/Wake button

MicroSIM slot   Home button   Speaker   Camera   Dock connector
Magnets

A BRIEF HISTORY OF THE TABLET

The iPad is not the first tablet-style computer to hit the market. In the 1990s, several computer manufacturers played with the idea of tablet computers, including Apple with the Newton. Microsoft got serious about tablet computing in 2000 with its Tablet PC initiative. Microsoft's strategy was to install Windows on a tablet-style PC and give users a stylus to interact with the operating system. Although Windows tablets had niche success (in doctor's offices, for example), they never found their place in the bigger PC market.

The iPad differed from previous tablet computing attempts in that the hardware and operating system were designed from the ground up as a mobile computing experience. Rather than use its Mac operating system, Apple created iOS, an operating system that starts with the premise users only have their fingers as an input device. Partly as a result of this new computing paradigm, and partly as a result of advances in hardware technology, the iPad landed in the market at exactly the right time and was wildly successful. Competitors are now marketing their own competing devices that more closely resemble the iPad than the Windows Tablet PC. Time will tell whether these competing devices will get a foothold.

When choosing how much iPad storage, your starting point should be 32GB. As demonstrated throughout this book, there is a lot you can do with your iPad. However, you can't work with data and apps on your iPad if there is no room for them.

Before stepping up to the 64GB model, consider the type of data and apps you intend to carry on your iPad. If you are a frequent traveler and like to keep movies on your iPad, the extra storage may be useful. Movie files often take several gigabytes each, so taking movies on a trip can fill up your iPad before you know it. Saving large pictures and video files is another reason for choosing the 64GB model. On a long trip, media files will fill up your iPad, so having the extra storage can make all the difference between capturing all your pictures and video and not. Finally, if money is not an issue, why not purchase the 64GB model? You cannot add storage to your iPad after purchase, and no one has ever regretted having too much storage in their computing devices.

Wi-Fi and 3G

All iPads include a built-in Wi-Fi radio. Wi-Fi is a wireless connection protocol that lets you wirelessly access the Internet at your home, office, coffee shop, or any place running a wireless Internet router. The iPad supports the 802.11n Wi-Fi standard, the fastest Wi-Fi connection speed currently in widespread use. I explain how to get the most out of the iPad's Wi-Fi connectivity later in this chapter.

In addition to Wi-Fi, some iPads ship with a built-in 3G radio that lets you connect to the Internet with a cellular data plan. (The term "3G" means third-generation cellular technology.) In the United States, adding a 3G radio to your iPad costs an additional $130. Having 3G releases you from the Wi-Fi leash:

WHICH 3G CARRIER?

If you decide to buy a 3G iPad, you must also choose a cellular carrier at the time of purchase. (Carrier connections are hard-wired into the iPad, so you can't change carriers.) There are three schools of thought for picking a 3G carrier:

The best-network approach. The most common method is to pick the carrier that has the best network where you work and live. In making this determination, avoid the cellular carriers' marketing materials and instead rely on your friends and co-workers. Ask what they use and how well it works.

The belt-and-suspenders approach. If several iPad networks generally work in your area (Verizon and AT&T in the United States), get your iPad network on a different network from that of your phone. This is what I did; my iPhone is on AT&T and my iPad is Verizon. This way, I have connectivity no matter which network chooses to have an off day.

The world-traveler approach. If you plan to use your iPad overseas, the AT&T iPad uses MicroSIM technology that allows you to change the MicroSIM card when abroad to work on a local GSM carrier — a significant money-saver over roaming abroad on your AT&T account. (GSM is the cellular technology used by most countries.) Note that the Verizon iPad uses the CDMA cellular technology, which is used mainly in North America and parts of Asia and Latin America, so when you travel abroad, the Verizon iPad effectively becomes a Wi-Fi-only iPad.

You can check e-mail from the park or surf the web at 60 mph on the highway (while someone else drives). 3G iPads also have a Global Positioning System (GPS) antenna not available on Wi-Fi-only iPads. Although a Wi-Fi-only iPad can determine your approximate location by looking at surrounding Wi-Fi networks, the GPS in the 3G iPad provides a more precise fix.

In addition to the $130 for the 3G radio, you also need to purchase a data plan for 3G access. As of this writing, in the United States, AT&T has data plans for $15 per month for 250MB and $25 per month for 2GB. Verizon Wireless's starting iPad data plan is $20 per month for 1GB and goes up to 10GB for $80 per month. These plans are not contracts: You can turn 3G off and on as you choose. If you plan to spend a month working from home with Wi-Fi, turn off your 3G and save a few bucks. If you are traveling, turn on the 3G; you'll love the connectivity as you traipse through airports, cabs, and hotels.

Setting Up Your iPad

Before iOS 5 was released in fall 2011, setting up a new iPad required plugging it in to a Mac or Windows PC with iTunes installed. With iOS 5, this is no longer the case. Now you can set up your iPad without a computer.

When you first turn on your new iPad, you see the iPad startup window. Use the Set Up slider to open the language-selection window. From there, the iPad takes you through a country selection and Wi-Fi network windows.

WHAT IS IOS?

Throughout this book, I reference the iPad's operating system, iOS. When iOS started in this world, it was called the iPhone OS. Apple grew the original iPhone operating system from a stripped-down version of the Mac OS X operating system used on Macs. After a few years, Apple changed the name of iPhone OS to iOS in recognition of the fact it was running on Apple devices other than iPhones.

Although both the iPhone and the Mac use much of the same underlying operating system, the user interfaces are quite different. Mac OS X is designed primarily for the keyboard and mouse, whereas iOS is designed specifically for the touch interface. When Apple released the iPad, it adapted iOS for the tablet's larger screen. As this book went to press, iOS was at version 5.

Next, the iPad asks whether you want to restore the iPad from an iCloud backup (covered later in this chapter), restore the iPad from an iTunes backup (also covered later in this chapter), or set it up as a new iPad.

If you are replacing an older iPad with a new one, restore from a backup. This lets your iPad pull down all data and settings from your iTunes or iCloud backup. (Make sure to plug it into your computer if restoring from an iTunes backup.) If setting up as a new iPad, input your MobileMe or iCloud account (covered in Chapter 5) to pull your data down from Apple servers. If you don't have an iCloud account, set up one here. iCloud membership is free and really useful, as explained throughout this book.

That's it. It just takes a few minutes and your iPad is good to go.

Using Your iPad

I just cover the basic iPad operations in this book; you can learn all the details from Apple's online manual (http://support.apple.com/manuals/#ipad) and from the iPad guide that comes with iBooks. If you don't know how to install and organize your apps, download Apple's manual and get those basics under your belt. There aren't many moving parts to an iPad. As shown in Figure 1-1, the front of the iPad includes the Home button at the bottom-center and a front-facing camera at the top-center. The rest is the iPad's multitouch screen.

The rim of the iPad 2, also shown in Figure 1-1, includes the Sleep/Wake button, side switch, volume rocker, dock connector, MicroSIM tray (in GSM 3G models only), headphone jack, and microphone. The back has the speaker and a camera.

The volume rocker increases or decreases the iPad's volume. Press and hold the volume rocker's down side (the lower side) to mute the audio playback. By default, the side switch mutes the iPad's audio, but you can change its behavior to lock the screen orientation in the Settings app's General pane, covered later in this chapter.

iPad power management

The Sleep/Wake button lets you put the iPad to sleep. Pressing this button turns off the screen, so you use much less power. But pressing the Sleep/Wake button does not turn off the iPad entirely; for example, iTunes music continues playing. Press the Sleep/Wake button or the Home button briefly to turn the screen back on.

To turn off your iPad completely, press and hold the Sleep/Wake button for a few seconds until the red slider appears on the screen; then slide the slider to confirm you want to turn off the iPad. To turn the iPad back on, press and hold the Sleep/Wake button again for a few seconds until the Apple logo appears.

Turning off the iPad every time you're done with it is not necessary; I sometimes go weeks without turning off my iPad. Instead, use the Sleep/Wake button to put the iPad to sleep when you're not using it.

The iPad ships with a 10-watt USB power adapter and dock-connector-to-USB cable. To charge your iPad, plug the adapter into an outlet and connect it to your iPad with the dock-connector-to-USB cable. Alternatively, you can charge your iPad by plugging it into your computer or USB hub with the same cable (but note that not all computers and hubs supply the required 10W of power; if they don't, the iPad will display the message "Not charging" at the top of its screen). When connected to the power adapter, the iPad will fully charge in three to four hours. The charge time from a computer or USB hub depends on the power output of the USB port on your computer or hub, but it generally takes between six and eight hours.

On a full charge, the iPad has about 10 hours of battery life. The battery life is one of the iPad's most remarkable features: It seems like it just keeps going and going. You can further extend the battery life by turning off the Wi-Fi, 3G, and Bluetooth radios (covered later). You can also use an external battery (also covered later in this chapter).

The iPad's home screen

Press the Home button to go to the home screen, shown in Figure 1-2. The home screen is the iPad's primary app launcher. Every app you add to your iPad appears on the home screen as an icon. You can keep multiple screens of apps and folders (covered later) on your iPad and move between screens by flicking left or right.

Flicking right on the first home screen opens the search screen. Tap in the Search bar and enter your search term to have your iPad search for apps, contacts, songs, and other data. The search screen also has options to search the web and Wikipedia. If you have a lot of apps and can't find the one you want, type a few letters of the app's name in the Search bar, then launch the app from the search results. (I do this often.)

Return to the home screen (by pressing the Home button or flicking the screen left from the search screen).

Tap and hold any app icon on the home screen to enter home screen edit mode. After a few seconds, all your apps start shaking, and a small Delete icon button (an X in a black circle) appears in the upper-left corner of each installed app. Tap the Delete

FIGURE 1-2

The iPad's home screen

FIGURE 1-3

Creating a folder on the iPad's home screen

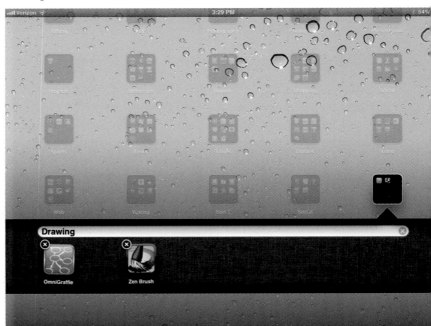

WHAT MAKES A GOOD IPAD APP?

If there is any problem with the App Store, it is that there are too many apps to choose from. As of this writing, there are more than 100,000 iPad-specific apps available. So how do you choose one? There is no single right way.

I start by taking a look at the associated screenshots. I love my iPad and I want my apps to look pretty. If the screenshots don't appeal to me immediately, I move on. I also spend time looking at the reviews, although this can be hit or miss. Some reviews are well thought out and rational, whereas others are completely nutty. You will find conscientious reviews if you look for them.

Also consider third-party sources. One of my favorite places to check on iPad app reviews is Macworld.com and, of course, MacSparky.com. Perhaps the best sources of information about new apps are your friends and co-workers. Find out what they like and play with the apps on their iPad.

Regardless, at some point you have to make a choice and leap. Fortunately, apps are not too expensive, so it's less annoying to discover you've bought a dud when it cost $2 rather than the $40 it would cost for a desktop app.

When you find an app you like or have constructive criticism, do send an e-mail to the app developer. Designing iPad apps is tough work, and the developers love to hear from users and often incorporate changes to future releases based on user feedback.

icon button to remove the app from the iPad. Note that apps that ship with the iPad can't be deleted and so won't display the Delete icon button.

When you delete an app, it removes both the app and its data. So, if you have been writing your 500-page novel in the Pages app (and have neglected to back up or sync with iCloud), deleting Pages also deletes the novel. You can reinstall the app using the App Store (covered later) or by syncing the iPad to your computer and having iTunes re-install it (also covered later), but reinstalling an app does not bring back your lost data.

There are several things you can do in home screen edit mode besides deleting unwanted apps. You can move your apps: Tap and hold on a shaking app and drag it to its new location or screen. You can even move apps off the dock — and put other ones on the dock — on the bottom of the screen this way. If, for example, you don't use the Photos app often, pull it off the dock and replace it with a different app. The iPad dock holds as many as six apps, and the dock's apps appear on every home screen.

You can also combine apps into folders while in home screen edit mode. To do so, tap and hold an app and drag it on top of another app. The iPad creates a folder for the apps and names the folder based on the categories of the two apps, as shown in Figure 1-3. (You can change that name in the open folder.) Once a folder is created, you can add additional apps to it by dragging them on top of the folder. You can also drag apps out of an open folder back to the home screen or into another group.

FIGURE 1-4

The Running Apps dock's screen rotation lock, brightness, audio, and AirPlay controls

When you are finished organizing your apps, press the Home button to exit home screen edit mode.

Switching apps

Tap an app to launch it. To go back to the home screen, press the Home button. Using this technique you can jump among apps on your iPad.

Another way to switch between apps is using the Running Apps dock, shown in Figure 1-4. To activate the Running Apps dock, double-tap the Home button. It displays the icons of the currently running apps along the bottom of the screen (you can scroll horizontally through that list).

iOS 5 adds a third way to switch apps: just swipe four fingers simultaneously to the left or right to slide to the next or previous running app ("next" and "previous" are determined by their order in the Running Apps dock). You can also swipe four fingers up to open the Running Apps dock from any app or the home screen, and you can pinch four fingers (three fingers and the thumb) to show the home screen from any app. (If these gestures do not work, go the Settings app's General pane and slide the Multitasking Gestures switch to On.)

For example, to copy text from the web into a text editor, you just copy the text in the browser, use the four-finger swipe left to switch to your text editor (assuming it is running), and paste the text in the desired location. This is much faster than switching apps using the Home button or the Running Apps dock.

You can tap any of the icons to launch its app. Because most often you will be jumping among apps you've recently used, switching apps this way is usually faster than exiting to the home screen, finding the new app, and launching it.

Also, while the Running Apps dock is open, flick right to expose additional iPad controls — rotation lock, brightness setting, and audio volume — shown in Figure 1-4. If you have an iPad 2, you also get the AirPlay control, which lets you send your screen to a TV or projector connected to an Apple TV (covered later in this chapter).

Exit the Running Apps dock by launching an app, pressing the Home button, or using a multifinger gesture (covered later).

The status bar

The top of the iPad screen shows the status bar, which is visible from the home screens and from most apps' screens. Several icons may appear in this status bar as you use your iPad. In addition to keeping you informed, the status bar also serves as a scroll-to-the-top button: Tapping the status bar in any app quickly scrolls the screen back to the top.

Airplane mode. Airplane mode turns off the 3G, Wi-Fi, and Bluetooth radios. This is most often used, not surprisingly, on airplanes. Airplane mode is also useful when you want to preserve your battery, though at the cost of losing all Internet and Bluetooth connectivity. I also use Airplane mode in court. (Judges get testy when iPads make noise in court.) Turn Airplane mode on or off from the Settings app.

Wi-Fi. This icon shows that your iPad has a Wi-Fi Internet connection. The more bars showing, the stronger the connection. Wi-Fi is covered later in this chapter.

3G. When the 3G icon appears in the status bar, your iPad is connected to the Internet through your cellular carrier's 3G network (HSPA on AT&T and CDMA EVDO on Verizon). Keep a wary eye out for this icon appearing when it shouldn't. If you are on your couch at home and see the 3G icon even though you know you should have a Wi-Fi connection, figure out why the iPad isn't on Wi-Fi. You are probably needlessly using up your 3G data allotment.

EDGE. If your current location does not have a strong 3G signal (or any 3G signal), your iPad may revert to a slower network called EDGE on AT&T.

2G. If neither a 3G nor EDGE network is available, the iPad may switch to the most basic type of cellular data network: 2G (second-generation), such as GPRS on AT&T or CDMA 1XRTT on Verizon.

If you see both the Wi-Fi icon and one of the cellular data icons, your iPad is using the Wi-Fi connection. Be sure to check that Wi-Fi is in use whenever possible so you don't unnecessarily use your cellular data allotment.

Activity. This icon shows network activity on your iPad. Additionally, some apps use this icon to indicate an activity in process.

VPN. This icon indicates your iPad is connected to a network using the VPN (virtual private network) protocol, a type of secure Internet connection used by many businesses.

Lock. This icon appears when your iPad is locked. I cover locking your iPad and other security concerns in Chapter 3.

 Screen orientation lock. This icon indicates your screen orientation is locked. I cover screen orientation later in this chapter.

 Play. This icon indicates a song, audio book, or podcast is playing on your iPad.

 Bluetooth. When this icon appears white, a Bluetooth device (most likely a headset or keyboard) is connected to your iPad. If the icon is gray, the Bluetooth radio is on but there are no devices connected. If there is no Bluetooth icon, the Bluetooth radio is turned off. You can adjust your iPad's Bluetooth settings in the Settings app's General pane.

 Battery. This icon indicates the battery status of your iPad, such as how much battery capacity is left and whether it is charging.

Location. This icon indicates that an app or service is detecting your current location.

Portrait and landscape modes

The iPad is a portable device. As such, there really is no "right way" to hold it. Indeed, most apps on the iPad automatically adjust themselves depending on how you are holding the device. You can hold the iPad upright like a portrait or on its side like a landscape picture. These viewing modes are referred to throughout this book as portrait and landscape modes.

Holding the iPad in portrait mode feels more like you're using a traditional clipboard and provides more vertical space on the screen. If you flip the iPad to landscape mode, you give up some of the additional vertical space in exchange for a wider horizontal view that usually also increases the text size.

Your iPad decides whether to display in portrait or landscape view depending on how you hold it. Sometimes, this becomes a problem. For example, if you're reading the iPad in bed in portrait mode and turn on your side, the iPad thinks you've flipped it to landscape mode and turns the display to match. To prevent this from happening, lock the iPad's screen orientation by opening the Running Apps dock, as explained earlier. Flick to the right to display the controls shown in Figure 1-4. Tap the Screen Orientation Lock icon button (the clockwise arrow on the far left) so the iPad's orientation does not change.

If you find yourself frequently locking the screen orientation, use the side switch instead. You can choose whether to use the side switch to lock the screen orientation lock or to mute audio (the default setting) in the Settings app's General pane.

If you want to capture an image of your iPad's screen, simultaneously press the Sleep/Wake and Home buttons. The screen flashes white for a moment and the iPad makes the sound of a camera shutter. The iPad saves screenshots to the Saved Photos library of the Photos app.

Change the brightness of the iPad screen in the Settings app's Brightness & Wallpaper pane. Alternatively, open the Running Apps dock and flick right to get the brightness slider.

From the Brightness & Wallpaper pane, you can also change the iPad's wallpaper for both the lock screen (which displays when you wake up your iPad) and the home screen. The iPad ships with several attractive wallpapers. You can also choose a wallpaper from your photo library or download one from the web.

iPad input

The iPad features a multitouch capacitive screen that detects human touch, including the number of fingers on the screen and what they are doing. (It can detect paws, too, and so there are iPad games for cats that actually work.) By and large, the screen replaces the traditional keyboard and mouse input on traditional computers.

There are several standard gestures used with the iPad screen. Read the conventions section in the book's introduction for a list of all the standard gestures and how they work.

In iOS 5, the iPad lets you set a custom gesture, as well as modify how gestures, the onscreen display, and audio feedback work to help those with disabilities or motor-coordination difficulties. You enable these assistive features and define the custom gesture in the Settings app by going to the General pane, tapping the Accessibility option near the bottom of the pane, and then setting your desired behavior in the Accessibility pane that opens.

Onscreen keyboard

The iPad's onscreen keyboard appears any time you need to type. The keyboard is what you use to enter text on your iPad.

The onscreen keyboard is largest in landscape view. In this mode, you can *almost* touch-type. The keyboard is only slightly smaller than a standard-size keyboard. In portrait mode, the keyboard is more friendly to "hunt and peck" typists. iOS 5 adds the ability to split the keyboard so it is more easily accessible by your thumbs while holding the iPad with two hands. Figure 1-5 shows the split keyboard.

There are a few additional secrets to using the onscreen keyboard. One is that you can add special or accented characters by tapping and holding on the related letter until the alternate characters appear in a contextual menu, as shown in Figure 1-6. Then slide your finger to the alternate character and let go. The iPad inserts the alternate character.

This trick works for more than just letters. For example, tap and hold the period to insert ellipses or the dash to add an em dash or en dash. Tap and hold the quotes to get curly quotes, or (in the United States) tap and hold the dollar sign to get other currency symbols.

Another trick: If you want to capitalize entire words, double-tap the Shift key to enable caps lock. Later, tap the Shift key again to turn off caps lock.

And a third trick: If you are often tapping the Numbers key (the .?123 icon) to open the numeric keyboard for just a single digit or punctuation mark, you know how tedious that gets. After opening the numeric keyboard, you have to tap your punctuation mark and then the Alphabet button (the ABC icon) to return to the

FIGURE 1-5

The iPad's split keyboard in portrait mode

alphabet keyboard. Instead, tap and hold the Numbers key to open the numeric keyboard. Then, without lifting your finger, drag to the desired punctuation, rest there for a second, and lift your finger. The digit or punctuation is inserted and the keyboard returns to the original alphabet view without any further work.

Auto-correction

The iPad keyboard uses predictive technologies to complete words and fix typos as you type. Specifically, the keyboard looks at where your fingers are touching the keyboard and compares that keystroke against words that would result from your typing pattern. As you type, the iPad predicts the word you are typing and offers to complete it for you.

If the iPad's suggestion is correct, tap the space bar, a punctuation mark, or Return to have the iPad fill in the suggested word. To reject the suggestion, tap the Dismiss icon button (the X icon) next to the suggestion. The iPad learns as you use

FIGURE 1-6

Inserting an accented character with the iPad's onscreen keyboard

this feature, so the suggestions get more accurate. The trick is to just go with it. As you learn to trust the suggestions, you get faster and more accurate.

But sometimes, auto-correction gets in the way. For example, when you type `its`, your iPad changes the word to `it's`. The trouble is I rarely type `it's` and often type `its`. This made me nuts until I figured out typing `itst` removed the apostrophe. Over time, my iPad has figured out my preference and now I don't even need to add the extra `t`. Table 1-1 shows how to bypass the common correctional shortcuts.

If you don't want to use auto-correction, turn it off in the Keyboard pane of the General settings.

In addition to toggling auto-correction, you can also turn on (and off) auto-capitalization, spell checking, caps lock, the period shortcut (tap two spaces for a period to appear), and the split keyboard covered earlier. The keyboard settings also lets you add global shortcuts, covered in Chapter 2.

When the iPad was first released, I was convinced the onscreen keyboard was useful for nothing more than filling in forms or typing short e-mails. As I've grown more accustomed to it, my opinion changed. I now routinely use the iPad's onscreen keyboard for typing projects of 1,000 words or less. Although I am a touch-typist, I find only a slight loss in speed using the onscreen keyboard with auto-correction turned on. For bigger projects, however, I still use an external Bluetooth keyboard. (I describe using an iPad with a Bluetooth keyboard later in this chapter.)

Bypassing the iPad Keyboard's Common Auto-Corrections

Shortcut	Output
`helll`	`he'll` instead of `hell`
`itst`	`its` instead of `it's`
`shell`	`she'll` instead of `shell`
`welll`	`we'll` instead of `well`
`weree`	`we're` instead of `were`

Cut, copy, and paste on the iPad

The iPad has an intuitive interface to cut, copy, and paste text. First, place the cursor by tapping and holding over the text. The iPad displays a magnifying glass showing where the cursor is located. With the magnifying glass visible, drag your finger around the screen to precisely place the cursor. When you let go, a contextual menu appears with options to select the adjacent text or select all the text in the active document or field. You can also select a word by double-tapping it (or an entire paragraph by quadruple-tapping it).

FIGURE 1-7

Selecting text on the iPad

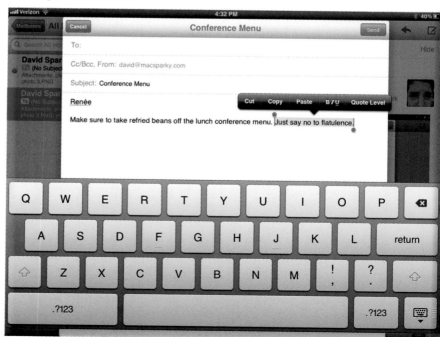

Once you select a word or block of text, a separate contextual menu appears with options to cut, copy, paste, or replace the selected text. The iPad also displays selection handles (the blue dots) at the beginning and end of the selection, as shown in Figure 1-7. To change the selection, tap and hold one of the selection handles and drag it to its new location in the text. Once you've set the selection just right, tap the Cut or Copy contextual menu options.

To paste text, insert the cursor at the desired location and tap Paste from the contextual menu. Alternatively, select a block of text and tap Paste to replace the selected text with the last-copied or last-cut text.

Using Wi-Fi and 3G

Getting the most from your iPad requires an Internet connection. This section explains how to use your Wi-Fi and 3G Internet connections.

Using Wi-Fi

Wi-Fi signals are increasingly available as the effort to provide Wi-Fi becomes easier for public entities, home users, restaurateurs, and just about anyone that serves the public. There is free Wi-Fi at McDonald's, for example. Nevertheless, not all Wi-Fi is created equal. Although some public places have outstanding Wi-Fi signal strength and speed, others throttle back to such an extent that it is only good for checking e-mail.

Moreover, using public Wi-Fi carries a security risk. Sitting in a coffee shop, anyone on the network could be using their computer to track your Internet connection and possibly obtain access to your data. (I cover Wi-Fi security in Chapter 3.)

For help finding a Wi-Fi signal, install the Wi-Fi Finder app on your iPad. This app, covered in Chapter 11, keeps a database of public Wi-Fi hot spots and uses your location data to point you to the nearest one.

You can make adjustments to your iPad's Wi-Fi settings using the Settings app's Wi-Fi pane.

Slide the Wi-Fi switch to turn on or off the Wi-Fi radio. The Wi-Fi radio, especially when searching for new Wi-Fi networks, uses a considerable amount of power. If you do not anticipate needing Wi-Fi access, turn it off and save some battery power.

The Choose a Network box lists all the nearby Wi-Fi networks your iPad sees. The right side of each entry includes a signal strength meter (the arcs). The more arcs filled, the stronger the Wi-Fi signal is. If the lock icon appears, the Wi-Fi signal is secured with a password.

Some Wi-Fi networks do not appear in the Choose a Network list, because they don't broadcast their network identification, to discourage unauthorized use. Tap the Other button to connect your iPad to a Wi-Fi network that does not appear in the Choose a Network list — you do need to know its name, though.

To get further details on a specific network, tap the Detail Disclosure icon button (a blue circle with a right-facing arrow inside). This opens the Wi-Fi details pane, whose information includes the IP address, subnet mask, router address, DN address, and search domain. If most of this sounds like mumbo-jumbo to you, do worry about it. You should never need to make adjustments to these settings.

The only button on the Wi-Fi details pane relevant to most users is the Forget this Network button. Once you connect your iPad to a Wi-Fi network, it remember those settings and automatically logs on when it sees that particular Wi-Fi network If you want your iPad to stop auto-connecting to a certain Wi-Fi network, tap this button when connected to it.

The Ask to Join Networks switch turns on (or off) a network-sniffing feature where the iPad actively searches for surrounding Wi-Fi signals and asks if you woul like to join when it finds one. I usually keep this option turned off. Having my iPac constantly ask me about strange networks is distracting, and continually searching for new networks drains the battery.

Using 3G

Make adjustments to your current 3G access in the Cellular Data pane of the Settings app.

To change your 3G data plan, tap the View Account button. This opens a window where you can enable, disable, or make adjustments to your 3G data plan with your carrier.

Turn on (or off) the 3G radio via the Cellular Data switch. Even if you have 3G enabled, turn off the radio to save battery power if you don't need Internet connectivity. I usually keep the 3G radio on until my battery gets down to about 20 percent.

Data roaming is a service that finds a 3G signal from foreign carriers when you are abroad. Although this seems like a great idea, you will question the wisdom of data roaming when you return home to find an $800 cellular bill in your mailbox. Data roaming is expensive, so keep this switch turned off at all times unless you are ready for an extraordinary bill. When traveling abroad with your iPad, you are bette off sticking to Wi-Fi or, if you have a MicroSIM-enabled iPad (like the AT&T model in the United States), swapping the MicroSIM for one distributed by a carrier in the country you are visiting.

Notification Center

One of the iPad's many tricks is notification support. App developers use notifications to send small messages ranging from the arrival of a new e-mail message to the deadline for an important task. Notifications are a popular feature in iOS. Indeed, it is so popular that Apple reports serving billions of notifications to iOS devices.

As users became more reliant on notifications, Apple revamped notification management with the addition of Notification Center in iOS 5.

Activate Notification Center by swiping down from the top of the screen from within any app or from any home screen. Shown in Figure 1-8, Notification Center gives you a list of recent notifications by app.

Tap on a notification to jump to the associated app. For example, in Figure 1-8, tapping on the OmniFocus entry opens OmniFocus. Alternatively, tapping the X on the right side of the OmniFocus entry in Figure 1-8 opens an option to clear the OmniFocus notification. When you're done with Notification Center, swipe it back up to the top of the screen so it goes away until you call it again. (On an iPhone, Notification Center also displays the weather at your current location and the price of your selected stocks. But Apple doesn't provide such apps on the iPad.)

You control which apps' notifications display in Notification Center in the Settings app's Notifications pane, shown in Figure 1-9.

This pane shows a list of all installed apps that have the ability to send notifications. Tap any app to change how it displays notifications. Figure 1-10 shows the notifications settings for the Calendar app.

For each app, you can choose to turn on or off the app's inclusion in Notification Center. You can also choose how many notification items to show at any one time. The View in Lock Screen switch determines whether notifications appear on your iPad while the screen is locked. (Tip: If a notification appears in the lock screen, slide the app's icon to the right to unlock the screen and jump to that

FIGURE 1-8

Notification Center's pull-down pane

FIGURE 1-9

The iPad's notifications settings

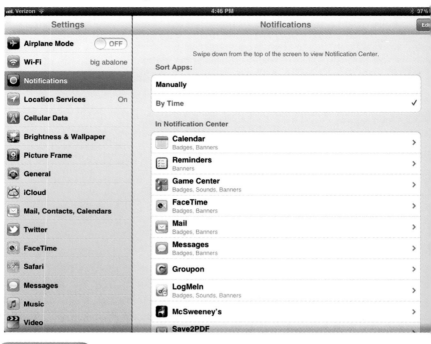

FIGURE 1-10

Customizing notification settings

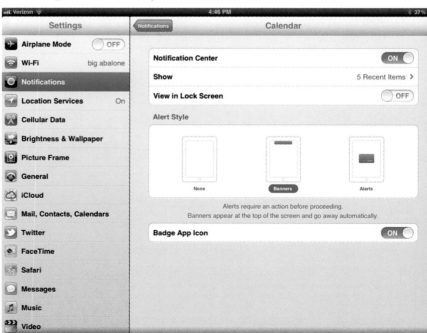

app and the specific notification in it. If your iPad has password protection, you'll be asked to enter your password before the app and its notification display.)

You can choose how the notification appears on the iPad's screen. For each app, you can set the notification to appear in a banner (it flips down temporarily in the top portion of the screen), in an onscreen alert window (which requires a tap to go away), or not at all. Although you may not need any notification about your Farmville crops, you may want calendar alerts front and center on your screen, and Twitter updates available less obtrusively in the banner.

Synchronizing apps in iTunes

iTunes is where you sync apps, music, video, and more. New to iOS 5 is the ability to sync over Wi-Fi, if you enable the Sync over Wi-Fi Connection option, shown in Figure 1-11.

Using the Apps pane, you can add and remove data — not just apps — from your iPad. If, for example, you use Pages on your iPad, you can copy Pages documents to or from the iPad and open them with Pages on your Mac. There are many useful iOS applications that take advantage of the ability to drag and drop files onto your mobile device.

To move files back and forth, simply click and drag data files from the Mac or Windows PC to the application's file window at the bottom of the Apps pane. The applications that let you transfer files require that the files are in a particular format.

FIGURE 1-11

Syncing an iPad to iTunes

Numbers for iPad, for example, requires that you transfer iWork Numbers files to your iPad device.

This iTunes sync is a frequently implemented solution for sharing data betwee iPad apps and your computer and referenced throughout this book.

Backing up

Every time you connect your iPad to iTunes via USB or Wi-Fi sync, iTunes mak a backup of all the data. This is really convenient. If you lose your iPad, you can ge new one and restore your data from the backup. To restore data, plug your iPad in iTunes and tap Restore in the Summary pane. iTunes does the rest. Restoring a 32G iPad takes about an hour.

If you are not using your iPad with a Mac or Windows PC, you can back up yo data to the iCloud service. An iCloud sync is not as good as one synced to your loc Mac or PC, as it doesn't back up media files you got from somewhere other than the iTunes Store, such as your home videos, the music you ripped from CDs, and podcasts you got directly from websites.

But even though you'll want to keep using iTunes backup for all those media files, you should turn on iCloud backup as well. (Do so in the Settings app's iClou pane, using the iCloud Backup switch.) The iCloud backup saves your iPad's setting any documents stored on it in your apps, your account information, and the photo in the Photos apps's Camera Roll library. That way should something go wrong when you are away from your computer, you can restore this core data from iCloud and then get back your media files from iTunes when you're back at your computer

Do note that backing up to iCloud also uses up 2.5GB of your iCloud account' free 5GB capacity (you can always buy more, of course, in the iCloud pane of the Settings app).

Printing from your iPad

These days, you can do a lot of work digitally without ever printing a hard copy Nevertheless, there are occasions when there is no substitute for the printed page. There are several ways to print with your iPad.

Apple AirPrint

AirPrint is Apple's iPad printing solution. AirPrint is built into iOS and lets you print wirelessly from your iPad to any AirPrint-supported printer. (As of this writing, the few available AirPrint printers are manufactured by Hewlett-Packard.)

The Printer Options popover is available in most apps where printing makes sense, including Safari and Mail. It displays any AirPrint-connected printers, as well as printing apps that register themselves with AirPrint. Figure 1-12 shows the Printe Options popover (from Safari).

Using AirPrint is easy. There is no software to download or drivers to install. AirPrint spoils you. The only setback is that you'll need a compatible printer.

FIGURE 1-12

The standard iOS Printer Options popover

Printopia

If you don't want to buy an AirPrint-compatible printer and you own a Mac, download Printopia ($20). This Mac app turns your Mac into an AirPrint server for any printer on your network. If you have a Printopia-equipped Mac, your iPad sees all your Mac-connected printers. Of course, this means you have to leave your Mac on all the time.

Printopia has features not available with AirPrint. In addition to sending your documents to a printer, you can also save the file as a PDF to your Mac or Dropbox storage. As of this writing, there were no products similar to Printopia for a Windows PC.

Print n Share

Print n Share ($9) is an iPad app that prints to most network-connected printers (as long as they're on the same network as the Wi-Fi router that your iPad is connected to). You use the standard iOS Printer Options popover but select Print n Share as the "printer"; doing so sends the data to the Print n Share app, from which you then send it to the desired printer. You can purchase, for an additional fee, modules for e-mail, calendars, and other functions.

Print n Share prints directly to most network printers. The app also prints to any printers attached to your Mac or PC if you install the free WePrint software for Mac or Windows. The WePrint software also works over a 3G connection so you can print while away from the office.

Print n Share is a bit awkward to use, but it does work with lots of printers.

Maintenance and troubleshooting

Although entire books are written on how to maintain Macs and Windows PCs, iPad maintenance involves remarkably few steps.

   1. If your iPad is acting wonky, close the current app and reopen it.

2. If your iPad is still acting wonky, turn off your iPad by holding the Sleep/ Wake button for several seconds until the red slider appears. Then turn on the iPad again by holding the Sleep/Wake button until the Apple icon appears.

3. If your iPad is still acting wonky, reset your iPad by holding the Home button and the Sleep/Wake button for approximately ten seconds until the Apple icon appears.

4. If your iPad is still acting wonky, take it to the Apple Store or call Apple support.

That's it. There are few troubleshooting steps to your iPad. The only additional point would be if the problem occurs in just a single app. In that case, try deleting the app and reinstalling it. This, however, is rarely a problem. Apple runs the apps through its diagnostic suite before putting them in the App Store and, by and large, the apps you download from the App Store are stable.

With this information, you have all you need to troubleshoot an iPad. Just wait to see how brilliant your co-workers think you are when you "fix" their iPads and all you really did was restart it.

iPad Accessories

The iPad provides a surprisingly accessory-free experience. Most days, I don't carry any accessories with my iPad. With the ten-hour battery life and onscreen keyboard, I get by just fine. There are, however, some accessories worth mention.

Apple iPad Smart Cover

There are many case manufacturers selling iPad cases. There are cases for every interest and budget ranging from boardroom-friendly leather to Half Dome-friendly rubber shielding. You'll have to make your own decision about what works for you. However, one case worth mention is Apple's iPad Smart Cover, which costs $39 for the polyurethane versions and $69 for the leather versions.

One of the design criteria for the iPad 2 was to get a better case. The iPad Smart Cover is one of the iPad 2's best features. Apple added a series of magnets to the inside of the iPad 2 that work with the magnets in the iPad 2 Smart Cover. The result is a case that magnetically snaps on and aligns itself to the iPad. The Apple Smart Cover folds back to provide support when typing or to prop up the iPad.

Magnets also alert the iPad when you close the Smart Cover and automatically put the iPad 2 to sleep. When you peel the Apple iPad Smart Cover back from the iPad 2's screen, the iPad detects that too and wakes up. The only negative point is that the Apple iPad Smart Cover affords no protection to the back of the iPad.

As this book went to press, other manufacturers were just starting to release their own cases taking advantage of the iPad 2's embedded magnets, giving you even more options.

Bluetooth keyboard

Using a Bluetooth keyboard, touch-typist can fly on the iPad. I use Apple's Wireless Keyboard ($69). It takes little room in my bag, and when I need to type a lot, you can't beat it. If you prefer a bigger keyboard, any Bluetooth keyboard should work.

To pair (connect) a Bluetooth device to your iPad, go to the Settings app's General pane and tap the Bluetooth option to open the Bluetooth pane.

Select the device you want to pair to your iPad, and the iPad provides instructions for doing so (in the case of the Bluetooth keyboard, you're asked to enter a code on the keyboard to complete the pairing).

When you are done using the Bluetooth keyboard, make sure to turn off the Bluetooth radio. Otherwise, random key presses against the Bluetooth keyboard in your bag may cause strange behavior from your iPad. I discovered this problem when my iPad once started playing *Star Wars: The Empire Strikes Back* in my bag while I was in a meeting. Although the John Williams score sounds good anywhere, I'd prefer that not happen again.

Even more troubling, if your iPad requires a security code (covered in Chapter 3), the random key presses on your keyboard with your iPad asleep may cause

INCASE ORIGAMI
APPLE WIRELESS KEYBOARD CASE

One of my favorite accessories is the InCase Origami Apple Wireless Keyboard case ($40), shown below. This case covers and protects the keyboard in transit. When you open the case, it makes a nice stand for your iPad. Thousands of words for this book were written on my iPad propped up in the Origami Apple Wireless Keyboard case.

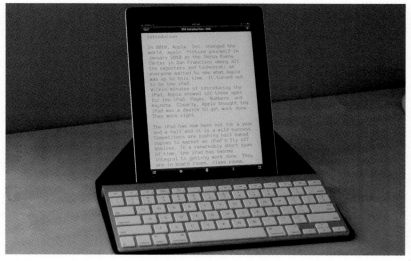

your iPad to think someone is trying to unsuccessfully log in, which could result in locking your iPad or erasing its data.

To avoid these problems, turn off the Bluetooth keyboard and the iPad's Bluetooth radio when they are not in use.

External battery

With a ten-hour battery life, the iPad should have no trouble lasting through most days. But what about the rough days that involve 14-hour flights and long cab rides? In that case, pick up an external battery. But be careful when purchasing an external battery: The iPad requires a 10-watt charger, and many of the older chargers and external batteries on the market are not powerful enough to charge an iPad. My favorite is the HyperMac Mini external iPad battery ($100).

The HyperMac Mini's 7200mAh lithium-ion battery (rated for 1,000 charge cycles) measures 5.2 inches deep, 3.1 inches wide, and 0.55 inches thick, and it extends your iPad battery's life by ten more hours. (It can also recharge an iPhone six times before the HyperMac Mini's battery itself needs to be recharged.) It is all wrapped in an aluminum casing and easily fits in your bag for those long days.

Camera Connection Kit

The Apple Camera Connection Kit ($30) includes two iPad attachments, one with a SD memory stick slot and the other with a USB connector. To get your media off the camera, plug in its SD memory stick or plug in the camera directly via USB. The iPad detects the connection and pulls up a menu with options to add the photos to your library. This works for pictures and video from just about any camera. If your work involves documenting anything with pictures, it is great having a portable 9.7-inch screen with you.

The Camera Connection Kit's name, however, is misleading. The kit is useful for much more than just pulling off pictures and video from your camera. The iPad reads SD memory sticks and USB thumb drives as attached storage. You can add media, such as movies, to a USB thumb drive or SD memory stick and later add them to your iPad using the Camera Connection Kit. For this to work, add a folder to the SD memory stick or USB thumb drive called "DCIM" and store your media files in this folder. (This tricks your iPad into thinking the attached storage is a camera.) For movies, make sure they are in the iPad-friendly M4V format.

One enterprising vendor took advantage of this trick to market its brand of external iPad hard-disk drives. The HyperDrive for iPad ($200 for 320GB) is a low power hard-disk drive that lets you pack media for the road. It has models with storage of as much as 1TB.

The USB connector has even more uses. You can attach all sorts of devices to your iPad, including some USB keyboards and USB microphones. It doesn't work with all devices (the sticking point is usually how much power the attached USB device draws from the iPad), but the USB connector does open your iPad to all sorts of possibilities.

Using an external display

Several iPad apps include support for output to external displays. Moreover, the iPad 2 supports video mirroring, which mirrors your iPad display on any external device. Using an iPad 2, you can share any app's display with an audience. (Using an iPad 1, you can share only the screens of video-out-compatible apps.) Apple sells two cables for hooking your iPad to an external display.

The Apple VGA Adapter ($30) connects the iPad 30-pin dock connector to a standard VGA connector used with external monitors and projectors all over the world. The VGA adapter does not supply power to your iPad, so if you anticipate using it for any length of time, make sure to charge your iPad first.

The Apple Digital AV Adapter ($40) works similar to the VGA adapter but instead interfaces with an HDMI cable, the preferred interface for high-definition televisions and monitors. In addition to carrying a video signal, the HDMI adapter also carries audio, allowing you to share both video and audio with one cord. Moreover, the Apple Digital AV Adapter includes a 30-pin adapter that carries power back to the iPad. You can charge and present simultaneously with your iPad when using this adapter.

The Apple TV

The Apple TV ($99) is sold as a home entertainment device. It essentially turns your television into an iTunes client to play your iTunes video and music from your computer. With the release of iOS 5, however, the Apple TV became a legitimate business device: The iPad 2's mirroring works wirelessly with an Apple TV with AirPlay mirroring for iPad 2.

Using an Apple TV and AirPlay mirroring, you can wirelessly stream from your iPad 2 to an HDTV. This lets you walk around the room with just your iPad and broadcast straight to the projector or monitor. For this to work, both your iPad 2 and the Apple TV need to be on the same wireless network.

iPad styli

One underlying design goal of the iPad was to create a stylus-free tablet. Apple wants everything to work with your fingers. Old habits die hard, though. Many mobile workers have been using styli since the days of the Palm Pilot. In researching styli for this book, I was nearly ready to give up. Most of the styli available for the iPad just felt cheap. Then I stumbled on the Cosmonaut ($25), which has the same dimensions as a dry erase marker. It feels great in your hand, so if you need a stylus for your iPad, look no further.

2

Useful Utilities

There are apps that, while not fitting any particular chapter in this book, are useful for getting the most out of your iPad. This chapter covers these useful utilities for text expansion, voice recognition, and storing files.

Text Expansion

Text expansion lets you type small phrases, like a51 that automatically expand to larger words or phrases, such as Area 51, Ltd.

Using text expansion, I save a lot of time. I have text expansion snippets for common contract terms, legal pleadings, and anything I write more than once. A snippet could trigger a short, difficult-to-type phrase or several thousand words. Because the iPad has separate onscreen keyboards for numerals and letters, snippets for bits of text that include both numerals and letters are also useful. For example, wkphn could expand text that reads (123) 867-5309 (Jenny's direct line). This five-letter snippet saves you the trouble of typing 36 characters split between two iPad keyboards. There are two text-expansion tools for the iPad: the TextExpander Touch app and the new Apple shortcuts feature in iOS 5.

TextExpander Touch

TextExpander Touch ($5), developed by the same company that publishes TextExpander for the Mac, is the best third-party text expansion tool on the iPad. Figure 2-1 shows the TextExpander Touch home window.

Tap Create & Edit Snippets to open the snippet window. The snippet window includes two panes. The left pane contains snippet groups and lists. The right pane displays snippets. Snippet groups let you combine similar snippets together. Grouping snippets by category makes it easier to edit and find them later. I use many snippet groups. To create a new snippet group, tap the New Item icon button (the + symbol) at the bottom right of the left pane.

The New Item menu also includes options to install predefined groups, including AutoCorrect Words, HTML, CSS, Accented Words, and Symbols. You can also download snippet groups from the web to share with friends. To do so, tap the Add via URL option in the New Item menu.

Tap a snippet group to see its snippets. Tapping any snippet displays the abbreviation and related content in the right pane, shown in Figure 2-2

Tap the New Item icon button in this view (located in the bottom-right corner of the left pane) to create a new snippet via the Add Snippet window. To create a snippet, type an abbreviation and the snippet content. In addition to standard text, you can add system data. For example, adding `%Y-%m-%d` inserts the current date in the `YYYY-MM-DD` format. There is a list of all the available abbreviations at the developer's website, `www.smilesoftware.com`.

Tap the TextExpander Touch icon button in the toolbar (the balloon with `te` inside) to open a menu with links to the notes view (covered later), help, sending a

---

FIGURE 2-1

The TextExpander Touch home window

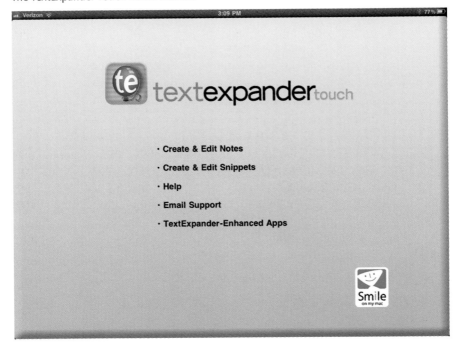

FIGURE 2-2

Displaying a snippet in TextExpander Touch

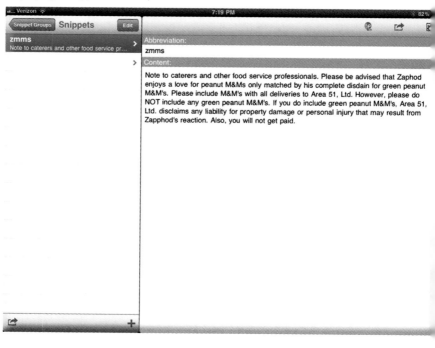

support e-mail, a list of the TextExpander-enhanced iPad apps, and returning to the TextExpander Touch home window, shown in Figure 2-1.

Tap the Settings icon button (the gear in a rectangle in the upper-right corner) for the Settings popover, shown in Figure 2-3. Here you can choose to ignore case when recognizing abbreviations, expand snippets immediately, play the expansion sound (a sort of a "plop" sound that I find quite satisfying), use auto-capitalization and auto-correction, and share your snippets and snippet groups. You can also set your default Twitter client, which is useful for sending snippets directly to Twitter.

Finally, TextExpander Touch can sync your snippets via Dropbox. Using Dropbox, it is easy to sync snippets between your iOS devices and Mac. For example, if you reset your iPad, you don't need to re-create your snippets, just sync TextExpander Touch to Dropbox and you are on your way.

The notes window, accessed through the TextExpander Touch home window or TextExpander icon button opens a simple text editor where you can compose snippets to use in other apps. When you are done, tap the Sharing icon button to send your text via e-mail, copy it to the iPad's paste buffer, or send directly to Twitter. For apps that do not recognize TextExpander Touch snippets (covered later), this provides a way to capitalize on your snippets. The notes window also lets you archive composed notes for reuse. For example, a collection of stored responses can be handy if you work in customer service.

FIGURE 2-3

The TextExpander Touch Settings popover

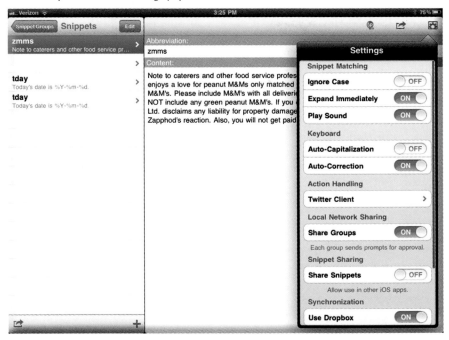

The challenge for text-expansion developers is the iPad's limited ability to multitask; the app runs while other apps are running, so they can use the shortcuts. Apple makes it difficult to run more than one app at a time. Multitasking kills batteries and slows down your iPad. Where the iPad does multitask, it is under controlled circumstances, like playing music in the background. There is no way to run a multitasking text expansion app. Or is there?

TextExpander Touch found a solution to this problem: Developers can access the TextExpander Touch program code and snippet library from inside their apps. It is not exactly multitasking but has the same effect. Your TextExpander snippets work in other apps. There are now more than a hundred iOS apps that do just this. Several of the apps covered in this book, particularly those in Chapter 13 on writing and iThoughtsHD in Chapter 17 include TextExpander Touch support. Notably missing from this support are the native Apple apps, including Mail and Safari.

TextExpander Touch is a powerful tool to automate text entry on your iPad. Someone at Apple must have noticed how useful text expansion is because with iOS 5, Apple added its own text-expansion tool.

Apple shortcuts

Apple shortcuts are Apple's text-expansion utility built into iOS 5. Apple shortcuts are located at the bottom of the Keyboard pane in the iPad's Settings app, shown in Figure 2-4.

FIGURE 2-4

Apple shortcuts in the Keyboard Settings pane

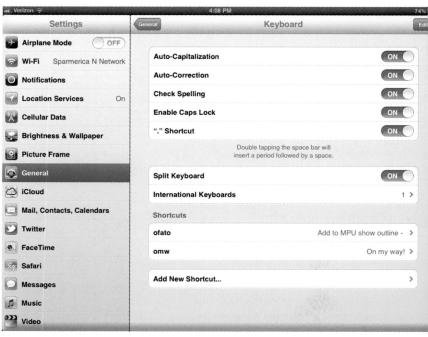

FIGURE 2-5

Adding a new Apple shortcut

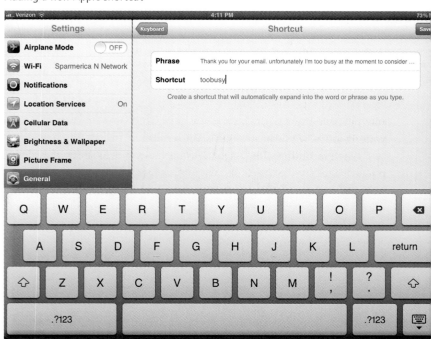

MY TEXT-EXPANSION WORKFLOW

I use TextExpander Touch snippets whenever possible. I like the additional features TextExpander Touch offers and love that the same snippets work on my Mac and my iPad. I do, however, keep a separate set of Apple shortcuts that I use in the iPad Mail app, where TextExpander Touch doesn't work.

To create a new shortcut, tap the Add New Shortcut button to open the window shown in Figure 2-5. Type the extended phrase and shortcut phrase and then tap Save in the upper-right corner — and you are done.

Apple shortcuts work just like iOS auto-correct for words. When you type the shortcut, the phrase appears below what you are typing and replaces the shortcut automatically when you tap the space bar, return, or any punctuation key.

Apple shortcuts do not have the deep feature set offered by TextExpander Touch. Your shortcuts don't sync over Dropbox (or even iCloud as of this writing). You can't auto-generate dates or sort your snippets into groups. You also can't download snippet libraries. The one thing Apple shortcuts has going for them, however, is that they work *everywhere* in the operating system, including Mail, Safari, and other apps that don't support TextExpander Touch.

Voice Recognition

Even if you have third-degree ninja iPad keyboard skills, sometimes it is just easier to dictate bits of text. iOS does not include extensive voice support. (This is an area of iOS that could stand further improvement.) On the Mac and Windows PC, Nuance is the king of all voice recognition. Nuance's Dragon Dictate for iPad (free), shown in Figure 2-6, brings dictation to the iPad.

Dragon Dictate's interface is sparse. To dictate, tap the red Listen icon button in the center of the right pane and start talking. When you are done, tap the screen again and the app sends your recording to the Nuance servers (so you need an active Internet connection), which convert your spoken words to text and send it back to your iPad. The whole process takes just seconds.

When recording with Dragon Dictate, make sure to speak toward your iPad's microphone. On the iPad 2, the microphone is at the top-center of the iPad, just behind the display screen. On the original iPad, the microphone is on the top-left of the device, next to the headphone jack.

Dragon Dictate works in small bursts: Dictate two or three sentences at a time. Many Dragon Dictate commands from the Mac and Windows PC versions also work on the iPad. Commands like "new line," "new paragraph," "caps," and "exclamation point" all perform as expected. You will find a full list of tips and commands available by tapping the Info icon button (a lowercase *i* in a circle) in the lower-right portion of the window.

FIGURE 2-6

Text generated by Dragon Dictate

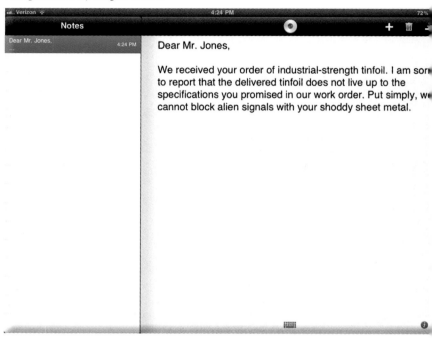

Make further modifications by tapping on individual words. You can also open a keyboard by tapping the Keyboard icon button in the bottom-center of the right pane.

There are three icon buttons at the right of the toolbar, shown in Figure 2-6: The New Dictation icon button (the + symbol) starts a new dictation. The Trash icon button (which looks like a trash can) deletes the current dictation. The Share icon button (the horizontal line with an arrow pointing down) sends your dictated text to a blank e-mail, Facebook, or Twitter, or copies it to the paste buffer for use in other apps. Dragon Dictate does a remarkably good job recognizing your words. I keep the app on my home screen and use it all the time.

Dictation only works from the Dragon Dictate app. You cannot dictate using the Dragon engine and other iPad apps. I suspect that one day Apple will include more dictation features throughout iOS, but for now, your best bet is Dragon Dictate.

File Storage

There are many ways to put files on your iPad. Chapter 1 explains syncing through USB using iTunes. Chapter 5 explains the many ways you can synchronize files using cloud servers including Dropbox and iCloud.

If, however, you are not willing to share your files through an Internet syncing service (perhaps because of security concerns), you can upload files to your iPad directly from your Mac or Windows PC with FileMagnet ($5). FileMagnet turns your iPad into a virtual traveling disk.

Using FileMagnet, you can copy any file from your Mac or Windows PC to your iPad using the iTunes USB syncing interface, covered in Chapter 1, or FileMagnet's wireless uploading app that installs on your Mac or Windows PC. The uploader, found at `http://magnetismstudios.com/filemagnet`, is free and works on both Mac and Windows PC. The uploader is easy to use: Just drag files you want to place on your iPad to the uploader. Then, when you open the FileMagnet app on your iPad, FileMagnet automatically downloads the files from your Mac or PC.

FileMagnet does not wirelessly upload files to your Mac or Windows PC once they are copied to the iPad; FileMagnet can only download files to the iPad wirelessly. To move a file from FileMagnet on your iPad to a different computer, you can e-mail the file from FileMagnet or sync the iPad through iTunes and then drag the file out of the FileMagnet documents list in the Documents section of iTunes's Apps pane.

The interface for FileMagnet is simple. In the main window, tap the Edit button at the top-right portion of the window to delete files from your iPad. Tap the Add Files button in the center of the bottom toolbar to open a menu with options to sync via iTunes or use FileMagnet's uploader.

Once you connect via the uploader, a button appears in the lower-left corner of the window to disconnect from your Mac or Windows PC. The Settings icon button (the gear icon) in the lower-right corner lets you set a password lock and includes options to automatically connect to your Mac or Windows PC at launch or, optionally, ban previously authorized computers.

In addition to holding files for transit, FileMagnet also displays several file types. Using FileMagnet, you can view PDF, Microsoft Office documents, iWork files, images, movies, and audio files. FileMagnet is a good place to collect reference materials not appropriate for cloud storage. For example, before going on a trip, you could load PDF files of your itinerary, Microsoft Word documents containing your proposal, and an iWork Numbers spreadsheets with your budget. All this is viewable (but not editable) from FileMagnet. (Other apps described in this book let you edit these file types.)

FileMagnet accepts any file in any format that you place in the uploader, including Zip files. If FileMagnet does not recognize the file type, it just holds the file as data for you to offload on another computer. I know several iPad workers who use FileMagnet to take files from their work computer to their home computer without using an Internet-based syncing service.

FileMagnet's utility is somewhat diminished with the growing adoption and sophistication of online syncing services, including those covered in Chapter 5. It is now easier to store files in the cloud making the extra steps to save files to your iPad unnecessary. However, if your work prohibits you from storing sensitive files on the cloud but you still need to get files to your iPad for reference or use elsewhere, FileMagnet is the way to go.

3

Security

Unfortunately, not everyone on the Internet — or in the corner café — is friendly. Keeping your iPad and its data secure is your responsibility. Just a few simple steps go a long way to a more secure iPad. This chapter covers the ins and outs of securing your iPad.

Passcode Lock

The single most important step to securing your iPad is adding a passcode. The iPad lets you set a four-digit number (or optionally a more complex passcode, as explained later) that keeps out any unwelcome user who might pick up your iPad.

To set a passcode, tap the Passcode Lock button in the Settings app's General pane. This opens the Passcode Lock pane shown in Figure 3-1.

From this pane, you can turn on or off the passcode lock. When setting a passcode, the iPad by default displays a ten-digit keypad, from which you pick a four-digit passcode. You're prompted to type the passcode twice; then your iPad is passcode-protected.

The Require Passcode window lets you pick how long the iPad waits after being put to sleep before locking. You can choose to lock the iPad immediately or wait as long as four hours. (If you've connected your iPad to a corporate server that enforces its own security rules, you may have different time-out options.) Setting the wait period involves balancing security versus convenience. If you use your iPad at home, you can set the delay for a long time. If you are in a crowded airport, you should set it to lock immediately.

The Simple Passcode switch allows you to change your iPad's passcode from a four-digit number to an alphanumeric password using the full iPad onscreen keyboard. Such complex passwords are more secure than the standard four-digit passcode. Again, deciding whether to use this approach requires balancing your interest in security versus convenience. I've always kept my iPad locked with a simple four-digit passcode. (Again, if you've connected to a corporate server, you may find you are required to use a password instead of a passcode. You may also have certain requirements imposed on that password, such as a minimum length, a required number of special characters such as numerals, and a maximum number of days before you must change to a new password.)

Your iPad automatically encrypts all the data stored on it, so it's harder for a thief to access your information. Entering a passcode or password unencrypts your data as you use it, but someone who gets to your iPad's storage directly will find only encrypted data. That encryption is not foolproof, but most thieves will be unable to access the data on the iPad unless they figure out your passcode or password.

The Picture Frame switch determines whether or not you'll need a passcode or password to activate the iPad's picture frame mode. (Your iPad, when plugged into a charging stand, can act as a digital picture frame, showing the pictures in the Photos app's Camera Roll.)

With the Erase Data switch turned on, ten unsuccessful attempts to enter the iPad passcode results in the iPad erasing all its data. (Again, if your iPad has connected to a corporate server, the number of permitted failed login attempts may be different.) I keep this feature turned on. I find something exciting in the fact that every time I get the passcode wrong the fuse starts burning down until the tenth attempt when the iPad scrambles its data. It makes me feel a tiny bit like James Bond.

Find My iPad

Have you ever lost your cellphone and wanted some way to track it on a map like they do in spy movies or maybe just make it play an alert because you had the ringer turned off the last time you set it down somewhere in your house? Apparently so did someone at Apple, because every iPad includes both these features with the Find My iPad service.

The Find My iPad service is free with every iPad. Find My iPad not only shows your iPad on a map, it can also display a message on the screen (like "I'm lost. If found please call 123-426-5678"), remotely lock the data, or remotely wipe all data.

You need an iCloud account for Find My iPad to work. (iCloud is free and covered in detail in Chapter 5.) Find My iPad requires that you consent to the iCloud service keeping track of your iPad. To do this, go to the iCloud pane in the Settings app, shown in Figure 3-2, and move the Find My iPad switch (at the bottom of the list) to the On position.

Flipping the switch tells the iCloud service it is okay to track your iPad. Once tracking is turned on, your iPad is ready to report in whenever the iCloud service asks.

FIGURE 3-1

The Passcode Lock pane

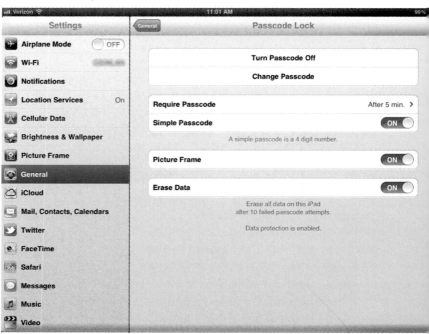

(This also means anyone with your iCloud login information and password could track your iPad, so any time you set a password, use one that is hard for someone else to guess.)

Apple makes it easy to track your iPad via Find My iPad: Just go to the web at www.icloud.com from any computer or device. Once you log in to the website, click the Find My iPad button to have iCloud display the iPad's last known location on a map.

The left side of the window shows a list of your devices. A red dot next to a device indicates iCloud can't find the device (usually because it is offline), and a green dot indicates the device was found. The right side includes a map with the location of the selected Apple device (iPad, iPhone iPod Touch, or Mac). A blue circle surrounds the iPad, showing iCloud's confidence in the location. The smaller the blue circle, the more precise the location fix.

In addition to displaying your iPad's location, you can also send your iPad instructions. Tap the Play Sound or Send Message button to send a notification message to your iPad and play a sound. (The sound plays loudly regardless of whether the iPad's volume is muted or turned down.) The sound plays for two minutes and is just the trick if you are looking for the iPad somewhere in your house or office.

The Remote Lock button secures your missing iPad. The web interface prompts you for a passcode and then locks the iPad, even if it is in use. The Remote Wipe is

FIGURE 3-2

Turning on Find My iPad

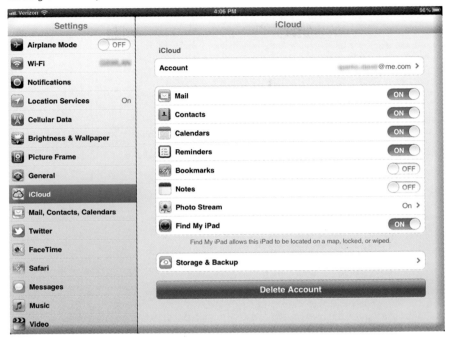

FIGURE 3-3

The Find My iPad app

LOCK IT UP — NO EXCUSES

I've heard all the excuses for not setting a passcode or password. It is inconvenient. It slows down access to your iPad. It's not "cool." None of these excuses work. The iPad's mobility makes it particularly susceptible to sticky fingers. Imagine your iPad, loaded with your work PDFs, key client spreadsheets, access to your banking website, and your address and telephone number (along with the address and telephone numbers of all your friends, family, customers, and colleagues) in the hands of some criminal wretch. Now does taking an extra three seconds to unlock it seem that big of a deal?

even more drastic: It erases all data from the iPad. Once you remote-wipe your iPad, you'll have to restore everything from a backup to get it running again.

If your iPad is turned off, the iCloud service keeps trying to find the iPad; when it does find the iPad (after the iPad is turned back on), iCloud sends the message, remotely locks the iPad, or remotely wipes the device as you requested. iCloud also sends you an e-mail confirming the mission was accomplished and telling you where the iPad was when it was turned on.

In addition to the web interface, Apple publishes a Find My iPhone app for the iPhone and iPad. (Even though the app is called Find My iPhone, it can find your iPad, Mac, or iPod Touch.) Shown in Figure 3-3, the app interface is similar to the website interface, with the same features and options. The Devices button in the top-left corner lets you pick which Apple device to track, and the Map, Satellite, and Hybrid buttons in the lower-right corner change the map format. Tap the Info icon button (the letter *i*) next to your device for options to display a message, play sound, remotely lock, or remotely wipe your iPad.

Even if your iPad is never stolen, you'll love the Find My iPad service the first time you realize your iPad is in your house or office, *somewhere.*

Insuring your iPad

It is expensive to replace your iPad, so insuring your investment may be a good idea. There are two types of insurance: AppleCare and third-party insurance.

AppleCare

AppleCare (www.apple.com/applecare) is Apple's insurance for your iPad. Every new iPad includes a one-year warranty. Purchasing an iPad AppleCare warranty ($80) extends the AppleCare warranty by an additional year. You can purchase an AppleCare warranty at any time within the first year of ownership.

An AppleCare warranty covers manufacturing problems and normal wear. If, after 18 months, your iPad screen fails and you have an active AppleCare policy,

Apple will fix or replace it. However, AppleCare does not cover accidental damage, such as if you crack the iPad's case or screen. It also does not cover theft or loss.

Theft, loss, and damage policies

Because AppleCare does not cover accidental damage, theft, and loss, additional insurance coverage may be appropriate. If you have a homeowner's or renter's insurance policy, you can often purchase an insurance rider policy that covers accidental damage, theft, and loss of your personal electronics (including your iPad). If you can't get insurance through an existing policy, you can purchase a specific policy for your iPad. There are several reputable insurance brokers that specialize in portable electronics. I keep one on my iPad that costs $65 a year. If I lose my iPad, or it gets run over by a truck, I get a replacement. If you travel with your iPad, the premium may be worth the peace of mind.

An important point is that AppleCare and a damage-and-loss policy cover two separate problems. Most accidental damage, theft, and loss policies do not cover warranty repairs. You should check with your insurer, but you may need both types of policies for full coverage.

Managing Passwords

In addition to locking your iPad with a passcode or password lock, you also need a reliable password and secure information system for the websites you use on the iPad.

Modern hackers are smart. If someone wants access to your online account, one of the first things they do is throw the entire dictionary at a password field. Gone are the days when "pencil" was a good-enough password. Many users don't give passwords enough thought and end up defaulting to the same two or three passwords over and over again. One of the most common passwords is, remarkably, "password." The trouble is that hackers know this: Once they get your password anywhere, they have it nearly everywhere. This problem is even more pronounced on the iPad where

PHYSICAL SECURITY

Often overlooked but critically important with mobile electronics is physical security. If a dirty rotten scoundrel gets physical possession of your iPad, there is a very good chance he or she will also get your data. Although this is a simple point, it bears consideration. What are you doing to physically secure your iPad?

Use common sense with your iPad. Keep it in a bag. When you go to the rest room at Starbucks, take it with you. The iPad sits in a unique position. It is too big to slide in your pocket but much more portable than a laptop. If you question whether to leave your iPad somewhere, you shouldn't.

1Password for iPad

you need to jump between onscreen keyboards to use numbers and letters in the same password, which encourages users to employ simplistic passwords.

Although Safari can hold your passwords, that is not an acceptable solution for anything important. It gives anyone with access to your iPad access to logins. Instead, use 1Password for iPad ($10), shown in Figure 3-4, to store your various passwords and auto-fill them on websites.

The idea behind 1Password is simple; use one password to remember them al Keeping all your account data inside the 1Password login system makes sense: You don't have to remember all your various passwords, but you also don't have to ma them easily discoverable through Safari auto-fill.

Using 1Password, you create one secure password that acts as a gatekeeper to access the 1Password database. This master password is separate from your passcod lock used to access your iPad. It creates, in essence, a second line of defense. If someone gets through your passcode lock and access to your iPad, they still need t get past the 1Password master password to get access to your most secure data in th 1Password database. Moreover, 1Password is beautifully designed and intuitive to use.

Figure 3-4 shows the 1Password interface. There is a strip down the left portio of the window with icon buttons for different categories of secure data. The right pane holds an alphabetized list and Search bar for the selected category. The large center pane holds the details for the selected record. When using the app, select th category of secure data in the far left pane and then use the right pane to select the particular record.

There are several categories of secure data supported in 1Password. Tap the Logins icon button for a list of website username and password data. This is where you may store login data for your secure websites, like your bank and PayPal. To log in to a secure website, copy the username or password by tapping and holding it in 1Password and then fill in the data in the Safari browser by pasting it. (To paste in iOS 5, tap and hold the destination field.) 1Password also has a Go & Fill feature (activated by tapping the ➡ icon button to the right of the website name, as shown in Figure 3-4), to automatically open the page in 1Password's built-in web browser, shown in Figure 3-5. 1Password fills in your username and password automatically. From 1Password's built-in web browser, you can also tap the Logins icon button to choose which 1Password login data to use at the current website.

The Accounts icon button in the left pane holds login information for several standard online accounts, including Amazon Web Services, databases, e-mail accounts, FTP accounts, instant messenger accounts, Internet service providers, router and server settings, and iTunes accounts.

The Identities icon button lets you add your identity details. The identity data fields include your name, birth date, occupation, and personal information.

The Notes icon button is one of my favorite categories of secure data in 1Password. These are freeform notes in which you can write any sort of data that

FIGURE 3-5

Using the 1Password Go & Fill feature

THE PERILS OF JAILBREAKING

Apple makes no secret of the fact the App Store is a closed system. To sell an app in the App Store, a developer must first make sure the app passes muster with Apple's review process. Generally, I think this is a good thing. It helps prevent malicious apps from finding their way to the iPad. However, it also means there are some apps that Apple does not approve.

Many of these apps were not approved for good reasons. They include tools to run pirated software and other apps most iPad users are happy to avoid. If you are tempted to unlock your iPad to run unapproved apps (called *jailbreaking*), be careful. Jailbroken iPads are not as secure. As an example, most jailbreaking procedures unlock root access (the underlying iOS command structure) to the iPad and don't lock up when they are done, leaving the iPad vulnerable. Also, the apps created for jailbroken iPads most certainly do not get the vetting afforded official iPad apps and could include malicious code. I recommend against jailbreaking your iPad. In addition to the security problems, jailbroken devices are not, in my experience, as stable, and you could be prohibited from future iOS updates.

Besides, there are more than 100,000 available iPad apps. There are plenty to explore without jailbreaking your iPad.

doesn't fit anywhere else. Any time you keep notes about something that should be private, open 1Password and save a secure note. I have notes ranging from my children's school details to the serial number for my MacBook Air.

The Software icon button opens a window with the software details and license codes for software you purchase. Although this is not necessary for App Store purchases (there are no serial numbers for iOS apps), it is useful for Mac and Windows PC software: It is nice having that list of license codes on my iPad when I rebuild a Mac or Windows PC.

The Wallet icon button lets you save financial information to your 1Password database, including bank accounts, credit cards, driver's license details, hunting licenses, memberships, passports, reward programs, and Social Security information. Again, all this is useful information to keep on your iPad that is much more secure with the 1Password master password than if it were kept on your iPad in an app accessible to anyone.

To create a new 1Password item for any of these secure data categories, tap the New Item icon button (the + symbol) in the upper-right corner of the window next to the Search bar. Figure 3-6 displays the 1Password window when adding a new wallet item.

Finally, the Settings icon button opens the application settings. 1Password includes settings to conceal passwords and show all login fields, backup and restore the 1Password database, change the 1Password master password, and sync the 1Password database with Dropbox. Because versions of 1Password also exist for the Mac, Windows PC, and Android, using Dropbox sync is a no-brainer with

FIGURE 3-6

Creating a new wallet item in 1Password

1Password. You can share your data across all platforms. When you add the login name and password for your favorite website on your Mac using 1Password, the data syncs automatically to your iPad. Your database is encrypted by 1Password before it gets saved to the Dropbox servers. Even if someone gets access to your 1Password database in your Dropbox account, he or she cannot read it. If you are still uncomfortable syncing your 1Password database with Dropbox, you can sync wirelessly over your Wi-Fi network.

The 1Password master password gives you the comfort of knowing access to your critical data is protected. Combined with the iPad's passcode or password lock, 1Password is just like wearing your belt and suspenders. I feel more secure knowing that my most secret data is behind this second wall.

Malware and Phishing

As Apple's competitors like to say, the iPad is a closed system. Particularly, every app you download from the iPad app store was vetted by somebody at Apple. Part of Apple's review process involves checking to make sure apps do not include any malicious programming code or misappropriate users' confidential data. Although no system is perfect and it is possible a shady app developer could figure out a way to get around Apple's checks, this hasn't happened yet to my knowledge. (By contrast, Google had to shut down several Android apps for harvesting private user data.)

In addition to Apple watching the gate for new apps, iPad apps are all separate contained in memory, preventing one app from accessing the data of another. This is called sandboxing. Even if a malicious app gets by Apple's screeners, it still canno get outside of its own sandbox without your permission. (You know that Open In menu in many apps that let you open content in another app? That's sandboxing in action. The apps in the Open In list broadcast to other apps what kinds of content they can access, and they appear in the Open In menu only when a user invokes th menu, if the app enabled Open In. Essentially, Open In is the only gate between sandboxes, and it requires explicit user action and developer permission.) Although a sandboxed app can still get access to plenty of personal data, like calendars and contact information that iOS automatically shares with other apps, it cannot secret access data belonging specifically to another app.

Sandboxing and Apple's measures do not, however, protect you from phishing attacks. Phishing (pronounced "fishing") is the fraudulent acquisition of your sensitive data. Phishing is not a virus. Instead it is a subterfuge where the bad guys masquerade as a trustworthy website or e-mail sender to convince you to provide credit card, financial information, or other sensitive data. Phishing attacks often start with you receiving an e-mail that informs you of some important change to your bank account. When you click the link, you are presented a website that *looks* identical to your bank's website but, in reality, is an entirely different site hosted, quite frequently, on the other side of the world. You dutifully type in your account information and password and — gotcha! — you are compromised.

These attacks aren't just limited to banking. Phishing attacks occur against many financial and shopping transactions including PayPal, iTunes, Craigslist, and anywhere the bad guys can get at your wallet. The iPad is just as vulnerable to phishing attacks as any other computer on the Internet.

The best defense to phishing attacks is user knowledge and distrust. No legitimate financial institution will e-mail you and ask you to tap a link to give sensitive data. When you get an e-mail from your bank or other financial institution don't tap any links. Instead open your browser and use your own bookmarks or type in the address yourself. Another clue is how the e-mail is addressed. When your bank writes an e-mail, it generally includes your account name in the e-mail. If the username isn't present and the e-mail is simply addressed to "valued customer," you defense shields should immediately go up. Finally, if you are ever informed of any account problems, turn off your iPad, pick up a telephone, and call the bank. I know this sounds paranoid, but don't call the number in your e-mail. Open your address book and call the number that you know is your bank's.

MY SECURITY WORKFLOW

I always keep a simple four-digit password lock on my iPad. It takes so little time to unlock my iPad, and the security it provides is so worth those lost seconds. I also keep all my iOS devices, along with those of my wife and children, connected to the Find My iPad service.

1Password is essential. All my sensitive data is locked behind a long, ugly master password, and that makes me happy. Although I'm not convinced I need AppleCare on my iPad, I do keep a theft, damage, and loss insurance policy on it.

Wi-Fi Security

Unsecured Wi-Fi is another security risk for your iPad. Whenever you attach your iPad to an open Wi-Fi connection, there is a risk of other people on the network watching your data packets to gain access to your online accounts. For example, if you fill out a web form with your banking username and password, those data bits travel through the air from your iPad to the Wi-Fi router. A sophisticated hacker could grab that data out of the air to maliciously log on to your banking site.

Stealing your login data is actually a lot harder than I describe. The iPad and smart financial institutions encrypt the username and password data so they don't travel through the air in a readable format. However, why take chances? I recommend not doing any sensitive Internet transaction while on an open Wi-Fi channel. Instead, wait until you are on a closed Wi-Fi network or use 3G (if your iPad supports it) and skip the "free" Wi-Fi altogether.

PART

Communications and Connections

4

The Internet

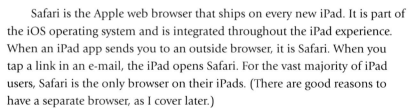

he Internet is such a part of our lives that it is only natural we've migrated to more Internet-friendly devices like the iPad. Perhaps the iPad's killer feature is its connectivity. If you don't believe me, go to your nearest airport and look around. You can take the iPad out of your bag anywhere and with Wi-Fi or 3G connectivity, plug into the world. This chapter covers some of the best ways to use your iPad for getting access to the Internet including web browsers, dedicated Internet apps, and social networking tools.

Safari

Safari is the Apple web browser that ships on every new iPad. It is part of the iOS operating system and is integrated throughout the iPad experience. When an iPad app sends you to an outside browser, it is Safari. When you tap a link in an e-mail, the iPad opens Safari. For the vast majority of iPad users, Safari is the only browser on their iPads. (There are good reasons to have a separate browser, as I cover later.)

Shown in Figure 4-1, the Safari user interface includes a toolbar, optional bookmarks bar, and browser window tabs.

The Safari toolbar

The toolbar icon buttons cover the standard browser tools. There are ← and → icon buttons to go backward or forward through your browser history. The Bookmarks icon button (the book icon) opens the Bookmarks popover and its bookmark management tools and Reading List, both covered later in this chapter.

The Sharing icon button (an icon of a rectangle with an arrow emerging) opens a menu with several tools to share and save websites. Tap the Add Bookmark button to add the current web page to your bookmark list. Tapping the Add to Reading List button adds the current website to the Reading List, also covered later.

Tap the Add to Home Screen menu option to create a link on your iPad's home screen to the current Safari website. That home screen link usually looks like an app on your home screen, but instead of launching an app, tapping the link opens Safari at the saved website. Although this doesn't actually turn the website into an app, it sure feels that way. If, for example, you are a power Gmail user and prefer to use the Gmail web interface, add your Gmail page to the home screen. Smart app developers even include a small piece of artwork in their web resources so when you add their page to your home screen, the iPad uses their custom artwork for the "app" icon image. There are many ways you could use this feature, ranging from monitoring a supplier's delivery status page to your daughter's gymnastics team practice schedule.

The remaining options in the Sharing menu let you e-mail a link to a page or send the active web page to your printer, as explained in Chapter 1.

The Safari toolbar also has an address bar and Search bar. Tap on the address bar to add a website URL. This opens the onscreen keyboard, shown in Figure 4-2.

FIGURE 4-1

The Safari web browser

Note that the onscreen keyboard is slightly different from the standard iPad onscreen keyboard. The Return key is now a Go key. Moreover, the spacebar is gone and in its place are several additional keys useful for typing website URLs, including a colon (:), backslash (\), underscore (_), and hyphen (–). There is also a button labeled ".com." Tapping this adds a .com to the current cursor location. Tap and hold this button for a contextual menu with other domain extensions, including .net, .org, .us, and .edu. (Extending the iPad keyboard using the tap-and-hold gesture is covered in greater detail in Chapter 1.)

The Clear icon button (a circle containing an X) at the right of the address bar clears the current address. If you want to copy a link from the address bar, tap the address and then tap Select All from the popover. Then tap Copy and paste the link where needed. Although this sounds like a lot of steps, it is not difficult once you try. Also don't forget you can e-mail a link directly from the Sharing menu, covered earlier.

Tap the Search bar and tap in your query to perform a search. You can set the default Safari search engine via the Safari settings, covered later.

You can also search the active web page. To do so, tap the Search bar but type your search query in the Find on Page Search bar that appears at the top of the onscreen keyboard, shown in Figure 4-3.

Tabs are a new feature to iPad Safari in iOS 5. (Before, you would switch among any open windows using the Pages icon button, which had two overlapping

FIGURE 4-2

Using the Safari address bar

rectangles with the number of open windows displayed in the foremost one.) Each tab represents a different web page. Tap on the tab to bring its web page to the front. Tap the Close icon button (the X icon) on the left side of the active tab to close it. Tap the New Tab icon button (the + symbol) at the right side of the tab bar to add a new blank tab. To rearrange tabs, tap and hold a tab and drag it left or right.

Navigating with Safari

Navigating a website with iPad Safari is intuitive. When using Safari while sitting on your couch, you realize that it seems the entire Internet was built for the iPad. It is so easy to flick, tap, and pinch your way through the web using your iPad that you'll wonder how you ever got along without it.

Drag the page up and down to scroll. Double-tap on an article for the iPad to auto-zoom the selected article's width to fill the screen. You can also use the pinch gesture to zoom in or out on a web page. If you want to quickly scroll back to the top of a web page, tap the status bar at the top of the window (the black bar with your battery and connection status icons).

Tap a link to open it. Tap and hold a link for more options from the Link contextual menu.

Use the Link contextual menu to open a link in your choice of the current tab or a new tab, add the link to Reading List (covered later), or copy the link for use elsewhere.

FIGURE 4-3

Searching the active web page

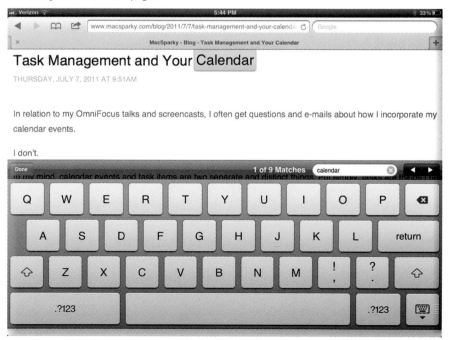

To stop a page from loading, tap the Stop icon button (the X icon) in the address bar. Once the page completes loading, the Stop icon button turns into the Reload icon button (the icon of a clockwise spinning arrow).

iPad-friendly videos play directly from the web page. If you want to see them full screen, tap the Full Screen icon button (the two diagonal arrows) that appears the video.

Tap and hold an image in Safari to open a contextual menu from which you c save it to your iPad's image library (in the Photos app).

Managing Safari bookmarks

Typing in a URL address on the iPad takes longer than it does on a traditional keyboard, even under the best of circumstances. Thus, creating a list of bookmarks for frequently visited websites makes a ton of sense on the iPad — and is easy to d

To make a bookmark, navigate to the website, tap the Sharing icon button, an then select Add Bookmark from the menu. This adds the current website to the Sat Bookmarks list.

To access your bookmarks, tap the Bookmarks icon button (the icon of an op book) to open the Bookmarks popover, shown in Figure 4-4.

Tapping the History menu option in the Bookmarks popover opens a list of recently viewed websites. This is a great way to get back to recent websites you haven't bookmarked.

Below the History menu option is a list of saved bookmarks and bookmark folders. Tap one to have Safari jump to it. Bookmarks are so useful that before lon you'll collect an unwieldy set of them. Fortunately, Safari has tools to organize bookmarks and sort them into folders.

Tap the Edit button at the upper right of the Bookmarks popover to arrange a delete bookmarks. Doing so alters the Bookmarks popover.

Tap a bookmark name or its More icon button (the > symbol) to open the Ed Bookmarks pane, from which you can edit its name and URL. You can also choose which bookmarks folder to place it in (using the Bookmarks option below the UR Tap Edit Bookmarks to return to the Edit Bookmarks pane, and tap Bookmarks to return to the Bookmarks editing popover.

In the Bookmarks editing popover, you can tap a bookmark's corresponding Delete icon button (a red circle with a horizontal line) to delete that bookmark. Ta and hold the corresponding Arrange icon button (three horizontal lines) to drag a bookmark up or down on the list to rearrange it. When you are finished editing th bookmarks, tap the Done button.

The Bookmarks bar, that line of bookmarks under the toolbar, is optional. You can turn this feature on or off in the Safari settings, covered later. Opinions are split concerning the Bookmarks bar. On one hand, using the Bookmarks bar makes navigation to your favorite pages super convenient. On another hand, the Bookmarks bar takes up even more pixels on an already small screen. I believe the trade-off is worthwhile, so I keep the Bookmarks bar turned on.

FIGURE 4-4

The Safari Bookmarks popover

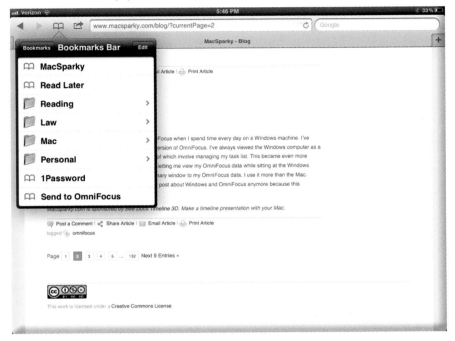

If you also use the Safari browser on your Mac, Windows PC, iPhone, and/or iPod Touch, iCloud syncs your bookmarks among all your devices.

Reading List

Reading List is a new feature in iOS 5. Reading List acts as an alternative to bookmarking a website. Bookmarks are great for keeping URLs you frequently revisit, but adding bookmarks to pages that you intend to come back to in the future just once (such as to read an article later on when you have time) can quickly junk up your bookmarks list.

That's why Apple has added Reading List to Safari in iOS, Mac OS X, and Windows. It lets you save those interesting articles in a list separate from your bookmarks, so your bookmarks don't get cluttered — and so you can actually find those articles you meant to read later. To add a web page to Reading List, tap the Sharing icon button and then the Add to Reading List menu option. To access the Reading List saved entries, open the Bookmarks popover and tap the Reading List option. With an iCloud account, Reading List links sync among your iOS devices and your Macs or PCs running Safari.

If you use Reading List often, try Instapaper (covered later in this chapter). Instapaper, which many consider to be Apple's inspiration for Reading List, adds several features not available in Reading List.

Reader view

Often, websites include a lot of extra content that gets in the way when working on such a small screen. Safari includes the reader view to remove that extra content and just display the key information on the web page. To enter this view, tap the Reader button in the address bar, shown in Figure 4-1. Safari then figures out the key text and displays it against a white background, as shown in Figure 4-5.

Reader view provides a cleaner interface to the web. When used with Reading List, you can easily read long-form articles on your iPad.

The reader view is, however, not without controversy. That extra stuff Reader strips out of the web pages often includes the advertisements that pay for the site's contents. So blocking the advertisements could ultimately result in websites shutting down. Moreover, some websites are designed for a pleasant user experience with colors and graphics. But Reader takes that away. Although I use Reader regularly, I make a point of subscribing and making donations to the websites I read.

Safari settings

With its minimal user interface, Safari has no settings inside the app. But fear not; Safari has its own pane in the Settings app. In that pane, you can tap the Search Engine button to choose among Google, Yahoo, and Bing as the default search engine.

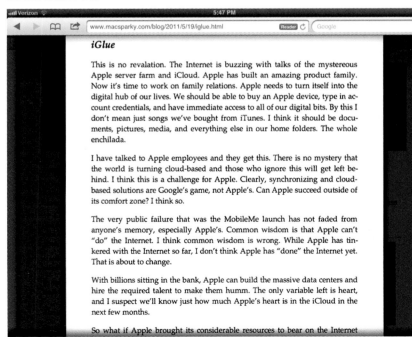

FIGURE 4-5

Safari's Reader view

Enable the AutoFill option to have Safari use your contact information when filling out web forms. AutoFill also remembers website names and passwords, and offers to fill them in for you. But be careful: Using this feature requires balancing security against convenience. Once you enable AutoFill, anyone using your iPad can access websites where AutoFill names and passwords are stored. I recommend you use AutoFill sparingly (and password-protect your iPad as well). Although it may be fine for logging on to a favorite news site to leave comments, it is most definitely not a good way to log in to your banking website. Instead, use 1Password, covered in Chapter 3, for storing more sensitive information.

The Safari settings also include switches to open tabs in the background and control whether to always show the Bookmarks bar. As explained earlier, I keep the Bookmarks bar visible.

There are also Privacy settings in the Safari pane of the Settings app. Private Browsing stops Safari from keeping track of your browsing history. To stop your iPad from accepting cookies from websites, disable that feature using the Accept Cookies button. (Cookies are bits of data sent to your browser from a website, such as to remember your account or personal settings for that site. But sometimes cookies are used to monitor a user's browser activity, which is bad.) You can also remove all website data stored in Safari using the Clear History, Clear Cookies, and Clear Cache buttons.

Finally, there are settings to enable a fraud warning, to control whether to use JavaScript (a web-oriented programming language many sites use for their interactive features), and to block pop-ups.

Atomic Web Browser

The Safari browser sets the bar high. It is fast, actively developed, and strikes the right balance of features and convenience for the iPad. Nevertheless, it is a good idea to have a second browser on your iPad.

Sometimes a website simply does not render properly in the Safari browser. Normally this happens with old websites that don't follow modern web standards or that use unique security protocols. If Safari hits a brick wall, I recommend Atomic Web ($1). Shown in Figure 4-6, Atomic Web is a meat-and-potatoes app that isn't particularly attractive but includes a ton of useful features that Apple would never let out the door.

The Atomic Web browser has its own pane in the Settings app. Atomic Browser has extensive privacy and ad-blocking settings. Its colors and user interface are also configurable. There are switches to turn on autofill forms, enable VGA-out (for the original iPad), and set compression with Google Mobilizer. You can even tell Atomic Browser to identify itself as a different browser, including Internet Explorer versions 6, 7, and 8. Sometimes when up against an old website, such spoofing of your iPad browser as Internet Explorer is exactly what you need to get it to display properly.

FIGURE 4-6

Atomic Web Browser

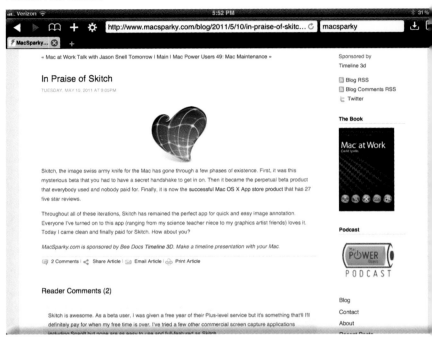

Whenever I'm able to access a website with Safari, I try Atomic Web and more often than not — with a little fiddling — I can open the site.

Flash and the iPad

One of the most common gripes against the iPad is its inability to run Adobe Flash. So what is Adobe Flash? It is a multimedia platform used to create animations, run interactive presentations, and show video on the Internet. It has been around for years, so the developer tools to create Flash video are widely used in websites. Until iOS, Flash Player was present on virtually all computers, assuring developers that everyone could view their Flash animations, games, and videos.

The problem is that Flash is not very efficient. Even on today's modern multicore computers with gigabytes of RAM, Adobe Flash can bog down the processor and wear down laptop batteries. Mobile devices such as the iPad and iPhone have only a fraction of the power and battery life of your computer. Flash is also persnickety in how it's coded, and poorly coded Flash objects are one of the most common reasons web pages don't open and browsers crash. As a result, Apple does not support Flash in iOS.

So what does that mean for you? It really depends. Much of the Internet is switching video formats from Adobe Flash to HTML5, an enhanced version of the basic presentation technology used on all websites. HTML5 is nearly universally deployed; every modern desktop and mobile browser uses it. But website developers are just starting to use the new HTML5 capabilities such as video presentation and interactivity support, so many websites aren't yet taking advantage of HTML5. And many that are using HTML5 still have lots of old content produced in Flash. That means many websites will give you an error message in iPad Safari saying Flash is required to view some content.

Over time, this Flash compatibility issue will diminish. Many websites are adding HTML5 content (in addition to or instead of Flash), and both Google and Adobe are developing their own tools to convert Adobe Flash to HTML5.

So today, Adobe Flash video doesn't play on your iPad out of the box. There is, however, an app for that.

The Skyfire for iPad browser ($5) exists for the purpose of playing Flash video on your iPad. Skyfire examines your current web page for the existence of any Flash video. If it finds any Flash video, the Skyfire servers download and convert the video to an iPad-friendly format and serve the video up to the Skyfire browser on your iPad. The whole process requires about a 20-second delay but if you are just watching Flash video, it gets the job done.

Skyfire does not solve the problem of playing Flash games on your iPad. As of this writing, that is not possible. But even if it could, I don't think you would be happy. Flash games are not designed around the iPad's touch interface, so they would be very awkward on an iPad (as they are on competing tablets that do run Flash). Besides, there are thousands of native, touch-optimized games available in the App Store.

Internet Apps

Your browser is no longer your only window to the Internet. Most native iPad apps also have their own connection to the Internet using an embedded browser called WebKit that iOS provides for them, so they can bring you information in ways no browser can.

I believe we are only at the beginning of this iPad revolution, and as app developers reimagine how we interact with the Internet, iPad apps will just get more innovative. There are already several great iPad apps that bring you the Internet without the browser.

Flipboard

Flipboard (free), shown in Figure 4-7, is a virtual magazine. Flipboard lets you choose among content channels that range from technology to fashion. Flipboard then collects the content for you from the Internet (usually from their websites). You flip pages with your finger and select articles by tapping them. Flipboard also connects to your Facebook, Twitter, and Flickr accounts. Flipboard collects links from your Twitter and Facebook friends and assembles pages and articles based on

FIGURE 4-7

Flipboard for iPad

those links. In essence your Facebook and Twitter friends curate a magazine just for you.

Really Simple Syndication

Remember when you first discovered the Internet and spent your days jumping among your favorite websites to see if there was anything new? As fun as "surfing" the web sounds, it is really inefficient and time-consuming. RSS (Really Simple Syndication) is a web standard that fixes this. Using RSS you can subscribe to your favorite websites and RSS creates a list of articles which you have, and have not, read.

An RSS reader app checks the websites for you and displays only anything new since the last time you checked. Most websites support RSS. Tapping the RSS icon, shown above left, opens the site's RSS feed. (A site may have multiple feeds, each with its own icon.)

The best way to manage RSS subscriptions for iPad owners is the Google Reader service (www.google.com/reader). Set up a Google Reader account on your iPad, Mac, or PC and add the RSS feed to it.

Although the Google Reader website renders just fine in the Safari browser, there are very good RSS apps that improve this experience. My favorite is Reeder.

FIGURE 4-8

Reeder for iPad

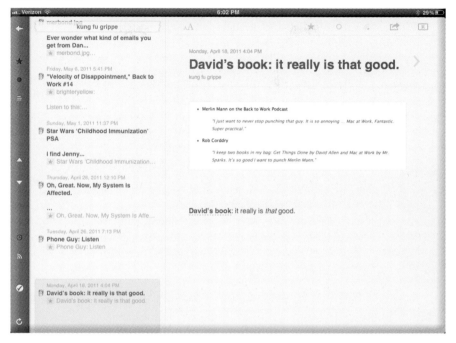

Reeder

Reeder ($5) is a Google Reader client with a minimalist bent. Shown in Figure 4-8, Reeder shows stacks of paper representing all your Google Reader folders with a toolbar down the left side of the page. There are three icon buttons on the toolbar. The Star icon button shows starred (flagged) articles. (You can star articles from inside Reeder or at the Google Reader website.) The New Items icon button (the dot) shows new items. The All Items icon button (the three horizontal lines) shows all articles (read and unread) for a given feed. The bottom of the toolbar has the Refresh button.

Tap a stack to open all associated articles or use the pinch gesture to open the stack to show individual feeds. Once you select a group of articles, Reeder adds icon buttons to the toolbar, including ↑ and ↓ buttons to navigate the articles. There are also icon buttons to change the sort order between chronological (the clock icon) and feed (the RSS icon). Finally there is the Read All icon button (the check mark) to mark all articles as read.

When reading feeds, Reeder has two panes. The left pane shows the article summaries and the right pane shows the selected article's text. Along the top of the right pane are additional icon buttons to star (flag) an article, mark it as read, and share an article with your Google Reader friends. The Share icon button (a rectangle with an arrow emerging) opens a menu with several options, including sharing the article via e-mail, opening it in Safari, sending it to Twitter, and sending the selecte article to Instapaper. Reeder includes support for most web-based sharing services.

Finally, the Readability icon button (a capital R) applies the Readability filter to the selected article. The Readability filter combines multipage articles and strips unrelated pieces of the website. It is based on the same technology as the reader vi in Safari, covered earlier in this chapter.

I follow several websites ranging from obscure legal writers to nerdy Mac bloggers. With Reeder, I can check my feeds in minutes and quickly sort the signal from the noise.

NetNewsWire for iPad

The Reeder interface reflects a minimalist design aesthetic that doesn't work fo everyone. An alternative RSS reader app with more interface bells and whistles is NetNewsWire for iPad ($10), shown in Figure 4-9.

NetNewsWire has a more traditional app interface but, like Reeder, is loaded with features. NetNewsWire also works with a Google Reader account. Although NetNewsWire is a credible alternative to Reeder, it loads the feeds noticeably slowe than Reeder does.

FIGURE 4-9

NetNewsWire for iPad

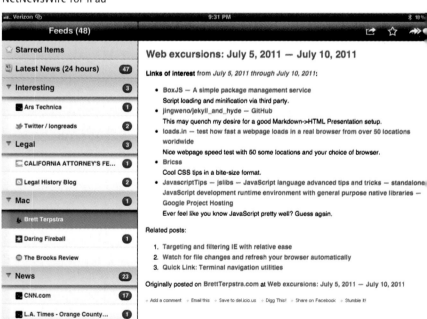

Instapaper

Instapaper ($5) is, without a doubt, my favorite app for consuming web content on my iPad. Instapaper is the ultimate tool to build your own customized iPad magazine of articles that interest you. Instapaper collects web pages you identify and strips out the excess formatting (like Safari reader view, covered earlier). Instapaper then saves the articles to its servers to sync with all your computers and mobile devices. You can read and archive the articles from your iPad, and Instapaper on your other devices automatically updates.

There are many ways to attach articles to your Instapaper account. You can install a bookmarklet in the Safari browser that sends the active page to Instapaper. (Do this by tapping the Install "Read Later" in Safari button in Instapaper's Settings menu.) Many newsreader apps — including Flipboard, Reeder, and NetNewsWire, all described in this chapter — include a Send to Instapaper feature.

Manage your Instapaper account at Instapaper.com, where you can organize your saved articles into folders. As an example, I keep folders for Mac, legal, and health articles, among others. You can arrange and edit your folders in the left pane of Instapaper's articles view, shown in Figure 4-10.

The articles view includes two panes. The left pane has a list of folders, and the right pane lists articles available in the selected folder. The article listings in the right pane include a brief preview and a series of dots indicating the article length and reading progress. (The solid dots represent how much you've read.) Tap an article in the right pane and Instapaper opens the reading view, shown in Figure 4-11.

Reading view displays the selected article. Using Instapaper, you can scroll through the article with your finger or, alternatively, tap the right or left sides of the screen to move forward or backward in the article. There is a setting for this behavior (settings are covered later), but Instapaper auto-detects your preference from your actions. For example, if you tap the right side of the screen several times, Instapaper asks if you want to enable pagination instead of scrolling.

The toolbar includes the Favorite icon button (the heart icon) to mark the current article as a favorite (explained later) and the Archive icon button (the trash can icon) to put the article in your Instapaper archive. The Typography icon button (it appears as AA) opens a popover in which you set the typeface, font size, line spacing, and margins.

Instapaper also has a "dark" mode that is useful for reading in a dark room when your spouse is trying to sleep and you know lighting the entire room with your iPad would come with dire consequences.

The Sharing icon button opens a menu with options to move the current article to a different Instapaper folder, print it, or open the page in the Safari browser. This menu also includes the Share button, which opens a separate menu.

The contents of the Share menu depend on the apps installed on your iPad. You can use this to e-mail a link or the full article text, or post the article to Twitter. You can also share the article with other Instapaper-friendly apps. For example, you can save

Instapaper for iPad's articles view

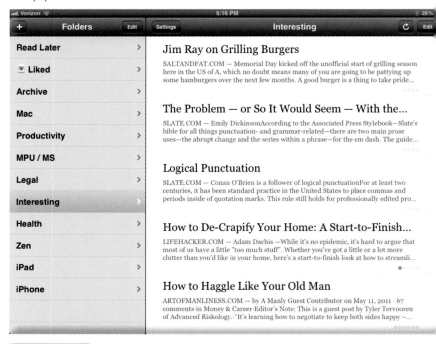

Instapaper's reading view

an Instapaper article as an OmniFocus task (covered in Chapter 19). I use this feature all the time. There are options to link Instapaper to your Facebook, Tumblr, Pinboard, and Evernote accounts. Make sure to check this menu on your iPad to see how nicely Instapaper plays with your favorite apps.

Instapaper for iPad downloads all articles in your Instapaper queue locally to your iPad. Once the articles are downloaded, you don't need an Internet connection to read them. This makes airplanes an excellent place to catch up with your Instapaper reading. The next time your iPad is hooked up to the Internet, Instapaper notifies its servers of the articles you read.

Instapaper also has light social features. You can mark an article as Liked and share that list of Liked articles with others. There is also the optional Browse bar that gives access to articles Liked by friends, selected editors, and your favorite websites. (Add the Browse bar from the Instapaper Settings popover.)

In Instapaper's articles view, tap the Settings button to open the Settings popover. This popover includes options for dark mode, rotation, scroll mode, sharing accounts, and the Browse bar (covered earlier). There are also buttons to install the Instapaper Read Later bookmarklet in the Safari browser and to add an Instapaper contact to your address book so you can add articles by e-mailing them to your unique Instapaper e-mail address.

I use Instapaper every day. The iPad is, without a doubt, the best Instapaper experience on any platform. Sometimes it feels like the iPad was built for Instapaper.

Wikipedia

It is easy to make fun of Wikipedia, the online encyclopedia editable by anyone with an Internet connection. Although Wikipedia entries sometimes more closely resemble battlefields than encyclopedia entries, it does have its uses. There are dedicated Wikipedia apps for the iPad, and my favorite is Wikipanion Plus for iPad.

Wikipanion Plus formats Wikipedia articles for the iPad. You control the typeface and the app handles the layout. Wikipanion Plus's left pane includes table of contents, bookmarks, and a queue mode that downloads Wikipedia content to your iPad. You can share your favorite pages via e-mail and Twitter. The queue mode is great for loading up on content before stepping on an airplane. Wikipanion Plus also uses your geolocation data to identify Wikipedia entries near you.

Social Networking

Social networking is about more than just finding old high school buddies. People use it all the time for business. There is no shortage of iPad apps supporting social networking platforms. Here are some of the best.

Facebook

Although Facebook has a custom iPhone app, the company did not make an iPad app. (As this book goes to press, screenshots of an iPad app are appearing on the web but there is no announcement by Facebook.) There are third-party Facebook apps but you may find you don't need one. Facebook renders quite nicely in the Safari browser, so you can easily log in, view friends and colleagues, and update your status. (Indeed, most third-party Facebook apps are nothing more than a glorified browser view.)

If you are a Facebook power user, check out Friended ($1). Friended adapts the Facebook interface to the iPad. The top of the window features icon buttons for friend requests, messages, notifications, and status updates. Friended also includes support for pictures and live chats.

LinkedIn

Like Facebook, LinkedIn has an official app for the iPhone but no native iPad app. Also like Facebook, LinkedIn renders great in the Safari browser. You can access your account and do anything with your LinkedIn account through the Safari browser that you could do on your laptop.

Unlike Facebook, there is no third-party app on par with Friended for LinkedIn. So stick with Safari.

FIGURE 4-12

Twitter for iPad

MY INTERNET WORKFLOW

I use the Safari browser nearly exclusively on the iPad. From Safari, I use the reader view to simplify reading web articles; I also send the articles of interest to Instapaper for offline reading later. I don't use Apple's Read Later service much because I prefer Instapaper's better features and its ability to read offline.

I spend a lot of time in Reeder keeping up with my favorite websites. I send any interesting articles from Reeder to Instapaper for reading and, where useful, linking to new OmniFocus tasks. For social networking services, I stick with the Safari-rendered versions except for Twitter, in which case I use Twitter for iPad.

Twitter

If Twitter, the 140-character microblogging site, fits into your work, there is no shortage of Twitter apps for the iPad. My favorite is Twitter for iPad (free). This is Twitter's own iPad app, shown Figure 4-12.

Twitter for iPad has a three-pane layout. The left pane displays Twitter accounts and filters, including time line, mentions, messages, and lists. You can access your account profile or conduct a search using these tools. The middle pane displays the active filter. If you tap @Mentions, the middle pane just displays tweets mentioning your Twitter name.

Tap the New Tweet icon button (a blank piece of paper with a pencil) at the bottom-left of the left pane to compose a new tweet. To compose a tweet, start typing. You can send the tweet to other Twitter users by tapping the @ icon button and typing their Twitter name. The # icon button opens a list of recent hash tags. (Hash tags describe the subject matter of a tweet, like #superbowl.) The Camera icon button lets you add a photo from your photo library or the iPad 2's built-in camera. Tap the Location icon button to add your location to the tweet. When you are done composing your tweet, tap Send and Twitter returns to its main window.

The Settings icon button in the lower-right corner of the left pane opens the Settings menu with options to add and remove accounts, adjust notifications, and set preferred services for photo and video sharing. You can also send tweets to Instapaper (covered earlier in this chapter) or Read it Later accounts to read later.

When reading your Twitter stream, tap tweets or links to open them in the third pane at the far right for closer inspections. Tapping a tweet with no link or conversation thread opens an account panel for the selected person. To get rid of the third pane, tap and hold the middle pane and pull it to the right. This displays an image of one pane falling off to the right in the center of the screen. When you let go, Twitter closes the right pane. Although this gesture is not intuitive, it becomes second nature once you know it exists.

5

The Cloud

One of the most salient complaints about the iPad after its initial release was how difficult it made file sharing. Although iOS's architecture of keeping data files with the apps provides many security and stability benefits, it also denies users the ability to easily store and organize data files. It felt like file management took a step backward with the iPad and we were back to sneakernet (using our shoes instead of the Internet to share files).

It didn't take long for Apple and several vendors to respond with cloud-based syncing and file-sharing services to take the work out of sharing files with your iPad, without the use of sneakers.

The cloud is a metaphor for the Internet. Cloud storage really means Internet storage. Cloud computing revolutionizes file sharing and synchronization. Where it used to be hard to keep files in sync among your various computers, it is now much easier with each computer pointing at shared storage or files in the cloud.

This chapter covers how to share files with your iPad using the Internet — or the cloud, if you prefer that term.

iCloud

iCloud is Apple's cloud computing initiative, released with iOS 5 in fall 2011. iCloud was not Apple's first attempt at Internet-based storage services. Apple went through several iterations of cloud-like services (most recently with MobileMe) before releasing the iCloud services. A basic iCloud account is free and includes 5GB of storage. (You can increase the iCloud storage for an additional fee.)

iCloud services

iCloud is not a traditional cloud file-hosting service as much as it is a collection of cloud-friendly services for syncing data among your iPad, Macs, PCs, and other iOS devices. (iCloud also can back up your iPad to its servers. I cover this in Chapter 1.)

Contacts and calendars

iCloud provides users a way to wirelessly sync their contact and calendar lists among computing devices. Changing a client's e-mail address over lunch is as simple as opening the Contacts app on your iPad and editing the contact. The iPad then informs iCloud of the change, which then propagates the change to your other iCloud-connected devices, such as an iPhone, Mac (if you use Apple Mail, iCal, and Address Book), and PC (if you use Outlook). Calendar changes are shared the same way.

Additionally, you can view your contacts and calendars from the web at www. icloud.com, where Apple maintains a web portal for iCloud contacts, calendars, and e-mail.

E-mail

iCloud users also get a free IMAP e-mail account. The domain is me.com, so your iCloud e-mail address will most likely be *your_name*@me.com. Because the service is IMAP-based (IMAP is covered in Chapter 6), any e-mail you receive and process on your iPad gets the same treatment on your other iCloud-connected devices. For example, if you delete an e-mail on your iPad, it gets automatically deleted on your other devices. It works the same way when you reply to an e-mail or save it to a folder. By using an iCloud IMAP e-mail account, your e-mail accounts remain in sync everywhere.

Chances are that your business e-mail will be handled not through iCloud but through a separate e-mail account, such as Exchange, corporate Gmail, or IMAP. Those too sync across devices automatically.

Safari bookmarks

iCloud syncs your bookmarks among iPads, iPhones, Macs (if you use the Safari browser), and PCs (if you use Internet Explorer or Safari). It does not sync bookmarks with other browsers, such as Firefox or Google Chrome.

Document storage

Document storage is where Apple makes a left turn from the rest of the cloud services available. The normal paradigm for document syncing is to have a cloud-based folder in which you keep documents for syncing among computing devices. You, as the user, store your data files (such as Word documents or Keynote presentations) in this cloud folder and then manually point your applications at the cloud folder or pull down copies to your local computer or device for use. It is up to you to access and maintain that cloud data folder. All the other cloud computing services covered in this chapter work just this way.

iCloud, however, is different. Rather than focusing on data files, iCloud focuses on apps. For example, saving a Keynote presentation from your iPad to iCloud doesn't require saving files to a particular cloud folder. Instead, when you save your Keynote file, it is automatically sent to iCloud and then synced with the rest of your devices and your Mac.

As you move among platforms, iCloud does the hard work of keeping the most recent changes distributed among all your devices. Thus, when you show up in the conference room to give the Keynote presentation from your iPad, you don't need to find the most recent changes in a cloud folder. Instead, you open Keynote on your iPad and the updated presentation is just there (assuming you've had your iPad connected to the Internet since the last changes).

Of course, for this to work, the apps must be iCloud-compatible, and iCloud sharing must be on. On the iPad (or iPhone), go to the Settings app's iCloud pane and make sure the Documents & Data switch is set to On. On a Mac (it must run Mac OS X Lion), go to the System Preferences application's Mail, Contacts & Calendars pane, and add an iCloud account (if you don't already have one) using the Add Account icon button (the + symbol). Then make sure Documents & Data is enabled in the iCloud pane.

Note that there is a downside to Apple's app-based document-syncing model. Common apps are the glue holding the sync together, not a shared folder and, as a result you have to use the same app on all the devices. For example, for Keynote presentations, you don't get the auto-sync goodness on your PC because there is no Keynote app for Windows — and iCloud does not sync between, say, Keynote and PowerPoint. The same issue occurs for PDF files, Word files, text files, and other formats that you use across multiple apps.

Even with these limitations, iCloud is a revolutionary cloud-syncing service. It gives novice users the ability to sync documents among iOS devices and Macs with no effort. People will be able to start a letter on their Mac and finish it on their iPad with absolutely no idea how it happened. I expect this is going to change the way users work for the better.

Photo Stream

Photo Stream is an iCloud service that synchronizes pictures among your iOS devices and your computer (both Macs and Windows PCs). If you take a picture with your iPad 2, Photo Stream saves the image to your iCloud storage, which then shares it with your iPhone and computer. (On the iPad and iPhone, photos in the Photos app are synced. On a Mac, photos in iPhoto or your Pictures folder are synced — you specify which. On a PC, photos in the My Pictures folder are synced via iCloud

This sharing removes the need to manually sync photographs among your iOS devices and your computers. Again, it happens automatically.

Photo Stream is intended as a temporary home for your photos. If Apple hosted all the pictures for all its users, its data centers would slow to a crawl. Photo Stream holds a rolling collection of your last 1,000 photos on your iOS device. Moreover, Photo Stream stores new photos for just 30 days. Before the 30 days are up, move the photos out of your Photo Stream to your picture library (like iPhoto on the Mac). Note that you need to turn on Photo Stream. On the iPad, do so in the iCloud pane of the Settings app. On a Mac (it must run Mac OS X Lion), go to the Mail, Contacts & Calendars system preference, create an iCloud account if you don't already have one, and be sure that Photo Stream is enabled in the iCloud services list. On a Windows PC, install the iCloud control panel (you can download it from www. apple.com/icloud) and enable Photo Stream.

Although Photo Stream is a consumer-aimed service, there is no reason it can't be useful in the workplace. If your job involves making inspections, for example, you can take photographs with your iPhone and immediately have them available on your iPad and computer.

iTunes in the cloud

iTunes in the cloud makes all your iTunes music purchases available to download on to your iPad and iPhone without syncing with your computer. Just make sure that in the Store pane of the Settings app, the Music switch is set to On for this auto-downloading to occur. In iTunes on your computer, go to the Preferences dialog box's Store pane and make sure Music is checked.

For an additional $25 per year, iTunes examines all the music in your library (even the songs you did not purchase through iTunes) and makes them available for download from iCloud, giving you an iCloud backup for all that ripped music — as long as you keep paying the $25 annual fee.

Apps and books

iCloud syncs apps and books purchased on other iOS devices or on your computer. If, for example, you buy an iPad app while using iTunes on your computer, iCloud automatically downloads it to your iPad. iCloud works the same for books. A book purchased in iBooks on your iPad also auto-downloads to your iPhone. Again, you have to enable this capability. Do so in the Store pane of the Settings app, the Apps and Books switches are set to On for this auto-downloading to occur. In iTunes on your computer, go to the Preferences dialog box's Store pane and make sure Apps and Books are checked.

iCloud storage

As you can see, you can do a lot with iCloud. An iCloud account is free and provides 5GB of storage. If you exceed the free 5GB, you can purchase additional storage: $20 per year brings your storage to 15GB, $40 per year brings it to 25GB, and $100 per year brings it to 55GB.

Setting up iCloud

Setting up iCloud is easy. When you set up a new iPad, one of the first promp is to enter your iCloud user data or set up an iCloud account. Based on all the additional functionality iCloud brings (even with the free 5GB account), I can't imagine why you wouldn't have an iCloud account.

Once the account is created, you can adjust your iCloud settings with the Settings app's iCloud pane, shown in Figure 5-1.

In this pane, you turn on (or off) syncing for the iCloud services, including mail, contacts, calendars, reminders (from the Reminders app covered in Chapter 19), bookmarks, notes, Photo Stream, documents and data, and Find My iPad (covered in Chapter 3). This pane also includes settings to set up the iCloud backu (covered in Chapter 1), add storage, and delete your iCloud account. There isn't much to operating iCloud. The point is for it to work in the background without a management on your part.

FIGURE 5-1

The iCloud settings

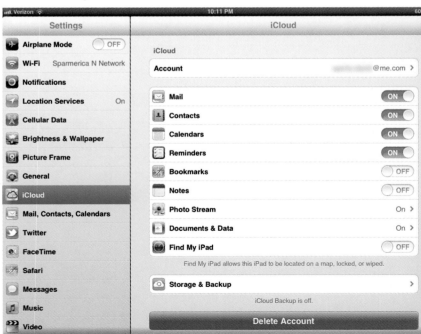

Dropbox

Dropbox is the reigning champ of online file-syncing services. In contrast with iCloud's app-based document syncing, Dropbox uses a file-based syncing model. With a free Dropbox account, you get 2GB of storage. (You can get more storage capacity if you pay for it: 50GB costs $10 per month and 100GB costs $20 per month.)

Your account includes a Dropbox folder accessible from your Mac, PC, iPad, and several other mobile devices. You can store any file you want in the Dropbox folder (or additional subfolders you create). Using this file-based syncing, you have control over what gets synced and where it is located.

A Dropbox account is just as essential to iPad users as an iCloud account. When the iPad was released, many of us were scratching our heads over exactly how we'd sync files to these shiny new iPads. Dropbox was at the forefront, having created a way for iPad app developers to easily access a user's Dropbox files from within their apps. This solved users' biggest gripe with the iPad, making it easy to get files on and off the device. App developers flocked to Dropbox and, as evidenced throughout this book, many of the best productivity apps use Dropbox as a file-sharing system.

There are two ways to use Dropbox on your iPad. The first is to access and save to your Dropbox storage from within your favorite Dropbox-enabled iPad apps. This method is covered throughout this book.

The second way to use Dropbox is through the Dropbox for iPad app (free), shown in Figure 5-2.

The Dropbox for iPad app features two panes. The left pane displays file lists from your Dropbox storage and the right pane displays the file contents. The bottom of the left pane includes the Dropbox, Favorites, Uploads, and Settings icon buttons, displayed a Figure 5-2.

Tap the Dropbox icon (the Dropbox logo) for the left pane to display your Dropbox contents. This gives you a complete view of all files saved in your Dropbox and any hierarchical folder structures.

The Favorites icon button (the star icon) filters your view to just the files you mark as favorites. You can mark a file as a favorite by tapping the Star icon button (it also looks like a star) in the upper-right corner of the right pane. When a file is marked as a favorite, its contents are downloaded and stored on the iPad's local flash memory so you can access it anywhere, even without an Internet connection. When I go on trips, I load PDF files of all my travel documents to my Dropbox storage and mark them as favorites. It allows me to quickly access necessary documents after I've just spent eight hours on a plane and am speaking with a cranky hotel employee.

Tap the Upload icon button (the folder icon) to upload pictures and video from your iPad to your Dropbox storage. Several of the screenshots for this book found their way to my Mac using this feature.

Finally, the Settings icon button (the gear icon) includes several Dropbox settings including upload quality, setting a separate passcode lock for the app, and the maximum size of local storage on your iPad for favorite files.

FIGURE 5-2

Dropbox for iPad

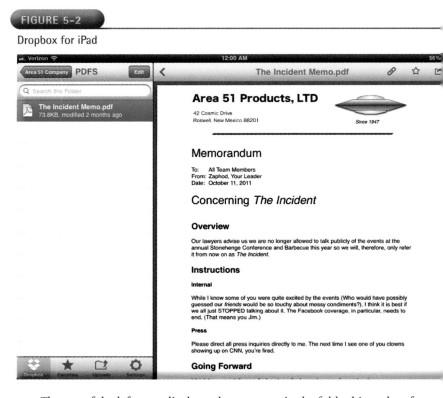

The top of the left pane displays where you are in the folder hierarchy of your Dropbox storage and an arrow button to move backward in the hierarchy. (For example, in Figure 5-2, I am in the PDFs folder and can move back to the Area 51 Company folder.) Tap the Edit button at the top of the left pane to delete files. Deleting a file from Dropbox on your iPad really deletes the file. It disappears from your Dropbox storage and all other computers connected to Dropbox. Finally, the top of the left pane includes a Search bar.

The right pane displays the selected file. Dropbox displays several file formats, including images, Microsoft Office documents, iWork documents, text files, and web pages. It even plays music and movie files.

The Link icon button (the icon of two chain links) at the top-right portion of the window provides a download link for a selected file. This is handy for sharing large files. For example, I often keep large PDF files with hundreds of pages in my Dropbox storage. These files are almost always larger than the e-mail download attachment limits so difficult to share with co-workers and clients. Using Dropbox I can send a link to the file and the recipient can download the file straight to her computer. I use this feature all the time. I upload large files to Dropbox for the sole purpose of sharing with download links.

The Open In icon button (the rectangle with an arrow emerging) is where the magic really happens in the Dropbox app. From the Open In menu, you can send your Dropbox uploaded files to any compatible app on your iPad.

CLOUD SECURITY

So how safe is your data in the cloud? It depends. The cloud services covered in this chapter all take security seriously. These companies understand that if you don't trust them, you will not do business with them. However, any data available on the Internet could be compromised. (This is true even for the data on that Internet-connected server sitting in a closet at your office.) Deciding to embrace cloud computing requires balancing its extraordinary convenience with its security risks. Take a close look at the security of your cloud service provider to make an informed decision. If your work requires absolute discretion, stay off the cloud entirely.

The Open In menu displays a few of the apps on your iPad that can open PDF files. Selecting any app from this list opens the app and loads the active Dropbox file into it. This feature gives you the ability to put any file into your Dropbox storage and inject it into your iPad workflows. Whether I'm sitting at my Mac, PC, or a friend's computer (Dropbox also has web access), I upload files to Dropbox all the time to get them into iPad apps.

Although Dropbox's usefulness is diminished with the arrival of iCloud, Dropbox still has features iCloud can't match. For one, Dropbox lets you open files in different apps, whereas iCloud keeps your files locked to a single app, as explained earlier. Dropbox also gives you more control over the files it stores and where they are located. For example, you couldn't keep a folder of travel-related documents in iCloud as I do with Dropbox.

Box.net

Box.net is another popular online collaboration tool similar to Dropbox. It allows you to securely upload and store your online files and folders using 256-bit encryption.

Box.net offers a free 5GB account for personal use, but Box.net is really aimed at businesses. Small businesses can set up a Box.net account for as little as $15 a month. There are also enterprise versions with advanced features, including file encryption and SharePoint-like file sharing and management for groups. Where Dropbox is best suited for a small office, Box.net is better suited for medium and large businesses with more need for security and file access control.

Box.net allows you to manage your files easily. You can create nested folders or even host your entire company file database on the Box.net server. You can then selectively set permissions for different users, such as edit, read only, or exclude from certain files. Using a business account, you can search the text in your Box.net files and access them from mobile devices such as the iPhone and iPad.

Once your files are located on the Box.net server, you can take advantage of several collaboration tools useful for business including commenting threads on

USING WEBDAV TO ACCESS DROPBOX

Although many apps adopted Dropbox integration, some do not. None of Apple's iWork apps (Pages, Numbers, and Keynote) use Dropbox storage. Neither do any of the Omni Group apps (OmniGraffle, OmniOutliner, and OmniGraphSketcher). Yet these are all great apps for which cloud storage would be useful. The good news is you can get to your Dropbox files in these apps with a little extra work.

The key is using WebDAV as an intermediary. WebDAV (Web-based Distributed Authoring and Versioning) is an Internet-based file-transfer protocol that lets users share and edit files from the web. Most computer platforms now support WebDAV, including the iPad. All the above-named non-Dropbox apps include WebDAV support.

Although Dropbox does not natively support the WebDAV protocol, there is a service called DropDAV that turns your Dropbox folder into a WebDAV account. Mixing Dropbox with WebDAV is something like mixing peanut butter with chocolate. Everything just gets better.

Setting up DropDAV is easy. Go to the DropDAV website and set up an account. DropDAV costs $5 per month. Once you've created your account, your Dropbox storage is accessible in any WebDAV-enabled iPad app. To access your storage, open the WebDAV option in your app and enter your DropDAV credential. That's it! Everything in your Dropbox storage is then available to your non-Dropbox iPad app.

documents and version histories. You can also set up tasks around specific files that all team members can review and update. Because Box.net tracks each team member who accesses its files, it can also send e-mail notifications when changes are made or if there is other activity in the Box.net account.

Box.net includes server administrative tools so you can manage user settings and permissions, manage passwords security, and get reports including an audit trail of all activity on any file in your Box.net storage. You can also customize the Box.net interface for your company account to reflect your company brand.

Box.net also has the Box iPad app (free), shown in Figure 5-3. The Box iPad app is similar to the Dropbox app, covered earlier. The left pane displays lists of files and the right pane displays file contents. Tabs across the top of the left pane provide filters to display the most recently updated, saved, or all files. The Manage button at the top of the left pane opens options to download the file for managing on your iPad while disconnected from the Internet. The bottom of the left pane includes the Refresh icon button (the clockwise spinning arrow) and the Settings icon button (the gear). Box.net settings include switches to cache recently viewed files on the iPad's local memory and setting a passcode lock.

In addition to displaying the selected file, the right pane also includes several icon buttons in the toolbar. The Full Screen icon button (a left-facing arrow) pushes the left pane off the window so the iPad can use its entire screen to display the selected file.

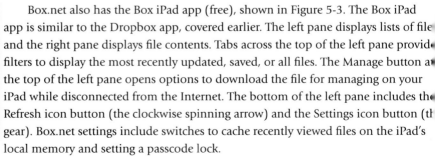

FIGURE 5-3

Box.net's iPad app

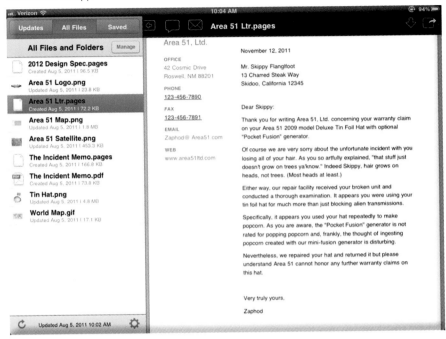

FIGURE 5-4

Using WebDAV with Box.net in Pages

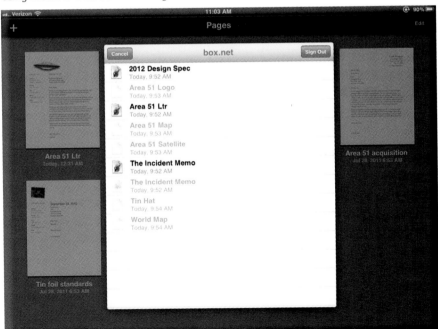

MY CLOUD WORKFLOW

I use and rely on both Dropbox and iCloud every day. Remembering the bad old days when syncing files required superhuman efforts, I revel in the ability to work on files on my iPad, Mac, PC, and iPhone without thinking twice. Moreover, having spent more time with Box.net preparing for this chapter, I'm seriously looking at the feasibility of dumping my business server and moving to Box.net for all my work files.

The Comment icon button (a cartoon bubble) lets you leave comments concerning the currently selected file that gets synced to Box.net for other team members. Dropbox does not have a commenting feature.

The Mail icon button (the envelope icon) mails a link to the selected file to e-mail recipients along with a message from you.

The Download icon button (the down-pointing arrow) downloads the active to the iPad's local storage so it may be accessed later without an Internet connectic

The Open In icon button (the rectangle with an arrow emerging) works just li the Dropbox Open In function (after all, Open In is a standard iOS feature). With you can send a file from your Box.net storage to any compatible app on your iPad.

Box.net makes WebDAV access even easier than Dropbox does. The Box.net WebDAV server is `http://box.net/dav`. Enter that URL along with your Box.n account name and password in your WebDAV-enabled app and you are in, as Figu 5-4 shows.

Although not as widely adopted as Dropbox, Box.net offers powerful cloud fi sharing features that make it ideally suited for businesses with multiple employees

We've come a long way since iPad's release and those early worries about returning to the sneakernet days. The iPad is now fully plugged into the cloud making file transfer, syncing, and storage a snap.

E-mail

The iPad *gets* e-mail. Using the iPad, you can check, process, and respond to e-mail from anywhere. Unlike most chapters in this book, there aren't a lot of alternative e-mail apps to Apple's built-in iPad mail client. Because the Apple Mail client is wound into the iOS operating system and most of the apps in this book, you really need to stick with it on the iPad.

Setting Up Mail Accounts

Before getting started with the Mail app, first you need to set up your e-mail accounts. Do this from the Mail, Contacts, Calendars pane of the Settings app, shown in Figure 6-1.

This pane shows a list of your online accounts (iCloud, Microsoft Exchange, and others) and a summary of what information they share with your iPad, such as calendars, contact lists, and e-mail.

To add a new account, tap Add Account to open the selection pane.

The iPad ships with built-in support for iCloud, Microsoft Exchange, Gmail, Yahoo, AOL, Hotmail, and MobileMe. If your mail account is with any of these mail services, tap the appropriate menu item and enter your account name and password. The iPad already knows the configuration details for these services and adds it automatically.

If your mail account is not with any of these services, tap Other, and then tap Add Mail Account on the New Account pane. Tap in your e-mail account details to have your iPad connect with the mail account. (If you are not sure about your e-mail account details, check with your e-mail service provider.) When you're done, you'll have a list of working accounts, as I do in Figure 6-1. The Mail, Contacts, Calendars pane also includes Mail's settings. I'll cover those later.

The iPad's Mail app

The Mail app, shown in Figure 6-2, includes two panes: The left pane includes the mail account and message lists and the right pane displays individual messages. (In portrait orientation, the left pane slides into view when you tap the All Inboxes button in the upper-left corner.)

The top of the left pane displays inboxes for all your accounts plus a single, unified inbox called, appropriately, All Inboxes. Tap All Inboxes to see all incoming e-mail from all accounts. Tap individual account inboxes to filter the inboxes to specific accounts.

When you tap an inbox, the list of inboxes slides out of view and the left pane instead displays a list of messages in the selected inbox. Figure 6-3 shows Mail displaying a list of messages in the left pane.

Tapping a message in the left pane displays the message contents in the right pane. (I cover this more later.) The message list in the left pane also adds a button to the top-left portion of the left pane, labeled MacSparky in Figure 6-3, that takes you back to higher folders or accounts. (In the case of Figure 6-3, tapping this button takes

FIGURE 6-1

The Mail, Contacts, Calendars pane

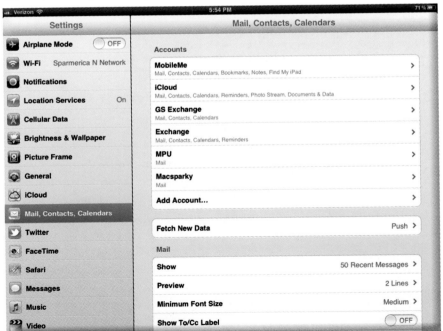

FIGURE 6-2

The iPad's Mail app

FIGURE 6-3

Displaying a list of e-mail messages in Mail

you back to the list of folders in the MacSparky e-mail account.) This method of navigating mail accounts works the same throughout the Mail app.

The bottom half of the left pane, shown in Figure 6-2, includes a list of e-mail accounts. Tapping any account opens a list of all its mailboxes along with its sent items and trash. For example, to see your sent items from your iCloud account, tap iCloud from the account list and then tap Sent. The left pane then shows a list of the cached e-mail messages sent from the iCloud account. (The iPad stores only a limited number of mail messages from your account, as configured in the Mail settings covered later.) From this left pane, you can access any folder from any of your e-mail accounts.

When displaying a message list in the left pane, Mail adds the Edit button to the left pane's toolbar. If you tap the Edit button, the message display alters. From the edit view, you can select multiple messages to delete, move, or mark them. (These actions are covered later.)

Mail adds a Search bar at the top of the left pane when displaying a message list, as shown in Figure 6-3. Tap the Search bar and type your search term. In addition to searching locally stored messages, Mail offers to search messages stored on the mail server.

THE POP AND IMAP E-MAIL PROTOCOLS

All e-mail is not created equal. The technology for managing and sending e-mail (called protocols) evolved over the years. POP and IMAP are the most common e-mail protocols. The POP (Post Office Protocol) e-mail sends your e-mail message to your computer and deletes it from the Internet server. This made a lot of sense when everyone used just one computer. All the messages came to one place, and you always had local access to all your mail. With the outbreak of e-mail capable devices, POP no longer works well: If your iPad pulls down an e-mail message from the server, your Mac won't see it. You'll end up with messages scattered separately across several devices.

The IMAP (Internet Mail Access Protocol) solves the POP problem. The idea behind IMAP is to keep the message on the server so it's available by any and all devices that check e-mail on that account. Because the server retains the e-mail, so every device you use can get that message — it's not deleted after the first device gets it, as in POP.

IMAP also synchronizes folders (POP does not). So, if you create an e-mail folder called Action on your iMac using an IMAP mail account, the IMAP server synchronizes that folder and its contents to your iPad. In addition to keeping your e-mail organized, IMAP synchronization helps you out with spam: Once you delete a spam e-mail on your iPad, it goes in the trash on the IMAP server, so you won't see it when checking e-mail on your other device

So use IMAP for your e-mail. Unless you check e-mail only on your iPad, the POP protocol will give you headaches. If your current e-mail services only offers the POP protocol, find a new one. A free iCloud account (covered in Chapter 5), for example, offers the IMAP protocol.

WORKING WITH WEB MAIL

Although there are no significant competing mail clients on the iPad, some e-mail services let you check your e-mail through the web browser. This generally works, as long as the web mail service doesn't use Adobe Flash or an antiquated web standard that the iPad doesn't support. The image below shows Gmail in the Safari browser.

But unless you can get your e-mail only through the browser, I don't recommend you do so. The Mail app is much easier to use, thanks to its iPad interface and fingertip-friendly buttons.

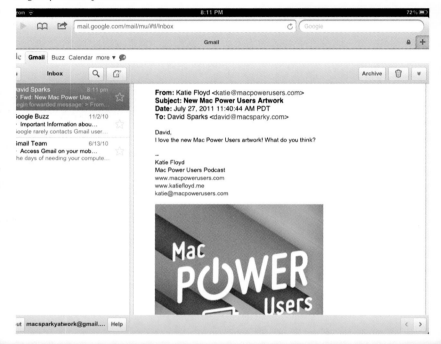

The bottom of the left pane displays the date and time of the last e-mail upda and the Refresh icon button (a clockwise circular arrow) to update your mail accounts.

The right pane displays the selected message. By default, the top of the messag displays just the name of the message sender. Tap Details in the upper-right corner the message, as shown in Figure 6-3, to see more information, including the messa recipients, and to flag a message (tap Mark), as shown in Figure 6-2. To remove the details, tap Hide in the upper-right corner of the message.

The iPad also uses the Mac's data detectors technology: Mail looks at an incoming message for dates and contact information, and then offers to add that data to your calendar and address book. For example, if a friend offers to take you to lunch on February 7, Mail underlines "February 7." Tapping "February 7" opens menu with options to create an event on that date, view that date in your calendar,

FIGURE 6-4

Creating a new message with Mail

and copy the date for pasting in other apps. Mail does the same with phone numbers, e-mail addresses, and physical addresses.

The right side of the right pane toolbar holds four icon buttons: Move, Trash, Reply, and Compose.

Tap the Move icon button (a folder with a down-pointing arrow) to move the selected message to a different mailbox.

The move window isolates the selected message (or messages, if you selected several using the left pane's Edit button covered earlier) and lists the folders in the current mail account. (You can move to another account's folders by tapping the account name button, which has the current account name, at the upper left of the window.) Tap a folder to have Mail run a fancy animation flinging the message into the folder. Mail then returns to the message display window shown in Figure 6-2.

To delete the current message or selected messages, tap the Trash icon button (the trash can). You can also delete a message by swiping across it in the left pane's message list.

The Reply icon button (a curved left-pointing arrow) opens a menu with options to reply, reply to all (if the selected message has multiple recipients), forward, and print the selected message. If you tap Reply, Reply All, or Forward, Mail opens a new message window with the contents of the selected message, ready for you to edit before sending.

The New Message icon button (a piece of paper with a pencil) opens the New Message window, shown in Figure 6-4.

The New Message window starts with the cursor in the recipient field. Start typing the name and Mail displays a list of possible matches using the iPad's Contacts app and recipients you've previously sent messages to from Mail; tap the appropriate entry. Alternatively, tap the Contact icon button (a blue circle with a + symbol) to select a name from the Contacts app. Finally, you can simply type in the full e-mail address; be sure to tap Return after each address you enter. Note that you can enter multiple names in the To field.

Use the Cc/Bcc From field to send the message to other recipients. "Cc" means carbon copy, an old-fashioned term that today simply means the recipient is getting a courtesy copy — an FYI, if you will. "Bcc" means blind carbon copy, a way of secretly sending the message (none of the To or Cc recipients can see who was Bcc'd). Tap the Cc/Bcc From field to have Mail display separate fields for Cc and Bcc recipients. Enter these recipients the same was as you do To recipients. (You can automatically Bcc yourself on all messages in the Settings app: Go to the Mail, Contacts, Calendars pane and turn on the Always Bcc Myself switch.)

If you have multiple e-mail accounts, you can select which to send the e-mail message from using the From field. (You set the default account in the Settings app's Mail, Contacts, Calendars pane using the Default Account option at the bottom of the pane.) To change the From account tap the From field and choose a different account from the menu that appears.

Next, fill in the Subject field and begin typing the body of your message. When done, tap the Send button.

Unfortunately, there is no way to add an attachment to a new e-mail message written in the Mail app. Instead, you have to create the message from the app that has the file you want to attach. For example, in the Photos app, you tap the Share icon button (the rectangle with an arrow emerging), select the photos you want to attach, click Share, and then choose Email to create an e-mail message with the selected photos. In Pages, you select tap the Tools icon menu (the wrench icon) and choose Share and Print ➪ Email Document to send the current document. The iPad uses techniques like these in many applications to send attachments.

When you type your message, you can format the text, such as to apply boldface or indent the text — if you're using iOS 5, that is. To apply formatting, select the text the usual way, then in the contextual menu, tap the More icon menu option (the right-facing triangle) for additional options, including one labeled "B*I*U" to open a new contextual menu with options for boldface, italics, and underline, and Quote Level to get a new contextual menu with options to decrease or increase the indentation.

Mail settings

To change the Mail app's settings, go to the Settings app's Mail, Contacts, Calendars pane (shown in Figure 6-1) and scroll down for the Mail settings, shown in Figure 6-5.

FIGURE 6-5

Mail's setting

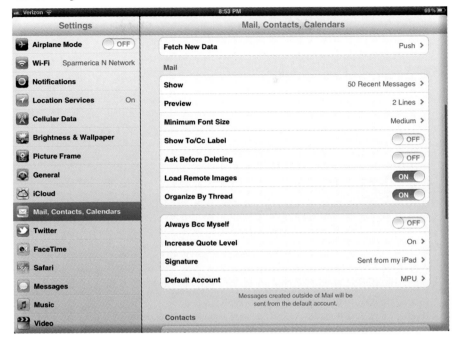

Tap Fetch New Data to change how your iPad receives mail. The Push option receives e-mail on your iPad as soon as it is sent; note that only some e-mail servers, such as Microsoft Exchange, support this method. For non-push-enabled accounts, you can set the iPad to just check for e-mail every 15, 30, or 60 minutes.

You can also have the iPad only check for new e-mail when you manually ask it to (by tapping the Refresh icon button at the bottom of Mail's left pane). Checking e-mail manually isn't a bad idea. If you are working on a deadline and don't want any interruptions, switch to manually checking your e-mail and get back to work. Telling your iPad to stop regularly checking for new e-mail also preserves battery life if you are running low.

Tap Show to change the number of messages stored in your Mail inboxes. This defaults at 50 messages but can be increased to as many as 1,000 messages.

Tap Preview to change the number of lines displayed in the left pane message preview. Mail lets you preview between zero and five lines.

Tap Minimum Font Size to change the size of the e-mail font.

There are also switches to show the To/CC label, ask before deleting, load images, and organize e-mails by thread. Threaded conversations keep related e-mails together in one group so you can easily find the original e-mail plus each subsequent reply.

If your e-mail workflow requires keeping copies of your e-mail, tap Always Bcc Myself.

Tap Increase Quote Level to indent quoted text when replying to an e-mail.

You can also change the default sending account by tapping Default Account. The Mail settings also permit you to change your e-mail signature. A signature i a bit of text that automatically goes at the bottom of every e-mail you send. Althoug Mail's default signature, "Sent from my iPad," probably helps sell iPads, it isn't a useful e-mail signature. (The only good reason I've ever heard for keeping that defau message is so people understand you are replying from a mobile device and your messages will be shorter and more typo-intensive than if written on a computer.)

Tap Signature to change your signature or delete it entirely. If you need multip signatures (such as one for each account), delete the default signature and instead up your multiple signatures as Apple shortcuts, covered in Chapter 2. Then insert t appropriate signature via a shortcut.

Corporate E-mail on the iPad

The iPad ships with Microsoft Exchange support baked in. To set up an Exchange account, type in your username and password and the iPad (usually) do the rest. (With some installations, you may need to add more server details.)

Your corporate IT department may further configure your iPad, as covered in Chapter 12, such as to enforce complex passwords and used certificate-based authentication.

Although Microsoft Exchange is the most popular corporate e-mail server, it's not the only one. IBM's Lotus Notes is widely used in large enterprises, while Attachmate's GroupWise is widely used in government agencies.

GroupWise's web access works through the Safari browser. Moreover, GW Mai ($6) is a native iPad GroupWise mail client. GroupWise has an additional product

FIRST THING WE DO,
KILL THE NOTIFICATION SOUND

An e-mail setting not found in the Mail, Contacts, Calendars pane but absolutely critical is turning off the new-mail notification sound. In the Settings app's General pane, tap Sounds, then tap New Mail and change the sound to None.

Perhaps because of my own failings, I am able to do only one thing at a time. I love to focus on a project and give it my full attention. That e-mail notification sound is my nemesis. Every time it goes off, I stop thinking about what I am doing and instead think about the amazing possibilities of that unread e-mail. Maybe I just won the lottery? Perhaps I got offered a new job? The curiosity simply consumes me. So of course, I go and check the e-mail, only to find out my digital water bill arrived. Then I have to go back to whatever I was doing and steer my rambunctious mind back toward the job at a hand.

And just about the time I get focused again, "Ding." You'll be shocked at how much more productive you are when you kill the new-mail notification.

MY E-MAIL WORKFLOW

I manage all my e-mail accounts (including Gmail accounts) using Apple's Mail app. Apple really nailed it with this app, and I find processing e-mail more enjoyable on my iPad than any of my other electronic gizmos. For processing my e-mail, I use the workflow described in this chapter. I've never used mail flags. Although they are great for some users, I just don't need them.

the Data Synchronizer Mobility Pack, that lets your IT department configure GroupWise e-mail to work in the iPad's native Mail app.

Likewise, IBM Lotus Notes Traveler Companion (free) is a Lotus Notes-friendly iPad client.

iPad E-mail Best Practices

There are many ways to manage e-mail. Some people get by just fine with 10,000 messages in their inbox, while others absolutely require a Byzantine collection of folders, subfolders, and subsubfolders to keep track of everything. On the iPad, where there are no smart folders like those found on the Mac and PC, I believe keeping your inbox clear for new mail is more important than ever.

Although I certainly don't claim to have all the answers for e-mail, I can share how I process e-mail on the iPad. For me, the mail inbox is like the postal mailbox outside my door. It is for new mail and nothing else. When I go through the inbox, I take four steps:

1. **I get rid of junk mail.** If a message is junk mail or a message I never need to see again, I trash it.

2. **If no response is required, I archive it.** If I get an e-mail thanking me for lunch and no reply is required, I send it to my Archive folder. Out of sight, out of mind.

3. **If the e-mail requires a quick response, I quickly respond.** When someone asks if I can meet him or her for breakfast the next morning, I reply. It just takes moment. After that, I send the original message to the archive.

4. **I set aside the other message for later.** If a message requires a reply but I don't have time for it, I move the message to my Action folder. Later I go back and answer those or create OmniFocus tasks to address them in the future.

If you read my workflow carefully, you noticed that I referenced only three mail locations: the inbox, the Action folder, and the Archive folder. Everything else goes to the trash. I just use three folders. I've never been unable to find a message. Besides, Mail's Search bar does a great job of ferreting out old e-mail.

7

Contacts

I n addition to bringing entirely new tools to the mobile worker's bag of tricks, the iPad also needed to nail the fundamentals. After spending at least $500 on this combination of silicon, glass, and aluminum, can you ditch your tattered old address book and Rolodex? It turns out you can. The iPad offers several ways to manage contacts starting with Apple's Contacts app.

Apple Contacts

The built-in Contacts app may be the beginning and the end of the contact management story for many iPad workers. Because Apple designed it, the app (and its data) is a core part of the operating system and is thus used by several Apple and third-party apps. Moreover, the app offers nearly ubiquitous syncing with the most common address book apps on the Mac and Windows PC.

Setting up Contacts accounts

Before using the Contacts app, first set up contact syncing. Open the iPad's Settings app and tap the Mail, Contacts, Calendars option in the Sidebar to get the Mail, Contacts, Calendars pane that displays a list of accounts along with their synced data. The Contacts app syncs data with several cloud-based calendaring services, including MobileMe, iCloud, Gmail, and Exchange. To add an account, tap the Add Account button. This displays the Add Account pane.

Choose the type of service you want to add and tap the appropriate button. Figure 7-1 shows the pane for adding a Microsoft Exchange account.

Repeat this step for all the accounts in which you keep contact data. If you use a service not shown in the list of providers, tap the Other button to open a pane where you enter the details of an LDAP or CardDAV account. The Contact app's syncing options cover most contact database formats in use; if you are using an older contact database format, it is time to update anyway. Move your contacts to one of the supported formats and sync up.

Contacts does not require that all your contact information be combined into a single database format. For example, you might have separate IMAP, iCloud, and Exchange accounts all syncing contact data. As explained in the next section, Contacts partitions your data so, for example, you can see all your work contacts from a Microsoft Exchange database in one group and all your personal contacts from an iCloud database in another. (For anarchists, Contacts includes a view that merges the separate databases' display.)

Using Contacts

The Contacts interface is remarkably Spartan. There are no toolbars and very few buttons. Instead Contacts is designed to resemble a traditional paper address book. Opening the app shows a list of accounts and contact groups. Contacts breaks down

FIGURE 7-1

Setting up an Exchange server account

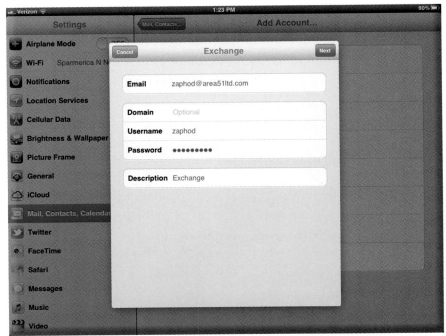

the contact groups by server, such as Exchange, iCloud, Yahoo, and Google contact lists.

Groups are a set of contacts created on your Mac or PC. Typical groups are Work and Personal, but you can go nuts. For example, when I have a business trip or speaking engagement, I create a group just for the trip and name it after the trip, such as "Macworld 2012." Then I put all related contacts, hotels, and restaurants in it so I can find them quickly on the trip. Afterward, I delete the group. (Deleting a group does not delete the associated contacts.)

You cannot create groups on the iPad. Instead, create them on your Mac or Windows PC; they automatically sync to your iPad. (Smart groups created with Ma

WHAT ABOUT GOOGLE CONTACTS?

Although the iPad can easily sync a Gmail account, it has no built-in support for Google Contacts. To sync your Google Contacts with an iPad, you need to sync the contacts to your Mac's Address Book contact list or Windows PC's Outlook contact list (through iTunes or iCloud), which then syncs the contacts to your iPad.

Alternatively, you can take advantages of Google Sync, Google's Exchange server for Google accounts. Google Sync uses Microsoft's ActiveSync technology to sync Google calendars, mail, and contacts. Google Sync turns Google's services into a Microsoft Exchange server.

Set up Google Sync by creating a new Exchange account (as described earlier in this chapter) with the Exchange server name, m.google.com. The full settings are shown below. Once complete, Google Contacts sync directly to your iPad.

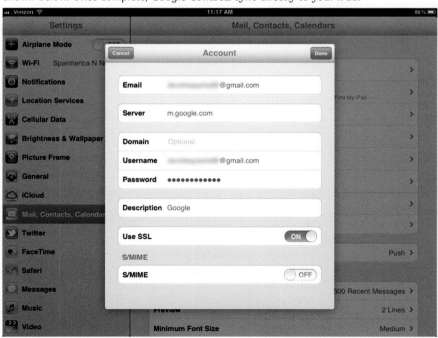

CAPTURING BUSINESS CARDS

Even though we live in the age of the iPad, we still share a bit of analog technology: the business card. Depending on which industry you work in, you may come across a few or a few hundred of these every week. Capturing business card information in your digital workflow is tedious. Typing in a new contact's name, title, company, address, and multitude of phone numbers and e-mail addresses takes a lot of time. Why not have your iPad do that for you?

There are several business card reader apps in the App Store. Most of them are built for the iPhone. (This is due to the higher-quality camera in the iPhone and the iPod Touch.) My favorite app for capturing business card data is CardMunch (free). Developed by popular business networking site LinkedIn, CardMunch takes a picture of the card with the iPad 2's built-in camera (or looks at a picture imported into your original iPad) and uploads it to the CardMunch service where real people, not computer algorithms, look at the card and manually type in the contact data for you. CardMunch then sends back the contact data to the app, which gives you options to add the contact data to your LinkedIn account or to the Contacts app. The whole process takes about five minutes.

Although this is an iPhone app (there is no native iPad version yet), CardMunch was the most accurate of all business card apps I tested. Now when I attend a convention or conference, I take pictures of all the business cards and let CardMunch input the data while I throw the cards away at the hotel.

OS X's Address Book, however, do not sync to the iPad.) Select a group in Contacts on the iPad to have Contacts display the group.

In this view, the left page shows an alphabetical list of all contacts in the group. If this list exceeds the page length, scroll up or down or use the alphabet tabs along the left side of the page.

The right page shows the contact details for the selected contact. By default, this view just shows fields that contain data. For example, the birthday field does not appear unless the contact has a birthday associated to it.

To add data to a contact, tap the Edit button. This displays the pane shown in Figure 7-2. Tap on a field to make changes or additions. To add a field, such as Phonetic Last Name, scroll to the bottom of the window and tap the Add Field button (not shown in Figure 7-2).

While editing a contact, you can also link two cards. This is useful if you have the same contact in, say, an Exchange address book (with the contact's work information) and your iCloud address book (with the contact's personal residence information). Linking two cards combines all the information into one card viewable in both accounts.

When your contact edits are complete, tap the Done button in the upper-right corner of the right page, and Contacts exits the edit view.

FIGURE 7-2

Editing a contact

FIGURE 7-3

Adding a new contact

MY CONTACTS WORKFLOW

I rely heavily on the Contacts app every day. I currently sync Microsoft Exchange, MobileMe, and iCloud contact databases with the app. I use the card-linking feature described in this chapter because many of my professional and personal contacts often end up merging. I constantly look up information in the Contacts database as I go through my day. Moreover, I use the Contact's Notes field to keep further details and notes on contacts that sync among all my devices automatically. In this sense, I use the Notes field as a sort of poor man's CRM system. Because everything syncs flawlessly with my iPhone and Mac, managing contacts and finding contact data is not a problem.

If you are a Twitter user, go to the Twitter pane in the Settings app and tap the Update Contacts button. Your iPad then uses the e-mail addresses and phone numbers from your Contacts data to automatically add Twitter names and photos to your contact lists.

A contact also includes buttons (which may be off the screen, so you may need to scroll to see them) to make a FaceTime video call to a contact, share a contact, or add a contact to your Favorites list. Tap the FaceTime button to open the FaceTime app (covered in Chapter 9) and initiate a FaceTime call. Tap the Share Contact button to open a blank e-mail with the active contact's information attached. (Normally, you do not need permission to share contacts. If you are connected to certain Exchange networks, however, permission to share may be required.)

The Add to Favorites button adds the selected contact to the Favorites list in the iPhone's phone app and the iPad's FaceTime app, covered in Chapter 9.

To add a new contact, tap the New Contact icon button (the + symbol) at the bottom-right corner of the left page to open the New Contact pane, shown in Figure 7-3. (Adding a new contact while viewing a specific group places that new contact in the active group.)

Although there are no settings in the Contacts app, there are settings for it in the Mail, Contacts, Calendars pane of the Settings app. There, you can change the sort and display order (using first name instead of last name), designate your default contact information, and set the default account for new contacts.

There are many good reasons to stick with the Apple Contacts app. It syncs with most common contact database formats and is integrated throughout iOS. As a result, any app that needs access to your contact database looks at Contact's data. Apple detractors often complain that using an Apple device requires you to work within Apple's "walled garden." There is some truth to this. But with Contacts, at least, this is a good thing. Because the hardware and the software talk to one another, using Apple's ecosystem for your key data makes a lot of sense.

Working with CRM on the iPad

Some iPad workers keep their contact data in a format not compatible with the built-in Contacts app. There were a lot more of these excluded users in earlier iterations of iOS. But at this point, iOS supports most contact database types, including Microsoft Exchange. As a result, most workers get by fine with the Contacts app.

Perhaps the biggest exception that remains is anyone that uses a customer relationship management (CRM) application. These applications track contacts, leads, and other tools to work with clients. They go beyond mere contact management to include tools to follow up on sales leads, track existing transactions, and better manage customer relations.

Two of the biggest providers in this space are Salesforce.com and 37signals' Highrise. Both services are web-based and do not involve installation of software on your iPad (or Mac or Windows PC). Both services have iPhone apps but not iPad apps.

There is, however, a third-party app for Salesforce.com, the free SlidePad HD.

In both cases, the developers of Salesforce.com and Highrise customized their websites so they display nicely on the iPad's Safari browser. Figure 7-4 displays Highrise in iPad Safari. Pricing varies on the number of users and level of service; the cost of each starts at about $25 a month.

FIGURE 7-4

Highrise in the iPad's Safari browser

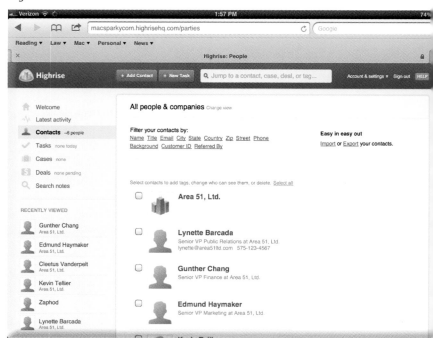

Both services also feature the ability to sync contacts with Microsoft Outlook and Apple's Address Book so you can view your contact data in the iPad's Contacts app as well.

Calendars

Just as Chapter 7 explained how to replace your paper address book with your iPad, this chapter explains why that paper desk calendar is a thing of the past. An electronic calendar has many advantages over a paper one. Because it is digital, you can share your calendar data between all your electronic gizmos. Moreover, you can share your calendar data with co-workers so they can view, edit, and add calendar events for you (assuming you let them). You can also back up electronic calendars so you know the data is safe. If the cleaning people accidently throw away that paper calendar on your desk, you are in trouble. The iPad's portability, combined with its large screen size (in comparison with a smartphone), put the iPad in that sweet spot which is perfect for calendar management. This chapter covers how to manage your calendar with your iPad.

Linking Your Calendar Data

Before working with the calendar apps on the iPad, you first need to tell the iPad where to find your calendar data. You do this the same way you identify contact data, as described in Chapter 7: Go to the Mail, Contacts, Calendars pane of the Settings app and create accounts for all services that provide you calendar data.

The iPad ships with built-in support for iCloud, Microsoft Exchange, and other calendar servers. Additionally, you can add subscribed calendars or any CalDAV account. To sync your Google Calendars account, use the Google Sync service, which shares your data through a virtual Microsoft Exchange server. (I describe how to set up a Google Sync server in Chapter 7.) Once you set up your calendar accounts, your calendar data is available to your iPad calendar apps. With CalDAV and Exchange support, you can sync most calendars with your iPad.

Apple Calendar

The iPad ships with Apple's Calendar app on every new iPad. Like the Contacts app covered in Chapter 7, designed to resemble a traditional address book, Apple's Calendar app resembles a traditional desk calendar. Shown in Figure 8-1, the Calendar app user interface that includes a top toolbar with a simulated leather border, date selection tools along the bottom, and a calendar in the center of the screen. A close examination of the top of the monthly calendar discloses the small bits of torn paper you would find on a traditional desktop calendar. (I always made a point of removing these bits of paper when I used a desk calendar and the inability to remove them from Calendar on my iPad makes me a little nuts.) This practice of copying a real-world object, called *skeuomorphic design*, is a recent trend from Apple showing up in iOS and Mac OS X 10.7 Lion.

The Calendar app toolbar

The Calendar app's skeuomorphic leather binding holds several buttons. The Calendar button (on the far left) opens the Show Calendars popover, shown later in Figure 8-3.

The Show Calendars popover displays each calendar your iPad sees from all the calendar syncing servers you've added. Tap each calendar you want to display. Although this may seem at first a "set and forget" popover, it is not. I use this popover all the time to filter my calendar view. When I'm going on vacation, I turn off the office calendar. Although I sync calendars with my wife and kids, I often keep their calendars turned off. Likewise, although I subscribe to several Internet-based calendars (like geek holidays), I don't usually keep them visible on my iPad.

Tap the Edit button in the Calendars popover to add calendars and change the display color for your calendar. Using contrasting colors for personal and work related tasks helps setting appointments and organizing your life.

WHAT IS THIS CALDAV?

CalDAV (which stands for Calendar Extensions to WebDAV) is an Internet standard that enables access to scheduling data on a centralized remote server. Because the calendaring data is on a server, multiple users can access the data. CalDAV lets users easily send invitations and share calendar data. Apple adopted CalDAV in Mac OS X 10.5 Leopard and made it the standard for its MobileMe service (which later became iCloud). Apple isn't alone. Many calendar services use the CalDAV standard. With respect to calendar data, standardization is a good thing.

The Invitations icon button (it looks like an inbox), next to the Calendar button, manages calendar invitations; I cover invitations later.

The top-right portion of the Calendar toolbar holds the Search bar. This is useful to filter your calendar to show just appointments related to a specific topic. an example, if I want to see my trial calendar, I type the word `trial` in the Search bar. The Search bar then opens a popover with a list of all events containing the word "trial."

Calendar views

The remaining buttons set the calendar display mode. Calendar includes five views: day, week, month, year, and list.

Day view

The day view, shown in Figure 8-1, displays two pages with the current date, a small monthly calendar, and a list of the selected day's events on the left page. The right page displays all the day's events against a time line.

There is a selection bar at the bottom of the day view listing each day of the current month and buttons for the months before and after the currently selected month. Tap any date in the selection bar to move the day view to that date. The Today button in the lower-left corner of the window selects the current date. Tap th New Event icon button (the + symbol) at the bottom-right portion of the window add a new event. New events are covered later in this chapter.

Tap and hold an event on the right page time line and drag the event up and down on the time line to move it. Alternatively, tap an event to open the Edit popove shown in Figure 8-2. Edit the event properties in the popover. You can change the length of an event by tapping and holding the event handles (small circles) at the top right and bottom-left portions of the event, also shown in Figure 8-2.

Week view

The week view, shown in Figure 8-3, shows the week in a grid-style format, wit each event appearing as a rectangle representing its length of time. This view is grea for finding overlapping events and blocks of open time. Tap an event to open the Event popover. To move an event, tap and hold it and drag it to its new location. I often spend part of my Monday morning moving events around the calendar.

The selection bar at the bottom of the week view displays links to the last two weeks and next seven weeks.

Month view

Month view displays the active month with one-line entries for each event. Ea event has a circle next to it with the color of its calendar.

Tapping an event in the month view opens a popover with further details and an Edit button, which opens the Edit popover for the event. To move an event, tap

FIGURE 8-1

Calendar's day view

FIGURE 8-2

Editing an event in day view

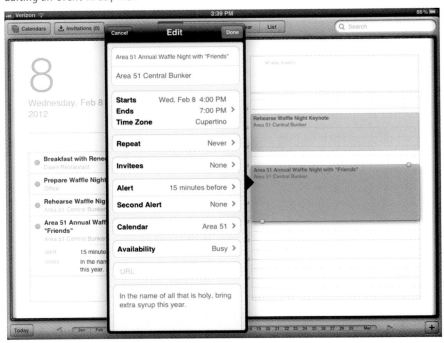

CALENDAR PRINTING

Neither Apple's Calendar nor MiCal include printing support. If your workflow requires you to print your calendar, use CalPrint for iPad ($7). CalPrint is a full-featured calendar app, letting you edit and view your calendar items. CalPrint really shines, however, with its ability to print your calendar to your iOS-attached printers with daily, weekly, monthly, and list formats.

and hold and then drag the event to a different date. When you move an event in month view, the start time and duration remain the same at the event's new date. You must open the Edit popover or switch to day or week views to change those properties.

The selection bar at the bottom of the month view displays six prior and futur months for quick navigation.

FIGURE 8-3

Calendar's week view, with the Show Calendar popover

FIGURE 8-4

Calendar's year view

FIGURE 8-5

Calendar's list view

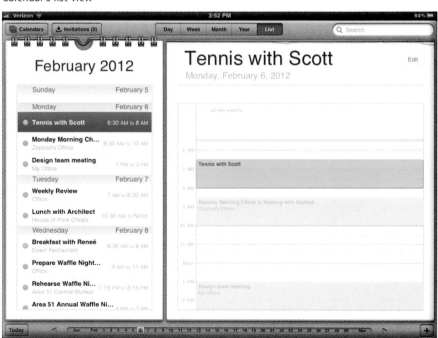

SET A MEETING WITH DOODLE

An age-old problem is scheduling a meeting with multiple participants. Every additional person invited to a meeting increases the difficulty in setting that meeting. Fortunately, the solution to this problem lies on the Internet: Use Doodle.com. Doodle is an iPad Safari-friendly website that lets you set a meeting with a group of people. You select available dates and times and Doodle sends a link to all participants (or gives you a link to send in your e-mail). The meeting participants go to Doodle and list their preference for the dates and times you propose. Once everyone has Doodled, you'll know exactly when to schedule the meeting. Doodle is a free service, but there is a premium option available with additional encryption and branding features.

Year view

The year view, shown in Figure 8-4, shows all months in the active calendar ye Each day's availability is indicated via color: There are no appointments on white days, and the color shifts to yellow, orange, and red for increasingly busy days. Tap the day in the year view to jump to day view and get further details.

The selection bar at the bottom of the year view displays links to the past two years and several years into the future.

List view

List view, shown in Figure 8-5, removes the calendar from the screen and instead provides a two-pane view with a list of all upcoming events in chronologi order in the left pane and a daily calendar in the right pane. Tapping a future (or past) date on the selection bar at the bottom of the window advances the left pan chronology and right pane's daily view appropriately. I use list view for a quick wa to see my appointments for the next several days.

Adding events

To add an event, tap the Add Event icon button (the + symbol) in the lower-rig corner of the window. This opens the Add Event popover, shown in Figure 8-6.

When adding an event, Calendar includes fields for the event title, location, s and end times, repeat frequency, invitees, alerts, calendar selection, URL, and note (These options vary based on the calendar you're using, because Exchange, CalDA Google Calendar, and so on offer different event parameters, and the iPad's iOS adjusts its options accordingly.) The Alert button opens a pane with options to ad alerts to your event.

Calendar includes full support for Calendar invitations. Tap the Invitees butto to add people to your event. Tap the Add icon button (the + symbol in the blue circle) in the Invitees pane to add people from your iPad's contact database — or just type in an e-mail address and tap the spacebar. When you finish creating the

FIGURE 8-6

Adding an event to Calendar

event, your iPad sends out e-mail invitations to the invitees. Calendar keeps track of confirmations and even provides the current status when you tap the Invitations icon button in the Calendar toolbar.

Calendar settings

There is no Settings button in the Calendar app. Instead, Apple added Calendar settings to the Mail, Contacts, Calendars pane of the Settings app.

The Calendar settings include a switch to turn on new invitation alerts. There is a setting for the number of prior events synced to your iPad, ranging from the last two weeks to all prior events. (Naturally, all future events always sync.) Turn on Time Zone Support if you travel outside your time zone. There are also settings for the default alert time and new event default calendar. Calendar lets you set different default alert times for birthdays, events, and all-day events.

MiCal HD

Apple isn't the only software developer for the iPad. If you don't care for Apple's Calendar app, try MiCal HD ($3). Shown in Figure 8-7, MiCal HD simulates the day planner of old (not unlike ToDo's task lists in Chapter 19).

MiCal HD's left pane shows the current date and time along with a list of the current day's events and upcoming birthdays. This view doesn't change, so you always know the current date, time, and the day's events no matter which view you are in. You can display additional days in the left pane via the Settings popover (covered later).

The right side of the screen displays day, week, month, year, or list views. To change views, tap the buttons across the bottom of the window labeled, appropriately, 1 (for day view), 7 (for week view), 31 (for month view), and 365 (f year view), as shown in Figure 8-7. From any view, a tap on any blank space of the calendar takes MiCal to the day view.

The list view displays a list of all events over the coming days along with color dots for their associated calendars.

Tap the Add Event icon button (the + symbol) in the lower-right corner to add a new event. This opens the Add Event popover, which includes several innovative features. For example, tapping the Title field opens several options, including a history of recently created events and a list of favorites such as "meeting," "call," and "appointment." Although you can add contacts to a new event, MiCal does no create CalDAV invitations as Apple's Calendars app does.

The Menu icon button (a rectangle with an arrow emerging) opens a menu wi Help, Calendar, Weather, Settings, and Birthdays option.

The Help menu option provides tips for using MiCal HD.

The Calendar menu option works similar to the calendar selection button in Apple's Calendar app: It opens a popover with options to select (and deselect)

FIGURE 8-7

MiCal HD's calendar replacement

calendars for display. MiCal can change the color of Microsoft Exchange-based calendars.

Tap the Weather menu option to add a weather report for your local area to the calendar.

Tap the Settings menu option to look under the hood. MiCal's Settings popover is one of those special popovers that cause nerds to dance with glee. The popover seems to scroll on forever. There are settings to tweak just about everything about MiCal, from the default meeting length (as short as five minutes) to the alarm tone for birthday reminders (including two versions of "Happy Birthday"). If you feel constrained by Apple's Calendar app, you'll feel right at home with MiCal.

COMBINE CALENDARS AND TASKS

If you are not happy with Apple's Calendar app and the task management tools in Chapter 19 aren't cutting the mustard, take a look at Pocket Informant HD ($15). Pocket Informant is a combination calendar and task management application. Shown below, Pocket Informant is a full-featured calendar and task management system (including some advanced "get things done" [GTD] task tools).

MY CALENDAR WORKFLOW

I was impressed with MiCal while researching this book but for my daily calendar routine, I use Calendar for iPad. Every Monday morning I open Calendar in week view and review my appointments. I also create events that are, in essence, appointments with myself for important research projects. The rest of the week, I spend my time jumping between the different Calendar views as required. I like Calendar so much that I use it nearly exclusively and rarely open iCal on my Mac. I also use Doodle constantly to set meetings.

The Birthdays menu option shows a list of all contacts with upcoming birthda and the number of days before you go from being Johnny-on-the-spot to that deadbeat who forgot your beloved's birthday, again.

The Today icon button (the analog clock icon) returns MiCal to the current da The Go To icon button (the pointing hand icon) opens the iOS date picker to jum to a specific date.

MiCal nails several details that Apple's Calendar app misses. Although it lacks some features found in Calendar (like CalDAV invitations), MiCal is a credible alternative to Calendar.

9

Video Conferencing and Messaging

E-mail is not the only way to communicate with co-workers and clients. We live in the digital age, and messaging and video conferencing are quickly transitioning from "strange and unfamiliar technology" to practical business tool in the workplace. This chapter covers some of the best messaging and video conferencing tools on the iPad.

Video Conferencing

A meeting used to require driving across town (or flying across the country), but using video conferencing technologies, you can virtually attend a meeting from your home or office. With the arrival of iPad 2 and its built-in cameras, app developers were quick to adopt this technology for video conferencing.

Although some of the apps mentioned in this chapter work on an original iPad, its lack of a built-in camera limits its usefulness for this conferencing (usually you can participate only via audio). If you intend to video-conference with an iPad, get an iPad 2.

FaceTime

Apple's FaceTime app ships on every new iPad 2. Shown in Figure 9-1, the FaceTime interface is nearly nonexistent. There is no toolbar. Instead, when you launch the app you see a preview from your camera and a list of available contacts. There are three icon buttons along the bottom of the contacts window for, from left to right, Favorites, Recents, and Contacts.

To initiate a call, find a co-worker or colleague on your list and tap the listing. The contact window then shows the details for that person. Tap his or her e-mail address and FaceTime initiates the FaceTime call. After your co-worker or colleague accepts the call, FaceTime displays him or her on your screen, as shown in Figure 9-1. A small, inset preview window shows what your camera is displaying to the other party.

There are few controls while making a FaceTime call. You can move your preview window to any corner of the screen by tapping and holding the preview and dragging it to the desired corner. The Mute icon button (the icon of a microphone with a diagonal line) mutes your voice, and the Camera icon button (the video camera icon) toggles between the iPad 2's front and rear cameras. The End button ends the call.

FaceTime's biggest limitation is that it works only on Macs and FaceTime-enabled iOS devices: the iPad 2, recent iPhones, and recent versions of the iPod Touch. Apple explained when it announced FaceTime that it was going to be an open standard and available for other platforms but, as of this writing, no other developers have adopted it. If your co-workers are on a PC or Android smartphone, FaceTime won't work as a video-conferencing tool.

Another FaceTime limitation is that you can use it with only one person at a time; you cannot have meetings with multiple participants. Finally, FaceTime works only over Wi-Fi connections. You cannot participate in a call using a 3G connection.

FIGURE 9-1

A video conference with FaceTime

Conferencing services

Several major meeting and conference providers act as hosts for electronic meetings, quickly releasing iPad client apps for their services. The best three are GoToMeeting, WebEx, and Fuze Meeting. It is a good idea to have all three on your iPad (all these client apps are free) so you are ready to attend any electronic meeting no matter the host.

The interface for each of these apps is simple: Tap in your account or meeting identification number to be added to the meeting — it's just like logging in from your Mac or PC. The distinction among these apps is not so much the app interface but the conferencing service.

GoToMeeting

GoToMeeting (free) is my favorite conferencing app. It is, in my experience, the most stable and widely adopted service. Many companies use it and, to use an Apple phrase, "it just works."

The GoToMeeting service has a $49 monthly fee for unlimited meetings, with as many as 15 attendees. You do not, however, need to be a subscriber to attend a GoToMeeting meeting, just to host them. The subscription allows you to set up meetings.

WebEx

Cisco Systems' WebEx (free) is similar to GoToMeeting, with monthly plans starting at $49. WebEx has more features than GoToMeeting, such as the ability to use multiple cameras and have as many 25 attendees per session. But with these additional features comes additional hardware and bandwidth requirements that can make WebEx less reliable than GoToMeeting, especially over a 3G connection.

Fuze Meeting

Fuze Meeting (free) is a relative newcomer to the iPad. Fuze Meeting's forte is the ability to host large media assets on Fuze's servers. If you are in a video conference that requires everyone to watch HD video, Fuze Meeting is the answer. The monthly service starts at $29 a month, with as many as 25 as attendees. For occasional use, you can also sign up for Fuze Meeting for $10 per day.

The iPad as a Telephone

In addition to video conferencing and meetings, the iPad can serve as a telephone in a pinch. There are two platforms for making calls with your iPad: Skype and Google Voice.

MY VIDEO-CONFERENCING WORKFLOW

When you write books about Apple technology, the people around you often end up buying Apple technology. As a result, I take advantage of FaceTime and iMessage with many of my colleagues, friends, and family. For multiperson meetings, I've never had a problem using GoToMeeting and, whenever I choose to use that service. I also use Skype on my iPad, especially on trips, to manage details and contacts.

Skype

The Skype (free) Internet telephony service enjoys global adoption, with millions of users. Although Skype got its start on the Mac and PC, it didn't take long for Skype to find its way to iOS.

The primary Skype interface shows a list of your contacts and call history. The New Contact icon button in the upper-right corner (the + symbol) opens a pane with options to search the Skype user directory, add a phone number, and import a contact from your iPad address book. The Call icon button (a dial pad with a phone headset on top in the upper-right corner of the window) opens a traditional telephone dial pad, which you use to dial phone numbers you want to connect to. Dialing actual phone numbers costs money, usually a few cents per minute, so you

FIGURE 9-2

Skype on the iPad

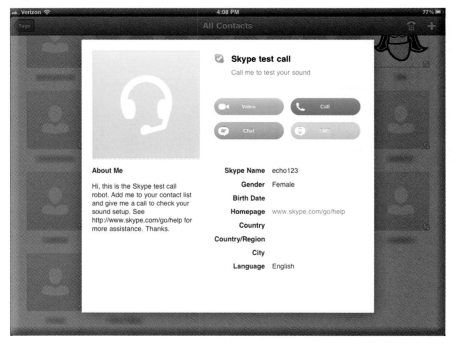

must have an account set up with Skype that is preloaded with at least $10. Skype provides an easy way to get cheap international calls when traveling — just find a Wi-Fi hot spot and place your call. The call quality improves if you use headphone with a built-in microphone rather than the iPad's microphone.

Tap on a Contact for options to initiate a video chat, audio call, text chat, or SMS message. With an iPad 2, the video chat uses the built-in cameras.

Google Voice

Google has its own Internet telephony service, which comes as part of your Google account, called Google Voice. (Google Voice currently only works in the United States, though you can call abroad from it.) Although Google has a Google Voice app in the iOS app store, as of this writing there is not a native iPad version.

Instead, download GV Connect ($3), an iPad-friendly app for managing your Google Voice account.

Google Voice does not let you initiate calls from your Google account in iPad Safari. (GV Connect can't initiate calls, either.) Talkatone (free), however, does support initiating calls with your iPad, and it works with GV Connect. (Enable the call using Talkatone in GV Connect's settings.) Although the process of using two separate apps to get a function from a Google service is messy, it does work.

FIGURE 9-3

iMessage for iPad

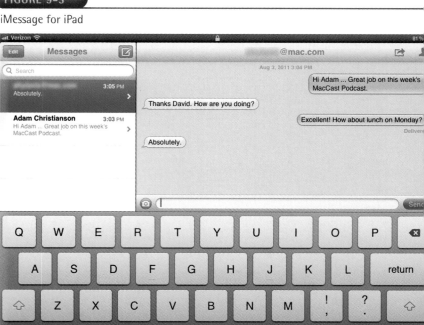

Messaging

With iOS 5, Apple released iMessage for iPad, shown in Figure 9-3. iMessage is not a new app to the iOS platform: It was one of the built-in apps on the first iPhone. The reason iMessage never found its way to the iPad or iPod Touch is because those devices had never been tied to a cellular telephone carrier. Without a cellular phone network, you can't send text messages, so there was no need for iMessage — until now.

With iOS 5, Apple created its own messaging network and extended iMessage to the iPad and iPod Touch. iMessage is a nice improvement over traditional text messaging. First, it helps you avoid getting gouged by your cellular phone carriers' SMS fees. Apple hosts the messaging system, and there is no fee to send iMessage.

iMessage also includes features not available with standard text messaging services. iMessage includes delivery receipts, informing you when your message is delivered. iMessage also supports live typing, which lets you see your friends and colleagues' typing as they draft messages. The downside of iMessage is that it works only with iOS devices, so if you want to send a message to your friend on his or her Android smartphone, you're out of luck.

To send text messages to someone not using an iOS device, try TextNow (free). The TextNow service lets you send and receive SMS messages to any SMS-enabled cell phone.

10

Remote Access

The iPad is so light and portable that it just begs you to leave your laptop at home. Unfortunately, the iPad also has its limitations. Using remote access apps, you can have your cake and eat it too. These apps access your Mac or Windows PC remotely from your iPad as if you were sitting at your computer. When you combine remote access with a Bluetooth keyboard, you'll be shocked at how easy it is to get that desktop computer experience on your iPad. This chapter covers some of the best options for getting remote access to your Mac or PC from your iPad.

LogMeIn Ignition

LogMeIn Ignition ($30) is my favorite remote access app for the iPad. LogMeIn works with Macs and Windows PCs. Whether you are running a macro-heavy Excel spreadsheet or a proprietary accounting package, LogMeIn makes it easy to get into your Mac or PC and get work done from your iPad.

For a remote connection to work, there needs to be a reliable handshake between the iPad and the computer. Specifically, the remote computer needs to know that the iPad knocking on the door is a friendly visitor and not an information burglar. LogMeIn Ignition takes the work out of this process by orchestrating the handshake from its own servers.

There are few steps to setting up LogMeIn. Download the app to your iPad (from the App Store), and download the PC client software (from www.logmein.com) on your Mac or Windows PC (or both). Then sign up for a

free LogMeIn.com account. Finally, add your new account details to the iPad, Mac, and Windows PC LogMeIn apps and you are done.

Once you enter your password in LogMeIn Ignition, the app displays the My Computers pane, shown in Figure 10-1. Computers online and available for connection appear with a blue monitor, as shown with the iMac and Office PC in Figure 10-1. Offline computers appear with the power button icon, shown with the MacBook Air in Figure 10-1. (For the connection to work, the remote computer needs to be powered up, and the local LogMeIn host software needs to be running.)

The Settings icon button (the gear icon) in the upper-left corner opens a popover with options to adjust and clear credentials, remove the display of offline computers, and adjust other connection settings for LogMeIn Ignition. The Screen Selection icon button (two overlapping screens with 2 on the top window), shown in Figure 10-1 in the upper-right corner, displays a list of available panes, letting you switch between the My Computers pane to other displays available in LogMeIn Ignition, including the Screen Sharing and File Sharing panes.

Tap an active computer to select it. LogMeIn Ignition slides in three icon buttons on the right side of the selected computer, shown with the iMac in Figure 10-1. The Screen Sharing icon button (the monitor with a mouse pointer) initiates a screen-sharing session with the selected computer, letting you see and control the remote computer as if you were sitting at it. The File Sharing icon button (two stacked pieces of paper) opens the file-sharing window, covered later, that lets you manipulate files

FIGURE 10-1

LogMeIn Ignition's My Computers window

on the remotely controlled computer without screen sharing. The Info icon button (the letter *i* in a circle) displays the connection details of the selected computer.

To begin a screen-sharing session, tap the Screen Sharing icon button; LogMeIn Ignition does the rest. Figure 10-2 shows LogMeIn Ignition remotely operating a Mac. The iPad screen mirrors the remote computer's screen. The blue toolbar along the bottom of the window contains several tools. The Keyboard icon button (the small keyboard) opens the iPad's onscreen keyboard. There is an additional row of virtual keys along the top of the keyboard, including Shift, Ctrl, Alt, and Command (⌘). (When screen-sharing with a Windows PC, the Windows key (⊞) replaces the Command key.) The Combo icon button (three boxes stacked in a pyramid) displays key combinations, including Command+Tab and Command+Shift.

The Mouse icon button (it looks like a mouse) alternates between left and right mouse button clicks, and the Magnification icon button (the magnifying glass) alternatively zooms in and out of the remote computer. The Settings icon button (the gear icon) opens the screen-sharing settings, including color quality, screen resolution, network speed, and mouse scroll settings.

You operate the remote computer using gestures. Tap and hold the screen and move your finger around to move the pointer. Use the pinch and expand gestures to zoom in and out, respectively. One tap with a single finger simulates a left mouse click, and two quick taps with a single finger simulates a double-click. Tapping once with two fingers simulates a right click or (for Mac users) a Control+click, and

FIGURE 10-2

Screen-sharing with LogMeIn Ignition

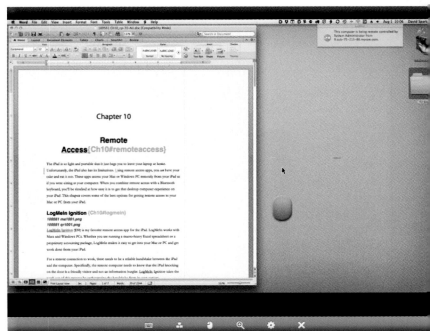

scrolling up and down with two fingers simulates using the mouse's scroll wheel. If the remote computer has multiple monitors, slide three fingers left to switch monitors. You can also drag up or push away the onscreen keyboard by moving three fingers up and down on the screen.

There isn't much more to screen sharing. Log on to your remote computer and start operating it as if you were sitting at your desk. When you're done with your screen sharing session, tap the End Session icon button (the X symbol).

In addition to sharing screens, LogMeIn Ignition also lets you share files with a remote computer. It is tedious logging onto a remote computer via screen sharing just to get a file: You need to open the Windows Explorer or Mac OS X Finder and drill to the appropriate folder. This takes time using the relatively small iPad screen. So LogMeIn Ignition includes a file-sharing tool to avoid such file management via screen sharing. Tap the File Sharing icon button in the My Computers pane, shown in Figure 10-1, to open the File Sharing pane.

From here you can easily navigate folders on your computer. Once you locate the file you want, use the buttons across the bottom of the window to open, copy, move, update, rename, delete, or e-mail the file directly. You can also share files from your local iPad storage to the remote computer using the File Sharing pane.

Jump Desktop

In addition to the hosted connection you get with LogMeIn, some workplaces use Remote Desktop Connection (RDC), a Microsoft technology that allows you to remotely log into a networked computer. Using RDC, the remote computer (in this case, your iPad) sees the desktop interface on the host computer (your office PC) as if it were accessed locally. So what does this mean? Using RDC, you can easily access a Windows computer and have the Windows desktop appear on your iPad.

Numerous computer platforms, including the Mac, use the RDC protocols to help users remotely access their Windows computers. There are several RDC clients available for the iPad. One of the best is Jump Desktop ($20). Shown in Figure 10-3, Jump Desktop puts Windows on your iPad.

WORKING WITH CITRIX

Some companies use the Citrix virtual desktop tools, a computing platform that lets IT departments control application deployment and data management from the data center, running the Windows desktops there but sending out the screen and taking the input from a remote computer or other device. If your job requires access to Citrix servers, download Citrix Receiver (free), an iPad app that lets your iPad access your Citrix virtual desktop and applications.

FIGURE 10-3

Windows 7 on an iPad using Jump Desktop

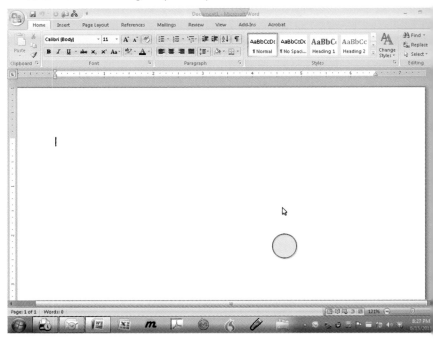

FIGURE 10-4

Setting up an RDC connection with Jump Desktop

To establish a remote connection, you must enable RDC on the Windows computer. Although not difficult for IT professionals, setting up an RDC connection on your Windows computer does take some knowledge of networking protocols. Setup requires creating exceptions to the network firewall and, if not done correctly, presents a security risk. Do not attempt setting up RDC on a Windows computer yourself unless you know what you are doing and have the blessing of your IT staff. Now having given the necessary warnings, once enabled, using your iPad with an RDC connection is surprisingly easy.

THE IPAD AS A MULTITOUCH DEVICE

Remote Conductor ($7) offers a different kind of remote control. Instead of viewing your Mac or Windows PC screen from your iPad, Remote Control creates a sort of command console for your Mac or Windows PC. Combined with the Remote Conductor server software installed on your Mac or Windows PC, the Remote Conductor app, shown below, displays icons for your installed apps and lets you launch the apps on your Mac or Windows PC using the icons displayed on your iPad. You can also use your iPad as the world's largest multi-touch trackpad. The experience is remarkable. Using Remote Conductor to control your computer feels like something you should be doing at the bridge of your spaceship, while traveling at light speed.

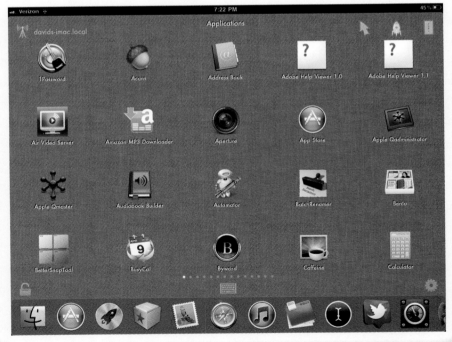

FIGURE 10-5

The Jump Desktop onscreen keyboard

Once you enable the RDC connection on the host Windows computer, take note of the host computer's IP (Internet Protocol) address. (An IP address is sort of an Internet phone number so other computers, and iPads, can find it.) To add the RDC connection to your iPad in Jump Desktop, tap the New Connection icon button (the + symbol) in the upper-right corner, and type in the IP address in the New pane, shown in Figure 10-4.

At the Setup pane, you can also designate the connection as a remote desktop connection (RDP) or a virtual network computing (VNC) device. (VNC is another remote access protocol, covered later.) Tap the RDP button and then the Save butt A connection is created and the IP address appears in the Jump Desktop connectic list.

Tapping the Detail Disclosure icon button (the blue circle with a right-facing arrow inside) opens the Connection Details pane. At this pane, you can customize the name of the connection, display type, login details, and other settings relevant to operating a Windows PC from your iPad. For example, you can choose to play t Windows audio over your iPad or not. You can also delete the connection from th screen. Once you have entered all the details, tap the Done button in the upper-rig corner to close the window and then tap the Jump button in the upper-left corner return to the Jump Desktop connection list.

Tap the desired connection to have Jump Desktop remotely log in to the RDC enabled Windows PC. Once the connection is established, you are prompted to lo

MY REMOTE ACCESS WORKFLOW

I tried most of the available iPad remote access apps in researching this chapter. At the end of this journey, I'm more convinced than ever that LogMeIn is the best one. Its clean interface, simple control scheme, seamless connection, and file sharing make it the clear winner.

I use LogMeIn for all remote access except for my office PC, which has an RDC connection. For the office Windows PC, Jump Desktop gets the job done. My office runs some proprietary Windows software, and every time I am able to operate it from my iPad, I giggle a little bit about the irony.

in with your Windows credentials, and after you provide them the Windows desktop appears on your iPad.

The controls for managing your Windows computer with Jump Desktop are not difficult to master. The two Keyboard icon buttons — at the upper-left and upper-right corners of the window — open the iPad's onscreen keyboard, shown in Figure 10-5. There is an additional top row on the keyboard for the Windows-specific keys, including Ctrl, Alt, and Windows (🐾), as well as the Shift, Esc, and Tab keys used by both Macs and Windows. The left portion of the keyboard's top row includes buttons to alternate between the standard keyboard, a numeric keypad, a function-key keyboard, and a pen tool. If, for example, you're working in Excel on Windows 7, you may find the numeric keypad more useful than the standard keyboard.

In the upper-left corner of the toolbar is the Disconnect icon button (a large X symbol) that disconnects your iPad from the Windows PC. Hide the toolbar by tapping the Hide icon button (the ↑ icon) in the center of the toolbar. The right portion of the toolbar also includes the Full Screen icon button (the small screen with four arrows) and the Tools icon button (the wrench icon) that opens a popover with view and input preferences.

When operating Windows with Jump Desktop, your finger replaces the mouse. To click on an item, tap it with your finger. A double-click is a double-tap. Tap with two fingers for a right-click. To perform a mouse drag, double-tap and then keep your finger down after the second tap and drag your finger on the screen to move an item. To use the scroll wheel, perform a vertical swipe with two fingers. To quickly show or hide the keyboard, tap once with three fingers. When you combine a remote connection with a Bluetooth keyboard, it gets even better.

Alternatively, Jump Desktop can connect to a computer via the virtual network computing (VNC) protocol. Although VNC is a different technology than RDC, it has the same result: You share the screen of another computer. Both the Mac and Windows support VNC hosting. If you are not interested in working with LogMeIn or RDC is not available, you can fall back on VNC with Jump Desktop.

11

Travel

Whether you are on a plane, train, or automobile, there is a lot to like about the iPad on travel day. With its ten-hour battery life, optional built-in 3G Internet connection, lightweight, and ability to instantly turn on, the iPad is the perfect traveling companion. This chapter covers some of the best apps and workflows for traveling with your iPad.

Travel Planning

You don't have to wait until travel day to start using your iPad. Plan your trip on your iPad. Most of my trips start with Kayak HD (free). Kayak HD is the iPad face of the Kayak.com service, where you can search multiple online databases to book airline tickets and make hotel reservations.

The Kayak interface is not difficult to master. There are icon buttons across the bottom of the window for flights and hotels. There is also the Explore icon button, covered later in this chapter.

Tap the Flights icon button (the airplane icon) to find a flight. Shown in Figure 11-1, its popover includes three panes. The left pane lets you set search parameters, including the origination and destination cities, the date of departure and return, and the number of passengers and type of flight (economy, business, and first-class). The left pane also includes settings to make the flight round-trip, one-way, or multicity. The right pane includes a list of hotels at your destination city. The center pane keeps the search history for past flights and additional searches from your origination city. Once you've entered the details, tap the Search button to locate flights.

In the search results, the left pane is a table of available flights matching your criteria. By default it is sorted by price, with the lowest price at the top. You can change the search criteria by tapping the appropriate column headings.

The smaller right pane in the Results popover includes filters you may add to the search. Available filters include the number of stops, airlines, airports, flight times, and prices. You can apply multiple filters to narrow your results; just check the applicable items in each filter column. Once your search is just right, tap the Share icon button (a rectangle with an arrow emerging) in the top-right corner of the window to e-mail a link to the search.

Tapping any particular flight removes filters from the right pane and replaces them with the flight details and links to book the flight. Using Kayak, your flight can go from a whimsical idea to a reservation in about ten minutes.

The Hotels popover, accessed via the Hotels icon button (the bed icon), works largely the same way. The left pane lets you set variables including the city, check-in and checkout dates, the number of guests, and the number of rooms. You can further filter by the number of stars, hotel brand, or a specific hotel name. After you set the search parameters, tap Get Rates to have Kayak return a list of hotels matching your criteria. Tapping a hotel opens a pane with further details, including an overview, photographs, reviews, and booking details.

The Explore icon button (the steering-wheel icon) is one of Kayak's most interesting features. With it, you can describe a time period (such as January 2012),

FIGURE 11-1

Entering search details in Kayak

FIGURE 11-2

Kayak's Explorer mode

desired activities (including the beach, skiing, gambling, and golf), and a maximum flight time to have the app find destinations for you. The top of the window includes a slider where you can set minimum and maximum prices. You could, for example, tell Kayak you have $500 and want to ski; Kayak figures out where you are and finds any potential destinations on your budget. Figure 11-2 shows this search.

Kayak is not the only app to make travel arrangements. Another innovative flight booking app is Hipmunk (free). Hipmunk only books airline flights, but does it with style. When you load the app, it presents the Search bar asking for the flight details.

Tap the Search for Flights button to have Hipmunk perform the search. Hipmunk then displays the results in a user-friendly graphical format, shown in Figure 11-3.

You can arrange the flights by cost, departure time, and length. Even more interesting, you can organize the flights by agony. This filter pushes the flights with the lousy departure times and seven-hour layovers to the bottom. Hipmunk also displays flights with in-flight Wi-Fi. If you like to travel with the Internet, you'll like Hipmunk.

Hipmunk does not include search features for hotels, automobiles, or other travel arrangements. However, no booking app I reviewed did a better job of visually displaying flight information than Hipmunk. Reviewing flight times graphically is a lot better than trying to sort a textual list of flights.

FIGURE 11-3

Flight search results displayed in Hipmunk

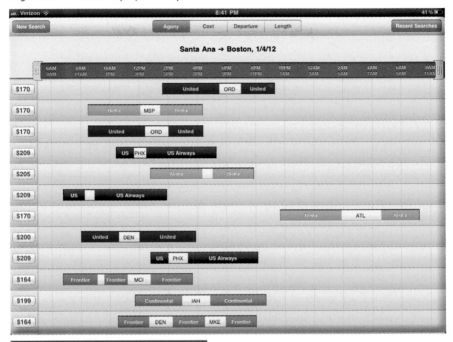

Tracking Your Flight

If you fly a lot, FlightTrack Pro ($10) is indispensable. Shown in Figure 11-4, the app features a left pane with tools to find a flight and a right pane with a map displaying the selected flight's progress.

To find a flight, tap the New Flight icon button (the + symbol) in the upper-right corner of the left pane to open the popover shown in Figure 11-4. This popover includes three panes to help you find a flight-by-flight number, route, or airport. The Flight # pane requires just the airline and flight number. The By Route pane finds your flight using airline, departure, and destination information.

If you tap the By Airport pane, FlightTrack Pro offers a $4 FlightBoard upgrade to the app that displays a digital flight board showing all arriving and departing flights for a given airport, as shown in Figure 11-5. I originally thought this feature was nothing more than eye candy, but when I encountered airline shenanigans in an airport with changing flight numbers and gates, it was really helpful.

You can also add flight information to FlightTrack Pro using the TripIt.com website. TripIt.com takes a forwarded plane reservation e-mail and parses the flight details from it. You can log into TripIt.com from inside FlightTrack Pro. (Tap the Info icon button, a lowercase *i*) in the lower-right corner of the left pane, shown in Figure 11-4.)

Once you find your flight, tap the Save button to have FlightTrack Pro rememb the flight. The left pane entry for the flight (which I call the Flight pane) shows the flight's date, departure time, and arrival time. The Tracking icon button (looks like eye) at the right of the Flight pane displays a real-time updated map for your flight the right pane.

The Flight Details popover, accessed by tapping the flight in the Flight pane, includes three panes: flight details, delay forecast, and flight notes. The Flight Detai pane displays the departure and arrival times with any changes from the original schedule (such as if the flight is taking off late or is landing early). This popover als displays the gate information at the departing and arriving airports. Tapping the Detail Disclosure icon button (a blue circle enclosing a right-facing arrow) opens a popover with even further details, including terminal maps, FAA notices, and weather forecasts at the departing and arriving cities.

The Delay Forecast pane of the Flight Details popover provides a detailed flight schedule and chart demonstrating how often the selected flight arrives on time. The Flight Notes pane includes fields to enter notes concerning a specific flight and, when available, provides terminal and seat maps. If things start looking bad, you can also search alternate flights from this pane. Finally, the Flight Notes pane includes option to override FlightTrack Pro's notification system for the particular flight.

No matter which pane you are in, the top-right corner of the Flight Details popover opens the Share Info popover. From here you can share your flight details via e-mail, SMS, Twitter, and Facebook.

FlightTrack Pro supports all the iOS 5 notification protocols. You can have fligh information appear as banners, alerts, and sounds.

In addition to using FlightTrack Pro when I fly, I also use it when picking up someone at the airport. Knowing arrival details, gate information, and delays make the airport run much easier.

The Info icon button (a lowercase *i*) at the bottom-right of the left pane flips the left pane around to disclose further options, including the ability to sync fight information to your calendar, set up a TripIt.com account (covered earlier), and giv developer feedback.

For $5 less, the non-Pro version of FlightTrack removes push notifications, terminal maps, weather forecast, and FAA airport delays and closures. I say go nuts and buy the Pro version.

Checking the Weather

Although the iPhone includes a built-in weather app, the iPad does not. Fear not. There is no shortage of weather apps available in the App Store.

Most weather apps fall in one of two extremes. The first type provides mountains of meteorological data. These are great for doing things like sailing around the world but are overkill for deciding whether to bring your umbrella. Th

FIGURE 11-4

FlightTrack Pro for iPad

FIGURE 11-5

FlightTrack Pro's FlightBoard upgrade

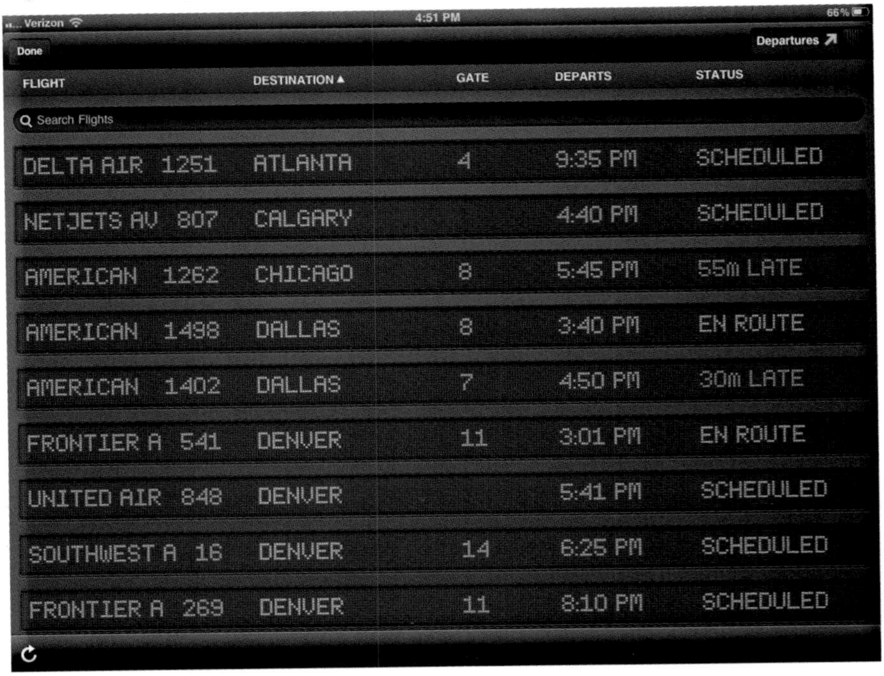

FIGURE 11-6

FIGURE 11-6

AccuWeather Platinum for iPad's forecast window

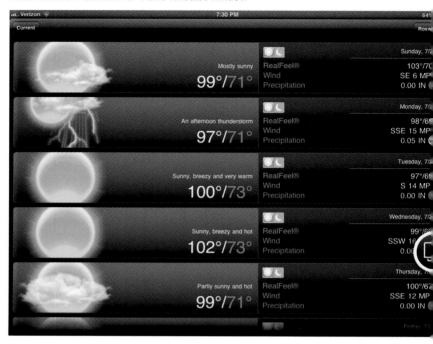

other extreme just tells you the temperature and nothing more. One of the best apps in the middle of those two extremes is AccuWeather Platinum for iPad ($1)

Shown in Figure 11-6, AccuWeather's Forecast pane shows a forecast for the ne five days. Each day includes a high and low temperature, along with wind speed, precipitation, and an adjusted temperature based on those variables.

Tap the Additional Screens icon button (the overlapping blank screens) in the lower-right corner and flick the screen left and right for the hourly forecast, video, maps, lifestyle, hurricanes, and settings panes.

The Hourly Forecast pane shows the current time and weather conditions. In this pane, you can tap and hold on the sun and drag it forward or backward aroun the clock to get the weather conditions at a specific time, such as tomorrow at 9 a.

The Lifestyle pane looks at the temperature, humidity, wind, and other meteorological variables to determine how well suited your current location is for variety of activities, and conditions ranging from jogging to hair frizz. In the Settin pane, you can edit and store locations and change between Imperial (British) and metric units. AccuWeather Platinum provides just the right amount of data and ha great user experience. It is the only iPad weather app I use.

MY IPAD TRAVEL CHECKLIST

So on travel day, what do you pack? With an iPad, not much. Here is my travel checklist.

1. My iPad, obviously.

2. Headphones. No matter how friendly the person sitting next to you is, he or she does not want to listen to a four-hour running battle of Plants versus Zombies. You can spend between $10 and $500 on headphones. I'm leaving this one up to you.

3. Bluetooth keyboard. I've never regretted bringing a Bluetooth keyboard along on travel day. You never know when you will have time to sit down and bang a few thousand words into your iPad. Indeed, I wrote several chapters of this book in airport lounges just this way. Chapter 1 covers Bluetooth keyboards.

4. 3G access. If you have a 3G iPad but don't normally keep the 3G plan turned on, do so before traveling. Having 3G Internet access has saved my bacon more than once. If you use an external device (like a cellphone or MiFi device) for 3G access, bring it and whatever you need to keep power in it.

5. Power. You really can get ten hours out of your iPad battery. But, depending on how far you are traveling, that may not be enough. If you think the battery life will be a problem and you expect to have access to power, bring the iPad charger and USB cable. If not, get an external battery like the HyperMac battery covered in Chapter 1.

6. Camera Connection Kit. Depending on your trip and layovers, it may be worthwhile to pack your Camera Connection Kit (covered in Chapter 1) so you can upload and organize your photos while waiting.

7. Your data. Remember to load your iPad with movies, books, music, and apps before leaving. This is especially true if you are leaving the country, as you may not have access to iTunes and the App Store once you depart.

If you can get by with just your iPad during the flight itself, do so and throw the chargers and other gear in your suitcase. It feels liberating.

Translation

If you are traveling to a foreign country, there are several translation apps to help you deal with language differences.

The best web-based translator is Google Translator (free). This app provides an interface to the Google Translator service in which you can type in any word or phrase and have it translate to any of a variety of supported languages, ranging from Tagalog to Latin. Alternatively, you can tap the Microphone icon button (looks like a microphone) and speak a word or phrase into your iPad to have Google Translator convert your speech to text and then translate the text to a different language. Google Translator displays the translation on the screen. (Tap the Expand icon button, which looks like four arrows pointing from the center, to fill the screen with the foreign language phrase.) For some languages, Google Translator even speaks the phrase for you.

Unfortunately, Google has yet to release an iPad-native version of Google Translator. As a result, you need to use the iPhone version. Nevertheless, it is still best web-based translation app on the iPad. Moreover, several web-based translati apps use the Google Translator service as their underlying engine, and Google recently announced it would start withdrawing support for such translation apps so use the real thing.

If you are traveling, you may not have access to Internet data and without the Internet, Google Translator can't work. In that case, you'll want a local translation app that keeps all the data on your iPad. There are several such apps, sold on a pe language basis, in the App Store. Ultralingua makes some of the best. As an exam its Spanish-English Translator ($20) supports both the iPad and iPhone.

Word Lens ($10) is another interesting translation app. With it, you can take a picture of a sign in Spanish using an iPad 2 to have the app translate the sign to English. At this point, Word Lens supports only Spanish, but it feels like technolo from the future.

If you're not satisfied simply having your iPad translate for you, perhaps you want to learn the language. In that case, check out the Rosetta Stone Totale Companion HD app (free) where you can subscribe, for an additional fee, to language modules that teach you to speak a foreign language. However, these modules rely on an Internet connection, so if you plan to learn the language whil in a foreign country, make sure you have a data connection there.

FIGURE 11-7

Finding a Wi-Fi hot spot with Wi-Fi Finder

LEAVING THE LAPTOP HOME

So exactly how far can you go with just the iPad? Can you take an iPad trip and leave your Mac or PC at home? It depends.

Take a look at the technology you'll be using and decide whether the iPad will cut it. For the most common tasks (e-mail, writing, and web browsing) the iPad is probably all you'll need. For presentation work, the iPad also may be enough. If you intend to do complicated Excel spreadsheets or need particular software not available on the iPad, bring the laptop, too.

Traveling with Data Caps

When traveling with a 3G iPad, give some thought to whether you have the capability to access data at your destination. Traveling domestically isn't a problem unless your 3G provider has poor service at your destination. But traveling internationally can lead to troubles. Your 3G connection may not work at all or, perhaps even worse, it may work just fine but subject you to exorbitant data charges: The Internet is fraught with horror stories of international travelers coming home to a $1,000 cellular bill.

The trick is foresight. Call your data provider before leaving the country and explain where you're going. Find out if there is data service available and, if so, how much it costs.

Chances are though, that it costs way more than you can afford. But there's a better option in many countries. If you have a GSM-capable iPad (meaning an AT&T iPad in the U.S.), you can buy a MicroSIM card in the country you're visiting for about $10, pop out your AT&T MicroSIM and replace it with the foreign one (keep your AT&T MicroSIM, as you'll need to put it back when you come home), and buy a pay-as-you-go plan for that

DINING ON THE ROAD

When you are in a strange city and looking for grub, a few of my favorite apps are UrbanSpoon (free) and Zagat to Go ($10). Zagat is a long-recognized authority on dining and has a large database of restaurant reviews. The iPad app delivers a great experience and the entire database is contained in the app so you can search for nearby restaurants without an Internet connection.

Although UrbanSpoon doesn't have Zagat's pedigree, it provides a unique experience with its slot machine-style interface for picking local dining options and a database of user reviews.

I have had delicious meals in far-away places using both apps.

country to cover your expected usage. (This option is not available for CDMA-based iPads, such as those tied to the Verizon Wireless network in the U.S.) This can drop your 3G costs in each country to well under $50. Note that in some countries, you can get a MicroSIM at a retail outlet, while in others it must be mailed to a local address. So check out your options before you leave.

Unfortunately, this MicroSIM-swapping trick doesn't work with an AT&T iPhone, as AT&T locks the iPhone to its network, regardless of what carrier's MicroSIM is installed. So you might consider buying an unlocked iPhone, either from AT&T or from a reseller in a country that forbids such locking. Although initially expensive, one or two trips abroad makes back the cost by the savings you get from not paying sky-high roaming fees.

If you can't get a reasonable 3G plan where you're heading, simply turn off the 3G radio in your iPad's Settings app before getting on the plane. And remember, Canada is a foreign country, and sky-high roaming fees will apply if you use your U.S. iPad there on a cellular connection.

So how do you get by without 3G data on your trip? The answer is Wi-Fi. Right now we live in a golden age of free (or nearly free) Wi-Fi Internet access. No matter where you go on the planet, chances are there is a nearby coffeehouse, library, or public facility where you can find a Wi-Fi connection. Even better, there is an app help you on your quest.

Wi-Fi Finder (free) tracks more than 320,000 public Wi-Fi hotspot locations in 144 countries. Shown in Figure 11-7, Wi-Fi Finder can even locate multiple hot spots in Roswell, New Mexico. If you can afford the extra space on your iPad, you can download the entire database to your iPad's memory so you can search the 38MB database offline. I always update this local database before leaving on a trip.

Currency Conversion

When you arrive in a foreign land, you may need to convert money. For this, use iCurrencyPad ($1). Shown in Figure 11-8, iCurrencyPad is a no-nonsense currency converter that can convert Lithuanian litas to Sri Lankan rupees — and just about every currency around. The app also graphs historical data on the selected currency.

Note that some news apps (such as Reuters News Pro) include currency conversion "pages" as well, so you may be able to forgo a dedicated currency app altogether.

Navigation

When traveling, it is a good idea to have navigation tools. Using the iPad's built-in Maps app, you can locate yourself anywhere on the planet. Shown in Figure 11-9, the Maps app displays map and satellite images of your surroundings. In addition to searching a location, you can also get directions by car, public transportation, or walking. If you are traveling with dodgy Internet access, take screenshots of the maps you'll need before you go. (To take a screenshot, press the

FIGURE 11-8

iCurrencyPad currency converter

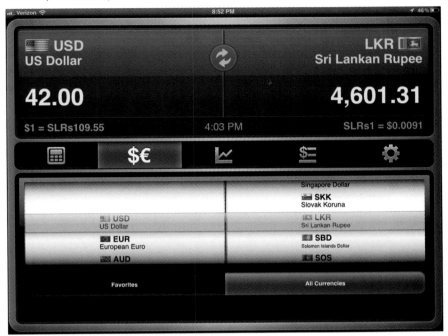

FIGURE 11-9

Navigating with the Maps app

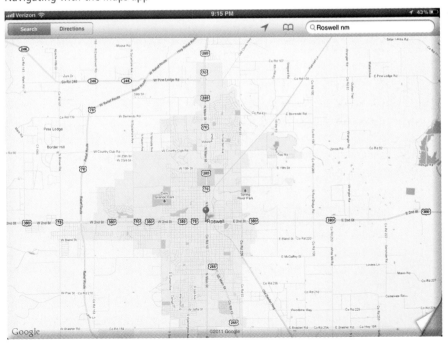

FIGURE 11-10

FIGURE 11-10

Motion-X GPS Drive for iPad

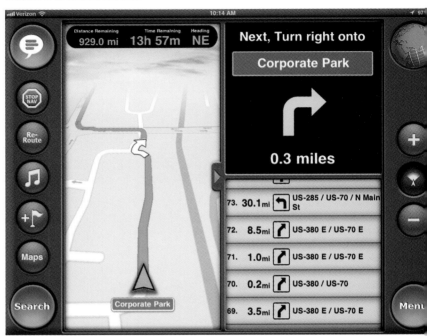

FIGURE 11-11

AllSubway HD for iPad

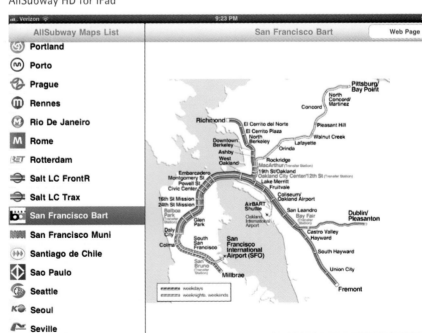

MY TRAVEL WORKFLOW

I've used all the apps listed in this chapter on trips at one time or another. With the ability to pull my iPad out of my bag at any moment and instantly turn it on, the iPad has become my secret weapon for conquering airports, public transportation, cranky waiters, and all the other perils that come with travel.

Wake/Sleep and Home buttons simultaneously.) The map screenshots are saved to the iPad's photo library, so you can access them at your destination, regardless of whether you can find an Internet connection.

For more active navigation, my favorite app is Motion-X GPS Drive ($1), shown in Figure 11-10. Motion-X GPS Drive downloads directions and maps as needed. It has a great user interface and gets you from point A to point B. You can optionally purchase (for $3 per month or $20 per year) a live guidance package that speaks the directions through your iPad speaker like a traditional GPS navigator.

Motion-X GPS Drive delivers with a deep feature list that includes driving and traffic options, custom live voice guidance, and alternate routes. I use it in my car and all my rental cars when traveling.

Navigation apps, as a rule, work much better on Wi-Fi + 3G iPads than on Wi-Fi-only iPads. The Wi-Fi-only iPad does not have a built in GPS receiver and thus is not nearly as accurate, which can throw your navigation app into fits. Be warned however, that constant use of the iPad 3G's GPS receiver is very taxing on the battery. If you plan to do a lot of navigation, bring a car charger.

If you travel to large cities, AllSubway HD ($1), shown in Figure 11-11, includes a full mass-transit map for most major cities in the world. It covers 132 cities as of this writing, but every update adds more.

12

The Enterprise

So what is the enterprise (in addition to a certain well-known spaceship)? Broadly, it's a large business with many moving parts, divisions, specialists, and generalists acting individually yet jointly in a complex environment. Unlike the sole practitioners and small businesses, the buck stops in many places, and unintended consequences can arise from each local decision on the rest of the enterprise. When it comes to computing, an enterprise has a distributed, managed computing environment built from many technologies. Like the people in the company, the technology in the company is both complex and diverse, and yet somehow coordinated, federated, and in some cases integrated. Enterprise computing deals with networks, security, software, and all the jigsaw pieces necessary to make information flow in big business.

What does this have to do with the iPad? Well, until the iPhone and iPad, the enterprise had little to do with Apple technology, which it viewed as not fitting into the norms and assumptions of the enterprise computing environment.

Before the iPhone and the iPad, mobile computing on the enterprise began (and ended) with the BlackBerry devices. Technology has advanced, however, and enterprise workers now realize mobile technology is capable of more than just e-mail and text messaging. Apple, too, is now more enterprise-friendly.

Historically, Apple computers were (and remain) aimed at users looking for a complete integrated solution — perfect for sole practitioners and small businesses. Apple never could (or tried) to compete with enterprise computer vendors, whose technology was designed to fit with enterprise standards so they could be managed jointly no matter who made them.

With mobile devices, however, Apple realized it had a chance to fit in the enterprise before the mobile enterprise standards became defined in a way that excluded it (as happened with the Macintosh), so Apple didn't take long to add enterprise-friendly features to the iPhone and then to the iPad, including mobile device management tools, enterprise app delivery, and corporate-level security features. As a result, the iPad is most certainly ready for the enterprise.

Enterprise management tools are specialized, having to be customized to each company's technology set and usage policies. You don't just install them and move on. So, instead of explaining how to implement enterprise management tools (a subject that could, and does, have its own books), here I summarize what companies can do with the iPad enterprise tools.

Enterprise Security

The iPad's iOS has a lot of security built in. Everything on the iPad is encrypted automatically, so if someone steals your iPad and takes out the internal storage, it's unlikely they'll be able to read your e-mail and other data. By default, the iPad also encrypts data sent through wireless networks, and it supports SSL encryption for e-mail, for corporate servers that use that technology. New to iOS 5 is the option to use the stronger encrypted e-mail standard called S/MIME, for corporate servers that use this technology.

The iPad allows users to set a password to use it, and as explained later in this chapter, IT can force the use of passwords, so if a device is lost or stolen, no one can get to its apps and data unless they know your password.

If your company uses a virtual private network (VPN), the iPad has you covered as well. (A VPN is a secure, private channel from an outside network such as your home's

SHAREPOINT ACCESS

Microsoft SharePoint is an enterprise-friendly web application platform. SharePoint is Microsoft's product for sharing web-based content, data, and files over the enterprise. SharePoint is modular and customizable, so many companies adopt and adapt SharePoint to their particular needs.

But Microsoft provides no real access to SharePoint from the iPad or other non-Windows devices; you can access SharePoint via the web in the iPad's Safari browser, but your access to SharePoint data is limited.

Fortunately, there's an app to get around these limitations. SharePlus ($15) is an iPad client for viewing SharePoint data. SharePlus syncs data from your SharePoint library for use and manipulation on your iPad. When you are done, SharePlus syncs the data back to the SharePoint server so it is available to the rest of your team.

DSL connection to the internal corporate network.) It supports all the common VP standards, which you set in the Settings app, in the General pane's Network subpa

Using mobile device management tools, the iPad also allows IT to control otl security aspects, such as whether the camera may be used, whether apps may be downloaded, and what Wi-Fi access points may be used. It can also install security certificates, which give your iPad a unique, proven ID that IT can use to ensure onl authorized iPads may access corporate data and systems.

Mobile Device Management

Mobile device management (MDM) tools let companies manage iPad deployment across their organization (as well as other mobile devices, from Apple and other companies) from a central location. Using the MDM tools, IT departme can securely manage all the iPads on the network. They can set limitations on app installation, camera usage, and network access; mandate specific password usage, lock or wipe lost or stolen devices remotely; and install preconfigured settings sud as for Wi-Fi, e-mail, network, and calendars.

All this occurs through the use of an MDM server. That can be the Microsoft Exchange server used by two-thirds of businesses today, or it can be a more sophisticated MDM tool from any of a dozen companies that supports more polic — the MDM term for rules and preset configurations — than Exchange does. Thos more expensive MDM servers also add capabilities like tracking the devices in use, such as to verify compliance with corporate standards (a big deal for government agencies and many regulated businesses).

For a user, this complexity rarely surfaces. Instead, once you connect to the corporate network, you may get a prompt to install a configuration policy that sets up your iPad as your IT department requires, or you may get a notice that you nee to enter a password to use your iPad each time you turn it on or unlock it. In some cases, you may have to use specific apps to access corporate resources (as a way of keeping your private apps and data separate from the business ones) — if that's th case, your company will tell you how to get those apps, and it may actually install them for you automatically.

Management via Microsoft Exchange

I explain in Chapters 6, 7, and 8, it is easy to use Microsoft Exchange to sync your e-mail, contacts, and calendars, respectively. But in an enterprise deployment, Exchange can do even more. For example, IT staff can enable company-wide security protocols over all Exchange data, such as a minimum password length, maximum failed password attempts before the iPad wipes its storage, and even requiring both numbers and letters in a password. IT staff can also remotely configure e-mail, calendar, and contacts accounts so users don't have to, as well as remotely wipe or lc iPads that have been lost or stolen. Figure 12-1 shows Exchange's management cons (via the Office 365 cloud version).

FIGURE 12-1

An example Exchange policy for iPad and other users

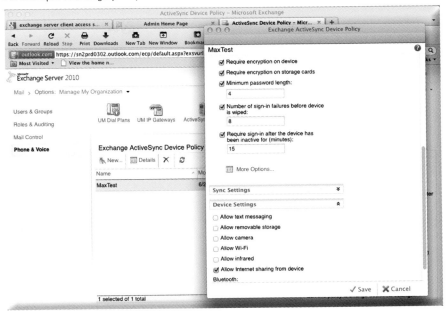

FIGURE 12-2

Mac OS X Lion Server's management tool for iOS and Mac OS X devices

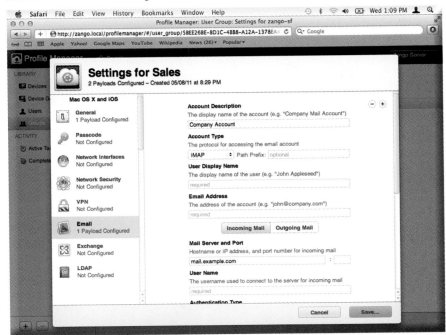

The iPad supports Exchange without any additional software; the configuration work happens on the Exchange Server end, using the same tools (such as Active Directory) that IT uses for desktop policy enforcement and delivery. In fact, these policies apply to iPads, iPhones, and a variety of other mobile devices, so IT doesn't have to do anything special for the iPad.

Management via Mac OS X Lion Server

Apple's Mac OS X Lion Server, a $49 add-on to Mac OS X Lion, also adds iPad (and iPhone and Mac) management capabilities similar to those in Exchange. Except that Lion Server offers more controls than Exchange does, so it can help an enterprise gain more control over iPads without the expense of a full-fledged MDM tool. Figure 12-2 shows Lion Server's management console.

In an enterprise, Lion Server can integrate with the Active Directory user-policy system that Exchange uses, so policies are defined just once even though used by multiple servers. Lion Server can also be used by itself, such as for a small business or a Mac- and iPad-heavy department.

Management with MDM tools

As previously noted, there are more than a dozen MDM tools aimed at large enterprises, with auditing tools in addition to the device management and security capabilities not offered by Exchange or Lion Server. Some also help manage expenses by preventing or alerting users about international roaming. These tools tend to have more complex security capabilities as well. And many can work with Lotus Notes and Attachmate GroupWise, for organizations that don't use Exchange.

Among the best known MDM providers are Boxtone, Good Technology, MobileIron, Sybase, Trellia, and Zenprise.

Enterprise App Deployment

IT can do more than manage iPads; they can create and deploy their own apps to iPad users. These are generally company-specific apps that give employees access to an internal database, such as a contact management system, inventory database, or product sales and information.

Apple provides two ways to do so. One is to let companies create their own iPad app and distribute it through the enterprise (using an intranet link or an MDM tool) not through the public App Store. The enterprise still needs to go through the Apple app approval process to get an electronic certificate that permits installation on iPads, and so the company must be a registered iOS enterprise developer, which costs $299 a year (individual developers pay $99 a year).

The other way is to hire outside companies to create the apps and then make them available through the new Business App Store, which works like the regular App Store except that IT sends users links to the authorized apps, which IT prepays.

That way, the apps can't be used by other companies but can be bought from outside developers.

PART

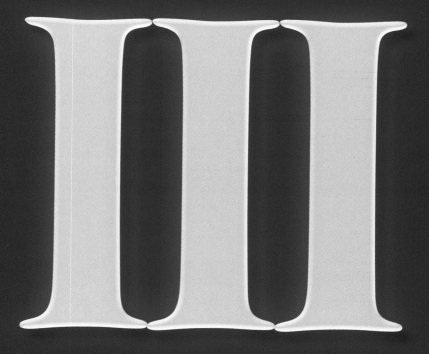

iPad Productivity

13

Writing

N o matter what your profession, you probably need a word processor. Words are the medium we use to solve client problems, make sales, and bring home the bacon. The iPad is a very capable portable word processor. When coupled with a Bluetooth keyboard (covered in Chapter 1), you can write on your iPad just as fast as on a Mac or Windows PC.

If you are easily distracted, the iPad may be a superior writing platform. On the iPad, you can only see one app at a time. When you write, you write. There is no distracting e-mail, Twitter, or Facebook window on the screen constantly beckoning your attention. This chapter covers how to write efficiently with your iPad using traditional word processors and its more nimble text editors.

Word Processing

Word processing applications are the traditional medium for writing using computers. Since the first desktop computers, software developers have cooked up applications that let you write, edit, adjust fonts, outline, and print to your heart's desire. It is only natural that with the arrival of the iPad, we all immediately sought ways to re-create that experience on this new device. Indeed, there are formidable word processors on the iPad, starting with Apple's Pages for iPad.

Apple Pages

Apple's iWork suite, which includes Pages ($10), was the first productivity application set created for the iPad. Apple demonstrated these apps before the iPad even started shipping. iWork answers the question of why, after ten years of tech companies pushing useless tablets on us, the iPad is special. Coming from Apple, Pages is the most polished word processor available on the iPad.

When you first open Pages, you're provided a selection window, shown in Figure 13-1 where you can open an existing document by taping the thumbnail version of the document.

Pull down the document-selection window (tap and hold anywhere in the window and pull down) to see buttons to sort the available documents by date or name, as shown in Figure 13-1.

Alternatively, you can create a new document by tapping the New Document icon button (the + symbol) in the top-left corner of the window. This opens a popover with icon buttons for creating a new document and copying a document from iTunes, iDisk, or a WebDAV server. Tap the Create Document button for the template-selection window.

Pages includes 16 document templates, ranging from letters to term papers. The templates are professionally designed and look great. They are also customizable, so you can use one as a jumping-off point for your own look.

FIGURE 13-1

Pages' documents-selection window

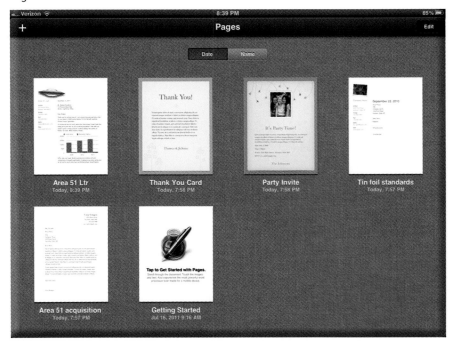

To copy a document from iTunes, you must have your iPad connected to a computer with your iTunes account, as covered in Chapter 1. The Copy to iDisk option works with Apple's soon-to-be-extinct MobileMe service, and the Copy to WebDAV option works with WebDAV servers. (WebDAV is a web standard used to share files. You can access documents stored in the Dropbox and Box.net cloud storage services, covered in Chapter 5, using Pages' WebDAV support.)

Note that the popover's label says "copy" not "sync." When you copy a file to your iPad from an external server, the result is a local copy on your iPad that stand apart from the original file. Any changes you make to the document are saved automatically, so you might want to work on a copy of the document instead, so you still have the original accessible on the iPad and so your changed version has a different name than the copy on the computer or server you got the file from; I explain how to make a document copy later in this chapter.

After making changes to a document using your iPad, you need to export the from the iPad when you are done. The iPad does not automatically sync its file wit the source file. I cover exporting from iPad Pages later in this chapter.

Pages works with the Apple's iCloud sync service, which does sync files with other devices. iCloud-synced documents share changes across all platforms, so changes you make to a document using Pages on your iPad automatically appear i Pages on your Mac and iPhone.

The Pages toolbar

Once you open a document, the Pages toolbar displays across the top of the window, as shown in Figure 13-2. Tap the Documents button to exit your current document and return to the documents-selection window. The Undo button works exactly as you would expect. (Tap and hold the Undo button to redo.) The remaining toolbar icon buttons at the top-right of Figure 13-2 are Info, Insert, Too and Full Screen.

The Info popover. Tap the Info icon button (the lower case *i* in a circle) to op the Info popover. The Info popover is contextually sensitive to the selected item. Fo example, when you have text selected, the Info popover displays the Style, List, and Layout panes, as shown in Figure 13-2.

The Style pane has buttons for formatting text, including bold, italic, underlin and strikethrough. This pane also lets you set the heading style. At the bottom of th Style pane are additional options to set point size, font color, and font family.

When text is selected, the List pane provides controls over list formatting (suc as bullets and numbering), as well as nice big arrow icon buttons you can tap to promote and demote items on the list.

Finally, the Layout pane for the text selected has buttons to set text alignment, the number of columns, and line spacing.

When you select text in Pages, the Text toolbar appears below the main toolba with several text-specific tools, as shown in Figure 13-3. Use the Fonts button (whi displays the current font's name) to open a menu where you can change the font.

FIGURE 13-2

The Pages Info popover

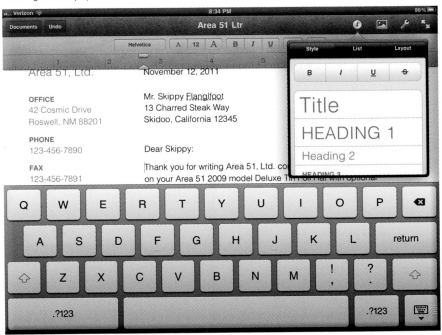

Next are three text-sizing buttons, a small and large capital A as well as a button with a numeral (by default, 12). Tap the small and large A buttons to decrease and increase the font size, respectively. Tap the numeral button to change the font size to a specified point size. The next three buttons (B, I, and U) apply character formats: bold, italic, and underline, respectively. The Text Alignment icon button (its lines show the selected text's alignment) opens a menu with options to set right, left, center, and full justification.

Finally the Breaks icon button (an arrow pointing at a vertical line) opens a menu from which you can set tabs and three kinds of breaks: line, column, and page. When you are done working with text, the Text toolbar goes away.

This context-sensitive toolbar is a feature borrowed from Pages for the Mac. But unlike the Mac version of Pages, on the iPad there's only a toolbar for text; selecting an image does not bring up any additional tools as it does on the Mac.

If you select an image in Pages, the Info popover changes, showing two image-related panes: Style and Arrange.

FIGURE 13-3

Pages' Text toolbar

The Style pane previews the selected image with various formatting options, including shadows, reflections, and frames. The selected image updates in your Pages document as you try various styles, giving you a preview of the selected effects. The Style Options button opens a popover with additional border options, including color, width, and line style.

The Arrange pane includes settings to change the order of objects on your window. If, for example, you have an image on the window that you want to appear behind text in the same space, move the image backward from this pane. (Drag the slider right to pull an object to the front.) This pane also lets you flip your images vertically and horizontally with one tap.

To mask an image, which limits the viewable portion of an image, press Reset Mask in the Arrange pane of the Info popover and handles appear around the image. Masking is useful when importing an image with sections you do not want in your document. When resetting the mask, you can zoom the image with the slider and adjust the viewable window by tapping and dragging the frame handles. Once you set your image and mask, tap the blue Mask button — and you're done.

Finally, the Wrap button in the Arrange pane opens additional options where you can select how your image will interact with the text surrounding it. Automatic wrapping, the default setting where the iPad figures out how to best place your text around your image, is usually best.

The Insert popover. Add objects to your document with the Insert popover. The Insert popover includes options to add photos, tables, charts, and shapes. To insert an object, tap and hold the object from the Insert popover and drag it into the body of your document.

Object manipulation in Pages is intuitive. Once the object is in your document, you move it by tapping and dragging. To resize an object, tap the object and then drag the resizing handles. Use the rotate gesture to rotate an object.

You can similarly insert tables, charts, and shapes. For each of these categories, Pages includes an assortment of colorful templates you can use in your Pages document.

Using the Charts pane as an example, shown in Figure 13-4, you may choose among several screens of charts and color schemes. (The set of six tiny dots in the bottom of the pane means there are six panes of charts to choose from.) By flicking in the pane, you can flip among the available options and, when you find one you like, tap and hold it and then drag it into your document.

Once the chart is in your Pages document, double-tap it to open a spreadsheet in which you may adjust its labels and data. One limitation to charts on the iPad is that they can be only two-dimensional charts; the iPad doesn't have the muscle to create three-dimensional charts.

Inserting tables works exactly the same way as inserting charts. Tap and hold and then drag the table onto your Pages document. To edit table data, double-tap the table after you insert it on your document.

FIGURE 13-4

Inserting a chart in a Pages document

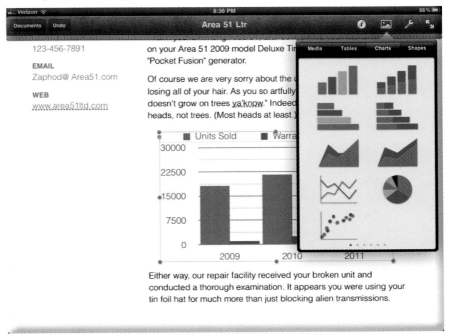

The Insert popover's Shapes pane includes six panes of shapes. Again, insert shapes in your document by tapping and holding, and then dragging the shape onto the document. You can create your own diagrams inside Pages, by inserting the prebuilt shapes and making adjustments with the sizing and rotation tools. Although not as powerful as OmniGraffle, covered in Chapter 21, Pages has enough shape tools and options to build a quick, basic diagram.

The Tools menu. The Tools menu is a "catch-all" menu for capabilities that don't fit with the other toolbar options.

The Share and Print option opens a submenu with options to share your document (covered later) and print. The Print option opens the standard iOS Printer Options popover. (Chapter 1 covers printing.)

The Tools menu's Find option opens a Search bar above the onscreen keyboard that searches the entire document for a word or string of text. Tap the Settings icon button (the gear icon) to the left of the Search bar to adjust the search parameters to match case or look for only whole words. And tap the Back and Forward icon buttons (the left- and right-facing triangles) to search for the next instance of the search term relative to the current location.

You can also set the Search bar to find and replace text; in that case, the Search bar divides into two sections, with one field for the search text and another for the replacement text.

FIGURE 13-5

Pages' Document Setup window

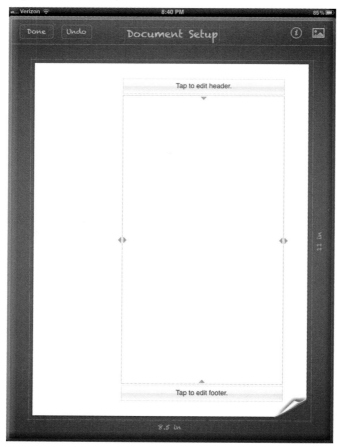

The Tools menu's Document Setup option opens the blueprint-style windows shown in Figure 13-5. Here you can adjust headers, footers, margins, and page size with your finger. Tap Done to close this window and return to the normal document view.

The Tools menu's Settings option opens a popover with several options, including spell checking (it displays a squiggly line below potentially misspelled words), word count (it displays a small box with the word count of the current document at the bottom-center of the window), and layout guides (which makes it easier to place and center objects in your document).

Finally, the Help option opens Pages' help window.

Full-screen mode. The final toolbar icon button is Full Screen (the icon of two diagonal arrows). Tapping it removes the toolbar and other user interface elements, presenting your document in full-screen mode. Use full-screen mode when you just want to write. I often use Pages' full-screen mode when tethered to a Bluetooth

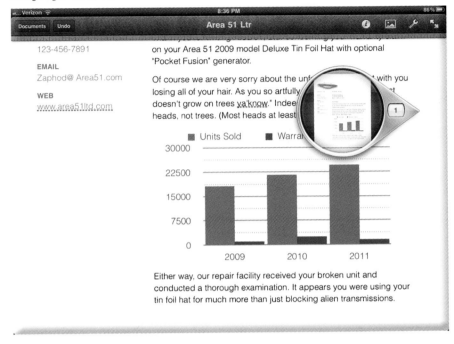

FIGURE 13-6

Using Pages' scroll bar

keyboard and hunkered down for the hard work of moving the cursor. To exit full-screen mode, tap the screen again to have the toolbar and other interface elements return.

Working with text in Pages is a snap. Tap the screen to get a blinking cursor and have the onscreen keyboard pop up. Then just start typing. If you have your iPad paired with a Bluetooth keyboard, tap the screen and begin typing on your keyboard. (Note that there are no keyboard shortcuts for boldface, italics, and so forth as there are on a Mac or PC.)

You move the cursor in Pages with your finger: Tap the screen where you want the cursor to be. If you double-tap on a word, Pages selects it. If you triple-tap a word, Pages selects the entire paragraph. Although the double-tap feature works throughout iOS, the triple-tap paragraph selection gesture is unique to Pages.

You can also use your Bluetooth keyboard's arrow keys to navigate text. Hold down the Shift key while navigating with the arrow keys to select text (just as on a Mac or PC). You can move forward and backward one word at a time by holding the Option key while pressing the right and left arrow keys (← and →), and you can move by paragraph by holding the Option key while pressing the up and down arrow keys (↑ and ↓).

You can also navigate your Pages document by tapping on the right side of the iPad window to display the scroll bar. When you do so, the navigator appears, showing a preview of the page at the location of your finger on the scroll bar, as

shown in Figure 13-6. Pages generates previews of each page as you drag your fing
up and down the scroll bar. This is one of the intuitive iPad features that I hope on
day finds its way to desktop word processors.

If Pages believes a word is misspelled, it draws a red squiggly line below it
(assuming you have spell checking turned on via the Tools menu, as explained
earlier). Tap a misspelled word to have Pages provide a contextual menu with
possible replacements.

Double-tapping a word opens a contextual menu with the Cut, Copy, and
Paste options. Tap the More icon button (the right-facing arrow icon) in iOS 5 or
the More button (in earlier versions of iOS) to display more options. Additional
options include Replace, Definition, and Style buttons. The Replace button provide
additional, alternative spellings for the selected word. Tap the Definition button fo
dictionary entry for the selected word. The Style button includes options to copy a
paste the selection's formatting style. If there are no words selected and you doubl
tap on the cursor, the More button exposes Insert and Style buttons. The Insert
button lets you insert a tab, line break, column break, and page break.

Sharing documents

Having covered the nitty-gritty of how to open files and make great looking
word processing documents, it is time to learn how to share your documents.

Go back to the Tools menu and tap the Share and Print option to open the
submenu with many options to get your documents to your colleagues.

Tap the Email Document option to send your document via e-mail. Pages give
you a choice of formats for the attachment, including Pages, PDF, and Microsoft
Word formats. (Pages is available for the Mac, and Microsoft Word is available for
both the Mac OS X and Windows platforms.) With these three options, just about
anyone should be able to open and read your word processing document.

If you want to send someone a copy of your document without giving him or
her the ability to edit it, use the PDF format. (I cover manipulating and creating
PDFs on your iPad in greater detail in Chapter 14.) Once you select the desired
format, Pages creates a new e-mail with the selected file attached. Set your recipien
and subject for the e-mail, type your message, and send it.

It is important to note that in sending a document via e-mail, you are creating
a copy of that document for the e-mail attachment. If the recipient receives that
document and opens and edits it on their iPad, Mac, or Windows PC, those chang
will not appear in the copy on your iPad. For you to see those changes, the recipien
needs to e-mail or otherwise send the document back to you. Creating multiple
copies of a document in this fashion can be dangerous: If you're not careful with
document tracking, you may find different revisions in different versions. Also, you
are at risk of forgetting which version is the most current. So take special care when
sharing documents.

The Share and Print submenu also lets you share a document with iWork.com
Apple's web-based collaboration service that shares documents created with the

iWork applications on your Mac or iPad. Once you finish a document in Pages, tap this option to send your document to the iWork.com website. Pages then opens a mail message containing a link to the iWork-hosted document. Depending on the permissions you set, recipients can annotate, modify, and download the document. Although the iWork.com tools are hardly the collaboration powerhouse you get from Google Documents, they are a step in the right direction and makes sharing your work a lot easier.

Tap the Send to iTunes option to send the file to iTunes (it will be transferred to your iTunes document repository the next time you sync, as covered in Chapter 1). Again, Pages asks you to choose among Pages, PDF, and Microsoft Word formats.

The Copy to iDisk option works only with the MobileMe service that Apple is discontinuing as of June 2012, so expect it to disappear from Pages in a future release.

Pages supports iCloud syncing, so your documents automatically sync across all devices that have Pages installed. For example, you can write several thousand words on your Mac and, using iCloud syncing, resume where you left off on your iPad. Your iPad will even know where you left the cursor in the Mac version. iCloud syncing is automatic across all iOS devices and Macs that have this feature turned on and that share the same Apple ID. (When you're in the document-selection window, you may see up-arrow icons appear next to documents; those icons mean that the document's changes are being sent to iCloud for syncing.)

There is no built-in Dropbox or Box.net support in Pages (or any of the Apple iWork applications). But you can add support for these cloud storage services. Pages, and the other iWork apps, include the ability to open and save files to a WebDAV server. WebDAV, which stands for Web-based Distributed Authoring and Versioning, is a protocol that enables users to manage documents stored on web-based servers. That means you can copy documents to and from a WebDAV server. Both Dropbox and Box.net provide WebDAV connectors.

Pages' limitations

By now you have probably figured out that Pages is a great word processor. Notice I didn't call it a mobile word processor or an iOS word processor. This application is a meat-and-potatoes word processor that can keep up with the best of them.

Like all apps however, Pages has its limitations. Pages is intended to be a "final destination" word processor. Often, you may write text in text editors (covered in detail later in this chapter) with the knowledge that the text will ultimately be formatted and printed from another application, like Pages. Although Pages provides many options to export its files to other formats, in their heart of hearts, the Pages developers intended you to finish, polish, and print your documents in and from Pages. I suspect this attitude is no different from the team responsible for developing Microsoft Word. The difference is that although Pages is, in many respects, a superior word processor to Microsoft Word, Pages does not have nearly the market penetration of Microsoft Word.

As a result, you will on occasion need to send your document to Microsoft Word. Although Pages provide this feature, it is not perfect. Several style formats, such as headings, simply don't translate to Microsoft Word format. If you meticulously set the style sheets for your document in Pages and export it to Microsoft Word format, paragraph style names and tags (often used for tables of contents, indexes, and layout programs' style sheets) are lost even though the character-level formatting is retained.

Likewise, Pages does not allow you to share a document in the RTF (Rich Text Format) file format (one that Apple has frankly never supported well), which often serves as an intermediary for word processing documents. (Ironically, RTF export is available in Mac OS X's Pages.)

Another missing feature in Pages is the TextExpander Touch shortcuts support covered in Chapter 2. Likewise, some of the more complex word processing tools are not available, such as tracked changes, footnotes, and endnotes.

All these limitations can prevent a business from letting you use Pages for documents used in standard business workflows. Still, even with these limitations, Pages remains a credible "final destination" word processor for documents whose final destination is not a business workflow. With the addition of iCloud, letting your files sync among your Mac and iOS devices, Pages becomes even more appealing. With little effort, you can create attractive documents on your iPad.

Working with Microsoft Word

What if you work in an environment where all word processing is done in Microsoft Word? Pretend your co-workers have nothing but disdain and revulsion for Pages and instead celebrate the endless features, options, and buttons available in Microsoft Word. In that case, can you still get word processing done on your iPad? Absolutely.

Although Microsoft has no Word application for the iPad (and given its stated intention of pushing Windows 8 to tablet computers, I suspect it never will), Apple

WORDPERFECT? REALLY, WORDPERFECT

In my day job as a business attorney, I am continually amazed how often I receive documents saved in WordPerfect format. Despite the fact that most of the world left WordPerfect behind ages ago, it seems that many lawyers still hold on to it. Although there is no iOS word processor that edits WordPerfect documents, WordPerfect Viewer for iPad ($6) at least lets you open and read WordPerfect files.

Pages does export to Word — with the limitations noted in the previous section that could cause issues in many business workflows.

Several developers also have created iOS applications that provide Microsoft Word compatibility. Moreover, as covered later in this chapter, you can create text files for later formatting in any word processor.

Quickoffice Pro HD

Quickoffice Pro HD for iPad ($20) is an office suite with components to read and modify Word, Excel, and PowerPoint files. Quickoffice opens with its file management system, shown in Figure 13-7.

Quickoffice syncs with several online services. Tap the New Service icon button (the + symbol) at the bottom-left of the window (as shown in Figure 13-7) to see available cloud syncing services, including Google Docs, Dropbox, Box.net, MobileMe, Huddle.com, and SugarSync. As this book went to press, the Quickoffice developers have not stated whether they will support iCloud, but based on their aggressive adoption of other cloud services, I suspect they will.

The file management system in Quickoffice is intuitive: Drag a document to the Delete, E-mail, or Send To icon button at the bottom of the window; the icon buttons grow large, providing an easy target for your selected file.

One disappointing aspect of Quickoffice is that the Send To menu works only with a few web services: Slideshare.net, Scribd.com, and Docstoc.com. Strangely,

FIGURE 13-7

File management in Quickoffice Pro HD

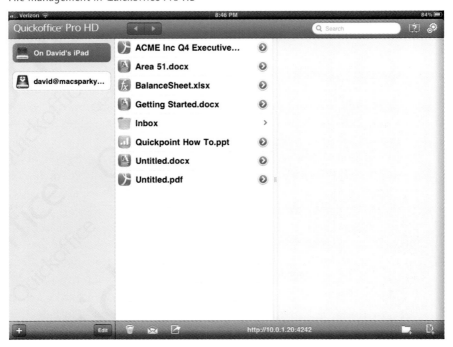

FIGURE 13-8

Quickoffice Pro HD's word processing tools

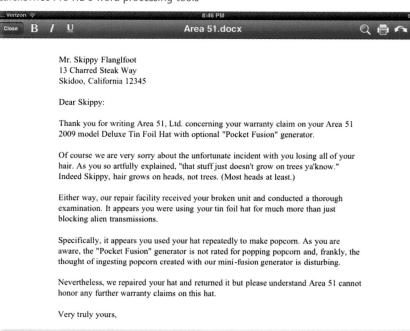

the application does not provide a way to easily share files with other applications on your iPad: Quickoffice doesn't support iOS's Open In facility for doing so. This design philosophy makes it easy to bring documents in but difficult to send out, an it seems counterintuitive on the iPad where most applications allow you to bounce files between them. (To get a file to another app on your iPad, e-mail it to yourself and then use Open In from the mail message to send the file to the other app.)

You can create folders and files with the New Folder and New File icon button in the lower-right corner (the folder and document icons, respectively). Quickoffice creates documents in your choice of the 2003 and 2007 versions of Microsoft Word as well as in plain text.

The Settings icon button (the icon of two gears) in the upper-right corner of the window opens the Settings popover with options to enable wireless file transfer increase the file cache size, disable the iPad's sleep mode while working, and set a passcode lock on the app.

Regardless, once you open a document, Quickoffice presents its word processir interface, shown in Figure 13-8.

The Close button in the top-left corner of the window exits the word processor and returns to the file management window. Also in the top-left corner are formatting icon buttons for bold, italic, and underline (B, I, and U, respectively).

The top-right portion of the Quickoffice editing window includes icon buttons for (from left to right) search, print, undo, and formatting.

Tapping the Print icon button (a printer icon) opens a menu where you choose between the standard iOS print tools and saving the document as a PDF file. This is a great idea, as generating PDFs on the iPad isn't necessarily easy (see Chapter 14). Unfortunately, although you can easily generate PDF files in Quickoffice, the built-in PDF viewer does not contain annotation tools or the ability to export the file to another PDF application on your iPad. Instead, to get the file in a different app on your iPad, you must e-mail it to yourself as explained earlier.

The Undo icon button (the two curved arrows) works with the last ten changes to the document. You can also invoke undo by shaking your iPad. Although I understand that shaking to undo is a common feature on the iPhone, it makes no sense to me on the iPad.

Tap the Formatting icon button (the letter A with a gear) for the Formatting popover, which is similar to the text-formatting tools in Pages. There are panes for font, paragraph, and color formatting.

Quickoffice does not include footnotes, tracked changes, or other sophisticated word processing features. There is also no support for TextExpander Touch text expansion, covered in Chapter 2. It does, however, retain Microsoft Word paragraph formatting (even though you cannot see or edit Word in the application). If a co-worker, for example, sends you a Word document with formatting codes (such as Heading 1, Title, and Salutation) embedded, you can edit the file, send it back to her, and the formatting codes will remain even though you could not see them on your iPad.

There are several slick usability features in Quickoffice. Using a two-finger pinch gesture, you can adjust the size of your document. As the document approaches the optimal width for the iPad screen, it snaps to that dimension. Like Pages, Quickoffice also lets you select an entire paragraph with a triple tap.

Documents to Go

Another contender for the title of Microsoft Office companion on the iPad is Documents to Go Premium ($17). Documents to Go (labeled DocsToGo on the iPad) has a long history of mobile applications, with Microsoft Office compatibility going back to the Palm Pilot devices.

Shown in Figure 13-9, Documents to Go includes more features than Quickoffice, but it also is more complicated. Like Quickoffice, Documents to Go opens in a file system view from which you can select text, Word, Excel, and PowerPoint files for modification.

From the file system window, you can link Documents to Go with a computer on the same Wi-Fi network for wirelessly syncing files using the free desktop syncing application (found at www.dataviz.com/iphoneinstaller). Likewise, you can pair your Documents to Go application with the usual list of cloud storage services, including Google Docs, Box.net, Dropbox, iDisk, and SugarSync. The file system window lets you sort files by name or display just the recently opened files. Again, there is no word on iCloud support.

FIGURE 13-9

Documents to Go for iPad's file system window

FIGURE 13-10

Documents to Go's word processing mode

Mr. Skippy Flanglfoot
13 Charred Steak Way
Skidoo, California 12345

Dear Skippy:

Thank you for writing Area 51, Ltd. concerning your warranty claim on your Area 51 2009 model Deluxe Tin Foil Ha
with optional "Pocket Fusion" generator.

Of course we are very sorry about the unfortunate incident with you losing all of your hair. As you so artfully
explained, "that stuff just doesn't grow on trees ya'know." Indeed Skippy, hair grows on heads, not trees. (Most hea
at least.)

Either way, our repair facility received your broken unit and conducted a thorough examination. It appears you were
using your tin foil hat for much more than just blocking alien transmissions.

Specifically, it appears you used your hat repeatedly to make popcorn. As you are aware, the "Pocket Fusion"
generator is not rated for popping popcorn and, frankly, the thought of ingesting popcorn created with our mini-fusio
generator is disturbing.

Nevertheless, we repaired your hat and returned it but please understand Area 51 cannot honor any further warran
claims on this hat.

Very truly yours,

Zaphod

Tap a document to open it. Figure 13-10 displays Documents to Go's word processing mode.

The top toolbar includes the Back icon button (the ← icon) on the left side that returns you to the file system window. There are icon buttons for undo (the left-facing curved arrow) and redo (the right-facing curved arrow) on the right of the toolbar.

In Documents to Go, you accomplish all the document formatting using the icon buttons in the bottom toolbar, shown in Figure 13-10. The File icon button (an upward-pointing triangle) opens a menu with the Save, Save As, Send, and Open In options. (The Open In option lets you open your documents in any application that recognizes the file type. Word documents, for example, can be opened in Pages, Quickoffice, GoodReader, or any app installed on your iPad that reads or modifies Word documents.)

The Font icon button (the capital letter A with several horizontal lines) opens a popover with font tools for changing the font, character formatting (bold, italic, and underline), color, and highlight.

The Paragraph icon button (the paragraph symbol with several horizontal lines) opens a popover with paragraph formatting options. You can set paragraph justification, indents (including first line and hanging indents), and line spacing.

The List icon button (the icon of two bullets with a series of horizontal lines) opens a popover with bullet and numbering options.

In all three formatting popovers, tap the More option to open the Formatting popover that lets you handle character, paragraph, and list formatting in one place.

Finally, the Tools icon button (the icon of the crossed hammer and wrench) opens a menu with options for word count, full-screen mode, and find and replace. If you choose Find and Replace, the Search bar opens at the top of the window in

COLLABORATION TOOLS

On the PC and Mac, there is an emerging gray area of web-based word processing typified by Google Docs (http://docs.google.com) and Microsoft's Office 365 (http://office365.microsoft.com). These are web-based word processors that are built around the idea of collaborative work. With Google Docs, a team of people can work on the same document at the same time.

Neither Google nor Microsoft has released client applications for these services for iOS (the smart money is on Google eventually doing so, but Microsoft, not so much). Google Docs can work with the iPad through the Safari browser but doing so requires some work. To edit a text field, for example, you must force Google Docs to its normal browser view (not the custom version for mobile devices). It really isn't worth the bother. If you need to work with Google Docs, you are better off linking to Google Docs with Quickoffice or Documents to Go (both support linking to your Google Docs account) and using their native iPad tools instead.

Microsoft Office 365 has no support for the iPad beyond Exchange.

MY WORD PROCESSING WORKFLOW

Although I spend a lot of time writing on my iPad, I don't do as much word processing as you might think. Because I share documents with other lawyers all the time, the ability to track changes is critical. Unfortunately, none of the iPad word processors have cracked that nut yet. When I do need to use a word processor on my iPad, I prefer Pages. It is heads and shoulders above its competition in terms of polish. With the addition of iCloud syncing, Pages is all that much better for me. Moreover I use Printopia (covered in Chapter 1) to print my word processing documents to my local network printer.

which you enter your search phrase. Below the Search bar is an icon button (a down pointing triangle) that expands the Search bar to include a text field for entering replacement text and switches for setting whether the search is case-sensitive and/or for whole words only. Note that the Find next, Replace, and Replace All buttons are at the very bottom of the document window, where they are easily overlooked.

Documents to Go retains tracked changes from the original word processing file and displays them on the iPad, but it does not track the changes you make on your iPad. Documents to Go also retains paragraph styles applied in Word when you save the file.

There is no support for printing in Documents to Go. Likewise, there is no feature in Documents to Go to generate a PDF file from your document. The application also does not support TextExpander Touch snippets, covered in Chapter 2

Choosing between Quickoffice and Documents to Go

There is no wrong choice between Documents to Go and Quickoffice. They both are stable but offer different features. Generally, Quickoffice is easier to use and Documents to Go has more features. Neither is as polished as Pages and neither offers a complete replacement for Microsoft Word on your Mac or PC.

If forced to choose, I prefer Quickoffice. I like the interface better but I find its inability to easily share documents with other iPad apps a disappointment. If you need to view (but not change) tracked changes, you'll need Documents to Go.

Although all the word processors in this chapter are credible tools, give some thought to exactly what type of writing you intend to do on your iPad. If you can get away with just writing plain text and doing the formatting later, that is perhaps the best solution.

Working with Text

As described earlier, there are limitations to word processing on an iPad. Some features, like tracking changes, simply are not available.

Underlying this problem is the fact that the iOS software development platform and hardware does not have the same processing power and resources you find on a Mac or Windows PC. Formatting is challenging across multiple operating systems. It *can* be done, but you may want to ask yourself if it *should* be done.

Why not skip formatting altogether and simply write and format later on your Mac or Windows PC? For many iPad writers (including myself), this is the preferred method.

There are several advantages to working with text files as opposed to traditional word processing files with embedded formatting. By their very nature, text files are simple and work anywhere. Any word processor on any platform can read a text file. Likewise, because they do not include complex formatting, the files are easily readable, even by people. So what do you put in all these fancy text files? Just about anything. I have hundreds of files containing everything from my favorite Latin quotes (*Sit vis nobiscum*, translated: "Use the Force"), to travel plans, legal forms, half-written articles, and half-baked ideas.

Depending on which text editor you use, there are several ways to get the text back to your Mac or Windows PC, ranging from e-mailing the text file to cloud syncing using services like Dropbox and iCloud. There is a word of caution however. Most of the iPad text editors sync text using the Dropbox service. (The only exception is Simplenote.) If your workplace does not permit Dropbox syncing (some don't), your ability to easily sync your text will be limited. Ditto for any apps that support iCloud syncing, which some companies may also disallow use of. You may be required to e-mail or use iTunes sync (covered in Chapter 1) to move text files between your iPad and your Mac or Windows PC.

The other big advantage of using the iPad to write text instead of "word processing" is that the device is ideally suited to the process of writing. You open one application at a time, and distractions are limited. Although your Mac or Windows PC may display the Internet, Twitter, Facebook, and mail while you write, the iPad shows just a blank screen and the blinking cursor. I find it a great way to focus on moving a cursor and forgetting about the rest. Don't do any formatting — just write.

As an example of just how productive this can be, on a family vacation I took my iPad and left my MacBook at home. Using a simple text editor, I was able to write 20,000 words for my last book, *Mac at Work*, using my iPad and a portable Bluetooth keyboard. It was the most productive week I had over the entire process of writing that book. And I never once opened a word processor.

I am not alone in recognizing the value of text files on the iPad. Several talented developers have created useful text editing applications for the iPad. There are many great ones. Each however has its strengths and weaknesses.

PlainText

PlainText (free with ads, $2 in-app purchase to remove ads) is the poster child for a simple, reliable iPad text editor. Shown in Figure 13-11, PlainText has a simple interface with a list of documents on the left and the writing area on the right.

PlainText for the iPad

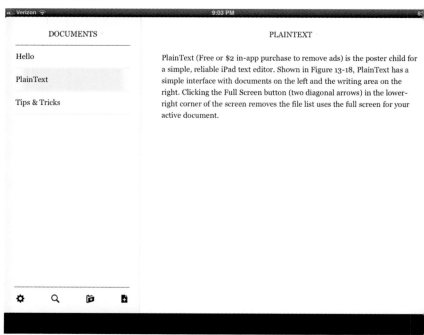

> PlainText (Free or $2 in-app purchase to remove ads) is the poster child for a simple, reliable iPad text editor. Shown in Figure 13-18, PlainText has a simple interface with documents on the left and the writing area on the right. Clicking the Full Screen button (two diagonal arrows) in the lower-right corner of the screen removes the file list uses the full screen for your active document.

Tapping the Full Screen icon button (two diagonal arrows) in the lower-right corner of the window removes the file list and uses the full screen for your active document.

The lack of features in PlainText is a feature. PlainText has an attractive layout with plenty of white space and exclusive use of the Georgia typeface. The typography and simple interface makes it easy to just write. It also includes TextExpander Touch support so your TextExpander snippets work.

PlainText does include a word-count feature that you access by tapping and holding anywhere in the white space in your document. Alternatively, if you select portion of your document's text and tap and hold, you'll get the word count for just that selection.

PlainText syncs text with your Dropbox account. Set up Dropbox in the Settings window, accessed by tapping the Settings icon button (the gear icon) in the lower-left corner of the window in Figure 13-11. When you sync with Dropbox, PlainText creates and defaults to the PlainText folder. You can, however, choose a different folder. You can also search your notes and organize them by filename or modification.

WriteRoom

WriteRoom ($5) is PlainText's big brother. Developed by the same company, WriteRoom keeps the clean PlainText interface while loading on the features: an extended

FIGURE 13-12

iA Writer for iPad

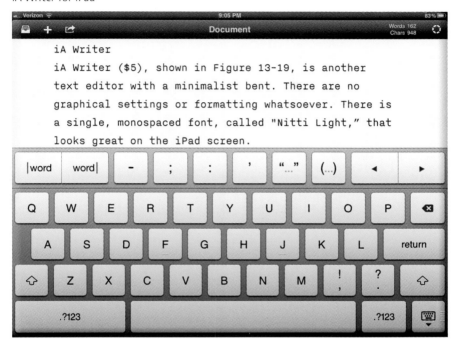

row, print and e-mail settings, and font and color customization. If you like the PlainText interface and want more features, look no further.

iA Writer

iA Writer ($5), shown in Figure 13-12, is another text editor with a minimalist bent. There are no graphical settings or formatting whatsoever. It has a single, monospaced font, called Nitti Light, that looks great on the iPad screen.

There is a running stat in the top right of the toolbar, shown in Figure 13-12, that displays the words and characters in the current document. If you tap the word count, it switches to display the estimated length of time required to read your document aloud.

There is an additional row of keys at the top of the iPad's onscreen keyboard in iA Writer with frequently used punctuation and navigation keys. This row saves you the several taps sometimes required to get to frequently used symbols, like the quotation marks and colon. Unlike Nebulous Notes, covered later in this chapter, you cannot customize the additional keys. iA Writer also supports TextExpander Touch.

Most interesting about iA Writer, though, is its focus mode, activated by tapping the Focus icon button (it looks like a camera aperture) in the upper-right corner of the window. Focus mode eliminates the entire user interface, giving you just the words and keyboard. Moreover, all remaining features are turned off. There is no auto-correction, spell checking, toolbars, scrolling, editing, or cut, copy, and paste. This is as close to an old-school typewriter as you are going to get with your iPad. Focus mode also blurs everything except the current three lines of text with the idea of keeping your attention. Focus mode doesn't work for me, but some iPad writers swear by it. To exit focus mode, tap the Focus icon button again.

You can link iA Writer to your Dropbox account. However, unlike PlainText, you cannot select the sync folder. Instead, iA Writer creates a Dropbox folder (called Writer) and syncs all the text there. iA Writer only sees text in the Writer folder. This is a limitation. If you want to edit text created with a different word processor or text editor not in the Write folder on your Dropbox storage, iA Writer can't see it.

Elements

Elements ($5), shown in Figure 13-13, is one of the best all-around text editors on the iPad. It includes more customization features than apps like PlainText and iA Writer but still provides a clean interface and enjoyable writing environment.

You have more typographical control with Elements than in PlainText and iA Writer. For example, you can specify the font and point size. Elements also displays data about your text file, including word, line, and character counts, accessed by tapping the Info icon button (the letter i in a circle) in the top-right of the window, as shown in Figure 13-13. Elements supports Dropbox syncing and TextExpander Touch snippets.

FIGURE 13-13

Elements for iPad

Elements includes other features worth mentioning. First is the Scratchpad. Tap the Scratchpad icon button (looks like a notepad) in the toolbar to have Elements open a small popover in which you can write additional text. You can also, for example, copy text from the web for reference as you type in Elements.

Elements also features built-in conversion for Markdown, addressed later in this chapter. Using Markdown, you can add formatting using simple, plain text syntax. When you tap the Markdown icon button (the star icon), Elements interprets that Markdown syntax and displays it as rich text directly on your iPad.

Notesy

Notesy ($3), shown in Figure 13-14, is similar to Elements, in that it provides a variety of typographical customization options but, at its core, is a simple-to-use text editor.

Notesy lets you specify fonts for both proportional and monospaced typefaces. This way, you can choose on a note-by-note basis how it displays. Notesy goes to some effort in letting you customize the typography and colors to your own preference.

You can search your notes and sort by filename, creation date, and modification date. Notesy also includes TextExpander Touch support and Dropbox syncing. The Info icon button (a lowercase *i* in the bottom toolbar) displays dates and details on the active note. Notesy also previews Markdown text, covered later.

FIGURE 13-14

Notesy for iPad

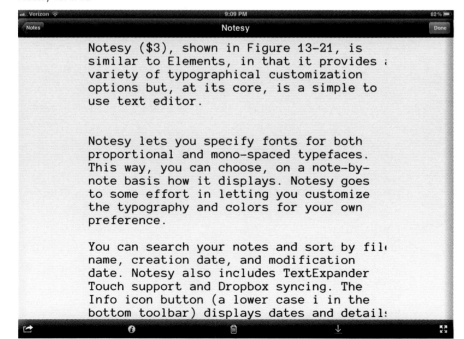

Writing Kit for iPad

Writing Kit ($5), shown in Figure 13-22, was built for power Markdown users. (Markdown is explained later in this chapter.) Writing kit includes a custom keyboard row with all of the most common Markdown syntax and gives a Markdown preview of your text, similar to Elements covered earlier. There is even a Markdown cheat sheet built right into the app.

Notesy's typography and ease of use have won me over. In fact, I used Notesy the primary text editor for writing this book.

Writing Kit

Writing Kit ($5), shown in Figure 13-15, was built for power Markdown users. (Markdown is explained later in this chapter.) Writing Kit includes a custom keyboard row with all the most common Markdown syntax, and it gives a Markdown preview of your text, similar to Elements covered earlier. There is even Markdown cheat sheet built into the app.

Writing Kit also features Dropbox sync, TextExpander Touch support, and the Quick Research popover that looks up a word in the dictionary. One of Writing Ki more innovative features is cursor navigation. Tapping one finger in the right or left margin moves the cursor forward and backward by one character. Tapping two fingers moves the cursor by one word.

Nebulous Notes

Nebulous Notes ($2), shown in Figure 13-16, stands at the opposite end of the spectrum from PlainText. Nebulous Notes provides a remarkable amount of customization. (Some would argue too much.) There are settings for font, point si and line spacing. You can also control the text and background colors so if you wa

FIGURE 13-16

Nebulous Notes for iPad

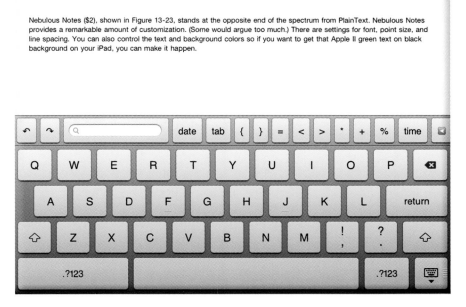

to get the Apple II's green text on black background for your iPad, you can make it happen.

Nebulous Notes' killer feature is the customizable bar at the top of the onscreen keyboard. If there's a particular glyph buried in the onscreen keyboard that you use frequently — braces ({}), for example — you can add them to the top bar for quick access.

Moreover, you can customize the entire top bar buttons with macros that include HTML code, reference macros (such as $day and $time), and navigation tools to jump around the window. This is the only text editor covered in this chapter to offer such flexibility. Nebulous Notes also syncs with any of your Dropbox folders.

Simplenote

In addition to being a text editor, Simplenote, shown in Figure 13-17, is a web-based text service that grew out of an iPhone notes app. Simplenote syncs all your notes with the Simplenote web servers. The app and service are free but there is a premium version ($20 per year) that removes ads, makes up to 30 backups of your notes, and lets you make formatted lists. A subscription account also syncs your notes to Dropbox (in addition to syncing the notes with the Simplenote account).

Simplenote was one of the first apps to feature syncing without iTunes; the developers created their own web-based syncing solution. (Simplenote's syncing came before Dropbox released its syncing protocols for independent app developers to use.)

FIGURE 13-17

Simplenote for iPad

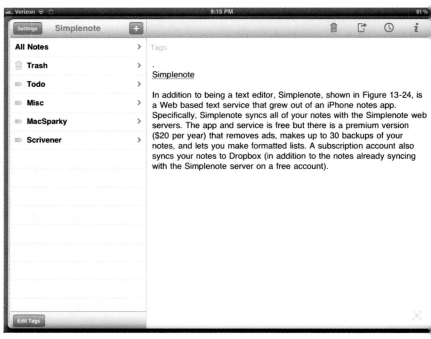

As a result, Simplenote is the only application in this chapter that does not sync with Dropbox by default. (The paid version of Simplenote can sync with Dropbox.)

This leads to certain advantages and disadvantages. Generally, I find syncing text through the Simplenote servers faster than using Dropbox. Also, there are apps designed for most major platforms that plug in straight to your Simplenote database disadvantage is that your data is limited to Simplenote and Simplenote-friendly apps If you want to try any of the other text editors covered earlier in this chapter, you nee to get your data into Dropbox, which requires a $20-per-year Simplenote account.

Because it started out as a notes app on the iPhone, Simplenote is good at searching your text. The Search bar looks at both the title and body of your text items You can also sort your notes by file name, creation date, and modification date.

Using the full-screen mode (activated by tapping the Full Screen icon button, which looks like a square with four arrows, in the lower-right corner, as shown in Figure 13-17), you can remove all the excess noise from the interface and just get to work. To bring the interface back, tap the lower-right corner of the window and the Full Screen icon button reappears. Simplenote also includes TextExpander Touch support.

Simplenote offers just one proportionally spaced font, Helvetica, and no monospaced fonts. You can display the type in four sizes (ranging from small to extra large) by tapping the Font Size option in the Settings menu. There are no other controls over the look and feel of the text. For example, you cannot adjust line spacir

MORE THAN A TEXT EDITOR

Because Simplenote (and the other cloud-syncing text editors) make it so easy to put your text on all your computers and mobile devices and effortlessly keep them in sync, you can use the apps for more than just writing. Two ways I repurpose these apps are to create text banks and databases.

If you write a lot, chances are there are bits of text you reuse frequently. These could be client proposals, contracts, or anything. The point is, you can use synchronized text to keep specimen copies of that frequently used text and then block and copy it into your word processor of choice whenever you need.

You can also use text files as a poor man's database. I keep text files for all my active client matters, and the contents vary. Sometimes I just keep my key client contact information. Other files have case numbers, court file references, and a running log with a date and description for every communication. The point is you can write anything you want in the app and always have easy access to it. Although not as advanced as a dedicated database application (covered in Chapter 22), text editors are easy, fast, and quite often the best solution.

This is, perhaps, the biggest shortcoming with Simplenote. Expanded typographical control over the application would make its use more enjoyable.

Tap the Info icon button (the letter *i* in the upper-right corner) to get a word and character count for your current note and options to pin the current note to the top of the list, removing it from the sorting preferences, and (with a paid account) the option to turn the current note into a list.

If you keep confidential information in your notes, you can passcode-lock the Simplenote app via the Settings popover (accessed by tapping the Settings button in the top-left corner of the window).

Choosing a text editor

Several of the very best iOS developers have thrown their hats into the ring for making the definitive text editor and, as you can see, there is no shortage of options for iPad workers who want to just write. Likewise, there is no single right answer for which text editor is best. It really depends on how you intend to use it. If you want to keep a large database of notes, you require a text editor that can easily search the notes. If you want to do a lot of writing but then send the text to a different word processor and don't care about search, you want one of the text editors with the best writing environment.

Moreover, because there are so many talented developers working in this space, there is an arms race of sorts that benefits all us users. All these applications are constantly iterating and adding new features. They are relatively inexpensive, so pick a few that look right for you and give them a try.

KEEPING A DIARY

If you would like to keep a diary on your iPad, look no further than DayOne,. This simple diary app covers all the bases and looks great doing it. Moreover, there is a companion Mac app that syncs your diary entries between your Mac and iPad using iCloud. Although I've never been a diarist, this app tempts me.

Syncing text to your Mac or Windows PC

When you're done working with the text file on your iPad, there are several ways to get it to your Mac or Windows PC. The easiest is to simply point your word processor at your Dropbox or other cloud service folder and open the desired text file. You can then format, proofread, and complete it. Just make sure to save the final document in the final word processor's format, since saving the file as plain text will not preserve your formatting. I recommend you save the document to a different location or with a different name, leaving the original file in its plain text formatting. That way, if you ever want to go back and use the text again, you can.

On the Mac, you can install Notational Velocity (free, `www.notational.net`) or Brett Terpstra's NValt (free, `www.brettterpstra.com/project/nvalt`) to search, edit, and create notes in a simple application environment. Notational Velocity is covered at length in my other book, *Mac at Work*. If you use Simplenote, you can similarly access, search, and modify your notes using Notational Velocity or NValt on the Mac or ResophNotes (free, `www.resoph.com/resophnotes`) on a Windows PC.

Formatting text with Markdown

There are a variety of useful text editors on the iPad. Working with text, however, has its limitations. You are restricted to just the words. There is no way to insert any sort of formatting. What if, while typing in a text file, you want to mark something as bold text or italics? You could wait until you import the text to a dedicated word processor on your iPad, Mac, or Windows PC. However, if you want to add that formatting while you type, there is a way. It is called Markdown.

Markdown is an open source text formatting syntax developed by John Gruber, publisher of DaringFireball.net. The original purpose of Markdown was to create an easy way to write for the web. Since the first days of the Internet, HTML has been the language of the web. However, it is difficult to write in HTML: The syntax is exacting, and if you get anything wrong, it breaks. Moreover, it is not easy to read. Here is a simple bulleted list written with HTML code:

```
<p>Warehouse supplies</p>
```

```
<ul>
<li>Tin foil</li>
<li>Antenna array</li>
<li>Pocket fusion device</li>
<li>Pizza</li>
<li>Beer</li>
</ul>
```

Here is that same bullet list written using Markdown.

```
Warehouse supplies
* Tin foil
* Antenna array
* Pocket fusion device
* Pizza
* Beer
```

As you can see, it is much easier to write (and read) Markdown. This was great for the non-geek types writing for the Internet. Many web publishers adopted Markdown.

That, however, is not where the story ends. With the explosion of multiple operating systems, like the iPad, people started looking for ways to painlessly write from all their devices and operating systems. It didn't take long to figure out plain text is the easiest medium for the mobile world. We just needed a way to insert formatting into plain text. The perfect solution already existed: Markdown.

The point is that Markdown, originally designed to generate HTML, is perfect for sharing text with formatting. The iPad didn't exist when Markdown first appeared but Markdown feels custom-made for writing in plain text on multiple devices.

Using Markdown, you can add basic formatting to these text files, including headings, bold, italic, and links. Later, you can convert that Markdown text to HTML code or RTF (Rich Text Format) for use in your word processor on your PC. (I'll show you how to do that in just a bit.)

Markdown syntax

So how do you learn Markdown? Markdown is ridiculously easy to learn; it takes only about 15 minutes.

Italics. To mark text for italics, surround it with single asterisks `*like this*` or underscores `_like this_`.

Boldface. To mark an item as bold, surround it with two asterisks `**like this**` or two underscores `__like this__`.

Headings. Headings are coded with a series of number signs (#) at the beginning.

```
# Here is heading one
## Here is heading two
### Here is heading three
```

You could also set headings one and two with lines underneath.

DICTIONARIES

No matter how you go about word processing or editing text on your iPad, there are notable dictionaries available on the iPad. There are two general classes of dictionaries on the iPad: 1) the traditional dictionaries, which are measured in pounds and (in the case of the iPad) file size; and 2) pesky upstarts that are smaller, faster, and generally cheaper. Two of the best examples are, respectively, the American Heritage Dictionary and WordBook XL.

American Heritage Dictionary for iPad

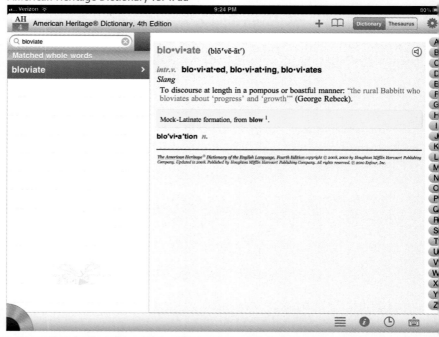

```
Here is heading one
==============
Here is heading two
-------------------------
```

Bulleted lists. To make a bulleted list, start each bullet line with an asterisk.

```
Here is a list of items for the campout:
* Toothbrush
* Bug Spray
* Hyperbaric chamber
```

American Heritage Dictionary ($25), shown on the opposite page, combines the original 300,000-word dictionary with Roget's Thesaurus. The application runs fast despite its large database size and features real-time progressive lookup. There are also 64,000 recorded pronunciation sound files. Everything is stored on your iPad, so no online connection is required.

Wordbook XL ($3), shown below, offers a smaller (and cheaper) alternative to the American Heritage Dictionary. It covers 150,000 words and a built-in thesaurus. The dictionary also includes etymologies for 23,000 root words and spoken pronunciations. WordBook XL is a good low-cost dictionary.

WordBook XL for iPad

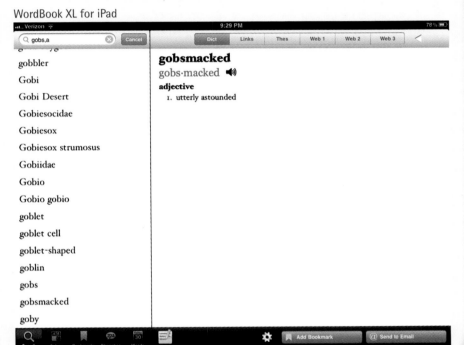

Numbered lists. Likewise, you can make a numbered list by substituting numbers for asterisks.

```
List of items for iPad adventure:
1. Deep sea iPad case;
2. External power supply;
3. Treasure map application.
```

Hyperlinks. If you are including links in your text, enclose the reference text in brackets followed by the link in parentheses. For example: `Here is a link to a [spectacularly nerdy Web site.](http://www.macsparky.com).`

WHAT ABOUT RTF?

RTF (Rich Text Format) is a document format that is meant to be word processor-independent. Using RTF you can embed codes for basic formatting in a document and most word processors read and understand it. (Note that Microsoft Word has better RTF support than Pages for Mac does.)

Apple added RTF support to iOS 5 and as this book went to press, there was likely to be a flood of new RTF text editors. Nevertheless, I prefer plain text for the reasons explained in this chapter. Using Markdown syntax, you can add formatting to plain text and still have all the advantages of plain text.

So you have the basics. If you learn these simple syntax rules and incorporate them into your text entry in your iPad text editor, you'll be able to add formatting to that text from your Mac or Windows PC. If you want to learn more about Markdown check out the full Markdown syntax guide on John Gruber's website, Daring Fireball (www.daringfireball.net/projects/markdown/syntax).

If you do technical or academic writing, you may want to investigate MultiMarkdown, an offshoot of Markdown that includes additional syntax for item such as footnotes, bibliographies, and related metadata. MultiMarkdown was create by Fletcher Penny, and you can learn more about it at his MultiMarkdown website (www.fletcherpenney.net/multimarkdown).

Converting Markdown

So let's say you've been working for weeks on a text file among your Mac, iPhone, and iPad using Markdown syntax. It is as good as it's going to get, so it is time to send that file to a word processor. How do you convert the Markdown to something your word processor understands? It's easy.

There are several software tools on Mac OS X for converting Markdown text to rich text or HTML. One of the best solutions is Scrivener ($45, www.literatureandlatte.com/scrivener.php), a very capable word processor that includes Markdown and MultiMarkdown support. Another option is TextMate (€39, http://macromates.com), one of the premier Mac OS X text editors that allows you to write in Markdown and MultiMarkdown and provides previews and syntax to make the job easier.

Mac OS X also has several free tools, including NValt, described earlier in this chapter. Finally, you can download the free Perl script from Markdown creator John Gruber's website at www.daringfireball.net/projects/markdown.

The Perl script also works on the PC. There are applications that convert Markdown text to HTML on the PC, including Softpedia's Text to HTML converter ($10, www.softpedia.com). The Windows text editor WriteMonkey (free, http://writemonkey.com) also includes Markdown support, allowing you to

MY TEXT WORKFLOW

I started using Simplenote before all the Dropbox-syncing tools existed. Perhaps I am a creature of habit, but I still prefer Simplenote as a text bank and text database. It syncs quickly and efficiently, and it has never failed me. Nevertheless, I am not a fan of Simplenote's writing interface. I've used all the text editors covered in this chapter, but my current favorites are WriteRoom, Notesy, and Writing Kit.

I have to admit that my preferred iPad text editor seems to change with the same frequency of my socks. This is a good thing. The developers are aggressively seeking our business and constantly making their products better. Any text editing app mentioned in this chapter is a good choice. Regardless of which editor I use, they are all constantly syncing to Dropbox, so anything I write on my iPad gets immediately backed up to the Dropbox storage cloud and is available on all my other computers. If I write something in a text editor that needs to get synced with my Simplenote database, I copy the text on my iPad and paste it into Simplenote.

With respect to formatting, I write everything in Markdown, so I'm free to write anywhere. The iPad is an excellent writing platform.

write in Markdown on your Windows PC and convert your text files to standard formatting.

An Example: My Workflow for This Book

This chapter covers a lot of ground about using text on your iPad for good reason: Text is an incredibly powerful tool for mobile workers. For example, looking back at the various iterations of this chapter as I wrote it, I used text in several ways.

To begin, I wrote large portions of the text using Notesy on my iPad while sipping overpriced tea at a local coffee and tea shop. All the text synced with Dropbox, and I edited it on my Mac with a nice Markdown-friendly Mac text editor. Each bit of text stayed there for several days as I tinkered with it on my iPad, iPhone, and Mac. Only when it was an acceptable first draft did I move the text into Scrivener on my Mac for final review, formatting, and submittal.

The iPad is liberating. Using it and the tools covered in this chapter, I can do serious writing just about anywhere. So go ahead. Take the plunge. Embrace the joy of text.

14

PDFs and Your iPad

Adobe PDF (Portable Document Format) is the *lingua franca* of the Internet. No matter which Mac or Windows word processor, spreadsheet, graphic, or other application you use, chances are you can save to PDF. Once the file is a PDF, you are aces. Your document can be read by any computing platform using nearly any operating system, including the iPad and its iOS. Indeed, the iPad is particularly well suited to working with PDFs. The iPad is a lean, mean, PDF reading machine. This chapter shows you how to manage, annotate, and create PDF files all from your comfy chair using nothing but your iPad and your finger.

Managing PDFs

The PDF format is so entrenched at the workplace that as soon as the iPad was released, the App Store was full of competing PDF readers slugging it out. Now that the iPad has been around a while, the PDF app market has settled and there is, in my mind, a clear winner: GoodReader ($5). GoodReader seeks to be the do-everything, be-everywhere PDF manager and reader for your iPad. It largely succeeds.

Although GoodReader's success is not a fluke, I was not originally a fan. The GoodReader interface is rough, partly as a result of the sheer number of GoodReader's tools and options. Regardless, if PDF apps were prizefighters, GoodReader would be the one with the crooked nose that has a knack for putting all its competitors, even the pretty boys, on the mat. Despite my initial reluctance, GoodReader's ever-growing bag of PDF tricks has made me a believer.

GoodReader's main library window, shown in Figure 14-1, includes two equal-size panes. The left pane shows a folder structure and the right pane a series of smaller panes (called *subpanes*). I think of the right pane as a toolbox, with each subpane holding its own assortment of PDF tools. The subpanes are named Preview, Find Files, Manage Files, Web Downloads, and Connect to Servers. Tapping on a subpane causes it to expand and display its associated tools.

The GoodReader toolbar is located at the bottom of the right pane, as shown in Figure 14-1. It includes icon buttons for a photo browser (accessing the iPad's Photos library), Wi-Fi sync, the application settings, and help. It also includes icon buttons for sending your GoodReader screen to an external monitor and locking the screen orientation.

Getting files in GoodReader

There is no shortage of methods to get your PDFs into GoodReader including USB cable sync (via iTunes), Wi-Fi sync, and cloud-based syncing (including iCloud).

iTunes sync

Using the USB syncing cable or a Wi-Fi connection (in iOS 5), you can copy documents to and from GoodReader via iTunes. To do so, select GoodReader in the

FIGURE 14-1

GoodReader's library window

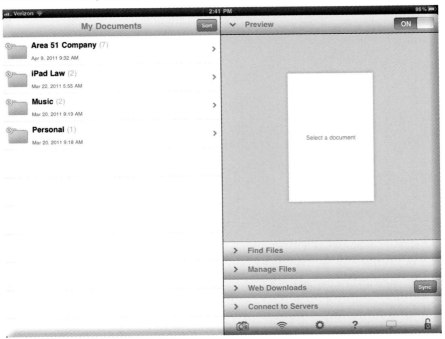

File Management area of the Apps pane in iTunes while your iPad is connected. You can then drag files to and from GoodReader. Unfortunately the file manager in iTunes is limited. For example, you have to create nested folders in GoodReader. I cover how to add and remove files from your iPad using iTunes in Chapter 1.

Wi-Fi sync

GoodReader can establish a Wi-Fi connection with any Windows PC or Mac on your network. Wi-Fi sync lets you bypass the tedious process of syncing PDF files through iTunes.

Tapping the Wi-Fi icon in the toolbar opens a window with instructions and the IP address for your iPad. It also points to the GoodReader website, which provides more detailed step-by-step instructions for linking your iPad to your computer.

To link GoodReader to a Mac, go to the Mac OS X Finder and choose Go ➪ Connect to Server or press ⌘+K. Type in the IP address from GoodReader in the Finder dialog box and click Connect. A Finder window opens, and you can now start copying files to and from GoodReader. Make sure to keep your iPad turned on and GoodReader active while downloading.

Syncing to a Windows 7 PC takes a few more steps. First, choose Start ➪ Computer and then click the Map Network Drive button at the top-right of the window. In the Map Network Drive window, choose the Connect to a Web Site That You Can Use to Store Your Documents and Pictures selection. In the new window, Add Network Location, click the Next button. Then click the Choose a Custom Network Location button in the middle of the window. Finally, you get a text field that asks for the Internet or network address. Type in the IP address from GoodReader and press Enter; you are now connected and can transfer files between Windows and your iPad.

If you've never linked your iPad through Wi-Fi, give it a go. It really isn't that difficult, and you will be surprised how handy it is to wirelessly copy PDF files back and forth. If the nuances of connecting your iPad to your computer via Wi-Fi is making your mind drift off to its happy place, never fear.

Syncing in the cloud

Cloud-based syncing is even easier. Selecting the Connect to Servers tab in GoodReader's right pane opens the menu to link GoodReader to your local and Internet-based servers. GoodReader supports most of the popular cloud-based services including iCloud (covered in Chapter 5), Google Docs, Dropbox, SugarSync, and Box.net. You can additionally link GoodReader to WebDAV, FTP, and Secure FTP servers. Finally, GoodReader syncs with mail servers such as Gmail, Yahoo, MobileMe, Hotmail, AOL, and any IMAP or POP service. Put simply, GoodReader syncs with just about everything.

Connecting to a server is easy. For example, to connect to your Dropbox account (you did take my advice and get a Dropbox account, right?), tap the Add button in the Connect to Server subpane. Tap the Dropbox icon button and insert your username, password, and an optional title. That is it. GoodReader then hooks in to Dropbox and appears in your server list. Tapping the connected server lets you browse its contents in the left pane.

So what does cloud syncing GoodReader do for you? A lot. It means that any data you copy to your Dropbox account (or other connected server) is available in GoodReader any time your iPad is turned on and connected to the Internet. Moreover, you can select and download documents to your GoodReader library from cloud services so they are available even when you are *not* connected to the Internet.

Take a moment to think about cloud-syncing GoodReader. If you work routinely with PDF files and want to have them available at all times on your iPad, you just need to copy them to your Dropbox folder or any cloud-based server, from any computer. Better yet, just *keep* the PDF files on the cloud-based server. Then you can access those PDFs from any Internet-connected computer.

At this point you are probably starting to worry about versioning problems. What if you make changes on your Mac and forget about it when returning to your iPad. That is a vexing problem for all iPad owners, but GoodReader has an answer: It syncs.

When I say "it syncs," I don't just mean you can access and download files. I mean that you can keep entire folders in sync across devices and computers. The syncing feature finally convinced me to get over the messy user interface and start using GoodReader. To enable syncing, pick any folder in your cloud service and tap the Sync button. Then choose a folder in your GoodReader database to hold the synced folder. There are no more steps. Now whenever you start GoodReader, tap the Web Downloads subpane and the Sync icon button next to the folder to have GoodReader go to Dropbox (or whatever cloud service you prefer) and check the folder contents in your GoodReader document library versus the same folder in the cloud; it syncs the folder as needed. You always have the most current versions. When you are done working in GoodReader, tap the Sync icon button again and GoodReader uploads the changes. Painless.

You can set the sync to be bidirectional, as just described, or unidirectional, so the iPad only receives files and doesn't upload them back. The unidirectional sync is perfect for distributing PDFs, such as memoranda and meeting agendas, to your team. They can then annotate their copies (for example, writing "fool" under the boss's name) and the annotations will not upload back to the server.

Although the iCloud service is fantastic, I find Dropbox syncing works best for PDF files. Because a single PDF may be used in four separate PDF applications, iCloud's app-based syncing paradigm (where the file is synced only with a single app) doesn't work with my PDFs.

Grab it from somewhere else

Using the Open In menu in other iPad apps (including Mail and other PDF applications), you can also open files and PDFs in GoodReader. The iPad then creates a new copy of the PDF in the GoodReader library.

A little known, but ingenious, way to get web pages into GoodReader is the "g trick." Navigate to any page in the Safari browser. Add a "g" to the beginning of the URL (like `ghttp://www.macsparky.com/`) to have GoodReader automatically open and import the page. This is particularly slick when viewing online PDF documents. The GoodReader Settings icon button (the gear in the toolbar at the bottom of the right pane) also includes an option to install a JavaScript bookmark in your iPad's Safari browser that sends the current web page to GoodReader.

File management and search

Now that you've collected your PDF files in GoodReader, it is time to organize them. GoodReader organizes your PDF files in the Manage Files subpane in the right pane. Tapping the Manage Files subpane adds selection bubbles to the files and folders in the left pane, shown in Figure 14-2.

File management then becomes a matter of tapping the selection bubble (it fi in green) and selecting the file-management task in the Manage Files subpane. For example, to move a file, tap the selection bubble in the left pane next to the target file, tap the Move button in the right pane, and select the destination in the menu. In addition to the basic copy and move functions, you can Zip, e-mail, rename, lin add tasks, and even open the file with other PDF applications on your iPad.

The Manage Files subpane doesn't stop there. GoodReader also helps organize your PDFs. You can add folders or star (mark as a favorite) a file so it is easier to fi

FIGURE 14-2

File management with GoodReader

(using the Find Files subpane covered later). You can also protect a file. Protecting a file locks it, requiring a password to be opened.

GoodReader provides several options to secure your PDFs. Using the Settings icon button (the gear icon in the toolbar at the bottom of the right pane), GoodReader provides options to set a password for starting the app (and accessing your entire library) or just for individually protected files. In addition to passcode-locking a file, GoodReader can also encrypt files.

The Preview subpane (located at the top of the right pane) displays a small preview of the selected document or file. To access it, select the file in the left pane and tap the Preview tab in the right pane. This is useful when your co-workers send dubiously named files like kmg365.pdf.

The Find Files subpane, located below the Preview subpane, searches the GoodReader library. GoodReader searches by filename (but not file contents) or displays only a list of your files sorted by last date read, last date added, or only those files you have starred in the Manage Files subpane.

Working with PDFs

So you've imported and organized your PDFs. What about reading and annotating documents? To open a PDF file, tap it in the left pane. The GoodReader interface then disappears and the app dedicates your iPad screen to displaying your PDF file as shown in Figure 14-3.

FIGURE 14-3

Reading a PDF in GoodReader

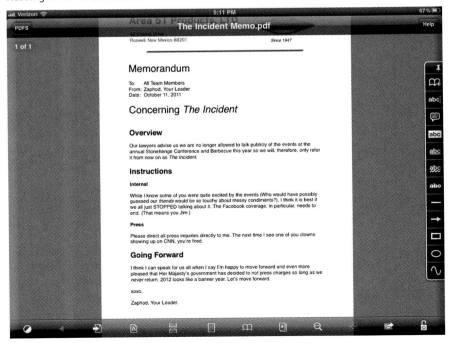

When you first open a PDF in GoodReader, there are three series of tools, one each at the top, bottom, and left side of the window, as Figure 14-3 shows. After a moment, the tools disappear. You can make them return (or make them disappear again) by tapping the center of the window.

When the tools are gone, your iPad screen is dedicated to displaying your PDF files. Multipage documents scroll left or right. You can tap and swipe to advance pages. Alternatively, you can tap on the right side of the window to move forward on the left side of the window to move backward. Double-tapping the window with one finger zooms in, and double-tapping with two fingers zooms out. Alternatively use the two-finger pinch gesture to zoom in and out.

If you just want to read a PDF book, GoodReader provides a perfectly acceptable environment to do so (although I prefer iBooks for this purpose, as covered in Chapter 15). You can swipe left and right to advance pages, and GoodReader does the rest.

If you want to modify your PDF file, tap the center of the window to bring back the PDF tools. The top of the window displays the Back icon button (an arrow icon in the upper-left portion with the active file's name). Tapping Back returns GoodReader to the library view. The upper-right portion of the window has the Help button that explains features and displays the tap zones on the window.

The left side of the window (when the tools are displayed) has a slider to help you navigate your document. Tap and hold the Scrub button (the white dot in the middle of the slider) and drag it up and down as needed. Sadly, this does not include the slick page preview function you get with the Pages word processor, covered in Chapter 13. Tapping the page indicator badge (in Figure 14-3, it reads "of 1") invokes the Go to Page popover. Type in your page number, and GoodReader jumps to the page.

All the remaining controls appear in the bottom toolbar. From left to right, the are as follows.

 Day/Night Mode: The Day/Night Mode icon button quickly dims the screen if you are reading in a dark room.

 Go Back: Consider this an undo button for PDF navigation. If you tap the wrong link or jump to the wrong page, tapping the Go Back icon button returns GoodReader to where you started. GoodReader remembers your last 20 positions.

 PDF Reflow: The PDF Reflow tool extracts text from the current PDF page and displays it on your screen. If you are reading a PDF with illegible text, PDF Reflow really useful. For this tool to work, however, the PDF file must have text embedded (Although GoodReader can read text from your PDF file, it cannot perform optical character recognition (OCR) for you on text that is scanned or otherwise not embedded in the file. That OCR needs to happen on your Mac, PC, or scanner before the PDF file gets to your iPad.)

 Rotate a File: The Rotate a File icon button opens a popover with rotation controls. If your PDF file is incorrectly oriented, use Rotate a File.

Page Layout: The Page Layout icon button provides options for single- and double-page layout. In double-page mode, GoodReader displays two pages next to each other on your iPad.

Crop: The Crop tool opens your PDF in a page with adjustable margins. You set the margin and crop the page. If your PDF has a large margin, crop it so you don't waste any of your valuable iPad screen space.

Locations: The Locations tool opens a popover from which you can access your bookmarks, outlines, and PDF annotations. You can also add bookmarks to your PDF files from this popover. If you work with large PDF files, take advantage of bookmarking and outlining. Bookmarks make you look brilliant when you can jump to exactly the right place while everyone in the room is fumbling with lots of scrolling, zooming, and cursing.

Go to Page: The Go to Page tool opens the Go to Page popover accessed by tapping the page badge, as explained earlier.

Search: Using the Search tool, GoodReader searches the text of your open PDF file. If the app finds more than one occurrence of your search term, you can jump among them.

Horizontal Lock: Do you ever find yourself reading a PDF file that is wider than the page and the file keeps drifting left and right when you only want to scroll up and down? If so, tap the Horizontal Lock icon button to stop that behavior.

Sharing: The Sharing icon button gives you several options for sending your file to a printer, e-mail, or a different iPad app.

Lock Rotation: The Lock Rotation tool works like the Lock Rotation icon button in GoodReader's library window. When it's active, the PDF does not change orientation while you are working on the couch. I find lock rotation particularly useful for proofreading briefs while watching baseball.

GoodReader is a champ in meetings. On a first-generation iPad (which doesn't have the mirroring functions of iPad 2) plugged into a projector, GoodReader displays your PDFs via that projector. Moreover, using all the GoodReader file-management tools, you will appear to have omniscient power over locating and displaying documents in front of your clients. You'll look brilliant.

Annotating PDFs

GoodReader includes some impressive annotation tools, including highlighting, markup (underline, squiggly line, cross-out, insertion, and replacement), popup notes, and drawing tools (lines, arrows, squares, circles, and freehand shapes).

There are several ways to annotate PDF documents in GoodReader. If you plan on doing several instances of the same annotation (highlighting, for example), tap the desired annotation in the annotation bar on the right side of the window, shown in Figure 14-3. Then use your finger as if it were a pen to make the annotations. For example, with the highlighter tool selected, you could draw your finger across lines of text to highlight at will. This is exactly how I make a first pass through important documents. When using this freehand annotation method, a small tool

Annotating a PDF document in GoodReader

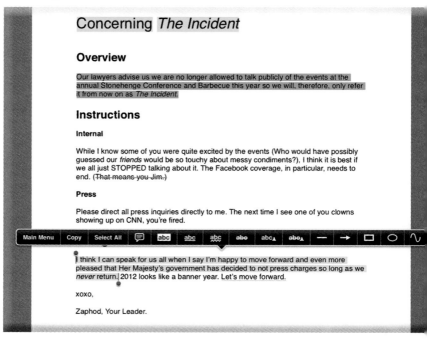

bar appears at the top of the window with buttons to cancel, undo, redo, and save the annotations as you make them.

You can also annotate selected portions of a PDF by selecting and applying annotations from a popover, shown in Figure 14-4. Tap and hold on any word; GoodReader then highlights that word and provides the standard iOS selection bar. Tap and drag the selection bars to select the desired portion of your text. While text is selected, GoodReader displays a popover with its annotation tools. Tap any tool from the popover to have GoodReader apply that annotation to the selected text. I annotate PDF documents this way when making small changes, like striking out a word when proofreading.

When you are done, you can send the PDF with annotations for use in a different app (such as Preview on the Mac or Adobe Reader on Windows, Mac, and Linux) or have GoodReader *flatten* your annotations into the file. Flattening embeds the annotations into the file's contents so you cannot alter or remove them. Flattening prevents others from altering or removing the annotations, even in a PDF editing tool.

Beyond PDFs

By now you can see why GoodReader is so popular. It does everything. You can also see why the interface can be confusing and overwhelming. *It does everything.* Although so far this chapter focused on GoodReader's PDF tools, the app can work with more files than just PDFs. GoodReader also views text files, pictures, iWork files, and Microsoft Office files, and it plays audio. There are application settings available for each file type, including, for example, font family and size for viewing text files (tap the Settings icon button in the lower-right pane). Because GoodReader opens so many file formats, it truly becomes the open-anything app on your iPad.

Signing PDF Forms on the iPad

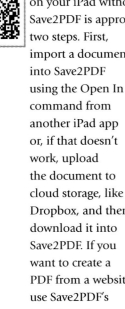

To digitally sign PDF documents on your iPad, look no further than PDF Expert ($10). By far, PDF Expert has the best implementation of a digital signature tool. Using PDF Expert, you can sign using the entire iPad screen and later apply (and resize) the signature to fit in your PDF document. You can even choose the ink color.

Creating PDFs

Although GoodReader is great for PDF management and annotation, what about creating PDFs on your iPad? You may one day be writing a document or looking at a web page and want to convert it to PDF. On a Mac or Windows PC, this is easy. Mac OS X lets you print anything to PDF. The iPad, however, does not. Once again, independent software developers come to the rescue. If your iPad is on a network with a Mac, you can use Printopia (covered in Chapter 1) to save any document as a PDF. (There are no similar options for Windows PCs.) To create PDFs on your iPad without help of a Mac, install Save2PDF ($10). Shown in Figure 14-5, Save2PDF is appropriately named: It saves to PDF. Creating a PDF with the app takes two steps. First, import a document into Save2PDF using the Open In command from another iPad app or, if that doesn't work, upload the document to cloud storage, like Dropbox, and then download it into Save2PDF. If you want to create a PDF from a website, use Save2PDF's built-in web browser.

Once you have selected the source,

GOODREADER ALTERNATIVES

If you don't need all the extra features of GoodReader, why not use a PDF app with a cleaner user interface? In that case, check out ReaddleDocs ($5). It doesn't have all of GoodReader's features (and doesn't try to) but is easy to use and looks great.

iBooks (covered in Chapter 15) is also a great app for reading PDF files. It doesn't, however, include any modification or annotation tools. If you are simply reading a PDF book, go for it. For working with a sales proposal or important contract, however, stick with the tools in this chapter.

FIGURE 14-5

Creating a PDF with Save2PDF

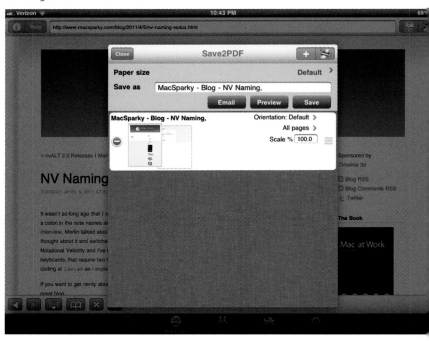

tap the PDF button in the upper-right corner of the window to open a popover wi options for orientation, scale, and other PDF preferences. Save the file directly to t Save2PDF document database or e-mail it. Although Save2PDF does not include a the features of GoodReader, Save2PDF gets the job done if you need to create a PL on your iPad.

As you can see, the iPad provides a complete platform for PDF management, annotation, and even creation. Indeed, once you work on PDFs on your iPad, it is

MY IPAD PDF WORKFLOW

So how do I work with PDFs on my iPad? I keep and manage PDF files in GoodReader using all the tools covered in this chapter. I bookmark and run optical character recognition on all scanned PDF files I intend to view on my iPad. I sync all my PDF documents to a common Dropbox account so I can access them on any of my computers or my iPad. (GoodReader's sync function is key to this working right.)

Once I finish any annotations, I sync the file back to Dropbox, and those annotations appear the next time I view the file on my Mac or PC. The only exception is when I have a PDF document purely for reference, such as a product manual or a book, in which case I put the PDF file in iBooks, as Chapter 15 explains.

difficult to return to a computer and keyboard for reviewing and annotating PDF files. Your iPad will spoil you.

15

Reading Books

One of the original complaints about the iPad was that although it had great potential as a content-consumption device, it was not suited for content creation. Essentially, critics argued (many without having touched an iPad) that the iPad was great for reading but it was not useful for writing. At least they got the first part right. As for the second part, read Chapter 13.

When it comes to reference materials, the iPad lets you cram a seemingly endless supply of documents and books in its skinny aluminum body. At any one time, I carry multiple books ranging from legal treatises to pulp fiction, and it still amazes me that I can access any one of those books anywhere as long as I have my iPad. The two best ways to manage reading materials on your iPad are Apple's iBooks and Amazon.com's Kindle for iPad apps. I cover both in this chapter.

iBooks

iBooks (free) is Apple's book reader application. For reasons more likely related to anticompetition laws than common sense, iBooks does not ship on your new iPad. You must download it from the App Store.

Like all things Apple, iBooks has plenty of polish. Opening iBooks, the bookshelf view, shown in Figure 15-1, is a virtual bookshelf right down to the quarter-sawn pine. Before long, you will fill those shelves with electronic books and references. The Grid icon button (the 2×2 grid in the upper-right corner) displays your books on the bookshelf. The List icon button (the three vertical lines) removes the bookshelf and instead organizes books in a list sorting by your choice of title, author, and category.

Getting books in iBooks

The easiest way to get new books is, not surprisingly, to buy them from Apple. Tap the Store button in the upper-left corner of the window, and your bookcase spins around, unveiling the Apple iBookstore. The shopping experience in the iBookstore is easy and painless. You can search for a specific title or author using the Search bar at the right of the toolbar. There are a series of icon buttons in the lower toolbar that display featured books and top sellers. The Browse icon button opens a window where you can skim through authors and categories. The Purchased button displays all the books you have purchased from the iBookstore and lets you download any purchased content not already on your iPad.

When you find an interesting book, tap it and a popover opens, providing more details, as shown in Figure 15-2. If you want to purchase the book, tap the price button ($19.99 in Figure 15-2) and that amount of money gets whisked out of your iTunes account. The iBookstore then flips back to the bookshelf view and adds your new book. The next time you sync your iPad to iTunes, your new book gets added to your iTunes library. Likewise, you can download the purchased book on another iOS device using the iBookstore's Purchased icon button and the iCloud service downloads a fresh copy.

FIGURE 15-1

The iBooks bookshelf view

FIGURE 15-2

Purchasing a book in the iBookstore

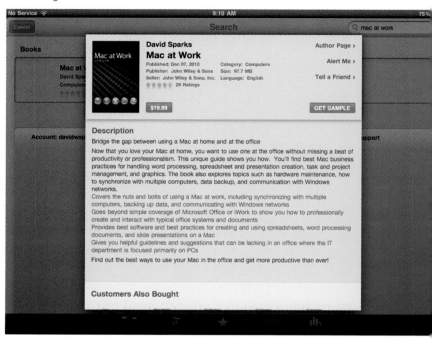

If you are not sure about a book, tap the Get Sample button in the iBookstore and, rather than getting the full book, you get a free sample, usually the first chapter.

If you don't find the book you're looking for in the iBookstore, tap the Library button in the upper-left corner to return to your bookshelf.

The iBookstore has an increasing number of publishers and titles, but it does not have the same exhaustive library offered by the Amazon Kindle Store (covered later in this chapter).

You can also load your own books into iBooks. iBooks reads PDF and ePub files. ePub, an open standard electronic book format, is quickly becoming the form of choice for several electronic book manufacturers, including Apple and Sony. ePub files can include digital copy protection (or not). ePub files can also be purchased from several vendors. If you are looking for a book not available in the iBookstore, you may find an ePub version from another online ePub bookseller. (The Kindle for iPad app, covered later in this chapter, does not read ePub files. Instead, it uses Amazon's own proprietary Kindle file format.)

With PDF files, the page layout of the file is fixed at the time the PDF file is created. The advantage of ePub over PDF is control: iBooks can control typography and other settings for the reading experience of ePub files. With PDF files, there is no control over font size or type. Sometimes this is a good thing: If the document includes complex diagrams and layout, the author may not want the book reader to change anything. iBooks distinguishes PDFs from ePub files in the bookshelf view adding black spiral binding to PDFs, as seen in the *Macworld* magazine and Rework PDF files in Figure 15-1.

To install your ePub or PDF books, import the files into iTunes by choosing File ➪ Add to Library in iTunes on your Mac or Windows PC, or just drag the file into your iTunes library. The next time you sync your iPad, the imported books are copied to your iPad and appear in your iBooks library.

You can also add ePub and PDF files directly to your iBooks library from your iPad. If you receive an ePub or PDF file as an e-mail attachment, tap and hold the file until the Open In menu appears, and then open the file in iBooks. The book then gets added to your iBooks library. Likewise, you can save directly to iBooks from your cloud storage services, such as Dropbox. To add a book from Dropbox, select the ePub or PDF file in the Dropbox app (covered in Chapter 5) and tap the Open In icon button in the upper-right corner of the Dropbox toolbar to open a menu from which you can send the file to iBooks. Finally, any books purchased from the iBookstore automatically sync among all iOS devices via Apple's iCloud service.

You can also add books from the web. From iPad Safari's browser navigate to a website with an ePub file and tap and hold on the file in the browser. The Open In menu appears, letting you download and open the file in iBooks. With little effort, you can quickly fill your iBooks library.

Organizing the iBooks library

To organize the books in your library, tap the Edit button in the upper-right corner of the toolbar, shown in Figure 15-1. Once you enter edit mode, the toolbar changes to offer Move, Delete, Select All, and Done buttons.

To move a book, tap and hold on it. After a few seconds the book grows slightly larger and appears to lift off the bookshelf. Drag the book to its new location, and the remaining books make room for it. Lift your finger and the book shrinks back to its normal size at its new location. Tap Done when you're finished to return to the regular iBooks menu.

If you have a lot of material in iBooks, use the Collections feature to group similar titles on one bookshelf. To create a new collection, tap the Collections

WHAT ABOUT BOOK APPLICATIONS?

Some book publishers are avoiding book readers on the iPad and instead releasing books as specific applications. You buy the application and it downloads a book wrapped in a custom reader app.

I am not a fan of this approach. These formats are proprietary, so you are unable to read these books on any other device. Also, often the book-reading app attached to this downloaded book does not receive the same love and attention given to the iBooks or Amazon Kindle apps. As a result, the reading experience is not as good. Buy these books with caution.

IBOOKS OR GOODREADER?

Although GoodReader (covered at length in Chapter 14) is an outstanding application for organizing, modifying, and annotating PDF files, iBooks' polished user interface makes it the perfect app for PDF files you just want to read. My iBooks library is full of PDF files I've downloaded or scanned in including user manuals, books, and articles I've torn out of magazines. I love having access to these materials anywhere.

button in the left portion of the toolbar, next to the iBookstore button, to get the collections view.

Tap the Edit or New buttons to add, modify, and remove collections. It is a good idea to add collections for your favorite subjects. Then return to the library window and tap the Edit button in the upper-right corner. Select the books you want to place in your new collection and tap the Move button in the top-left portion of the window. A popover appears with all your collections. Tap the destination collection and the selected books move to their new location. You can move just one book or multiple books at once this way. If you use iBooks on other iPads, iPhones, or iPod Touches, the collections appear on those devices as well after they sync.

If, despite your collections and organizational prowess, you still can't find your book, tap the Search bar found at the top-center of the top shelf (shown in Figure 15-1), and iBooks finds it for you.

Reading with iBooks

Now that your ePub and PDF files are installed and organized, it is time to read. To open a book, tap it. Your bookshelf disappears and the selected book fills the screen, as shown in Figure 15-3. iBooks faithfully reproduces a physical book with the pages curling into the virtual spine and exposed ruffled pages at the edges.

Reading a book in iBooks is a joy. Holding your iPad in portrait mode displays one page at a time. If you turn your iPad on its side to landscape mode, iBooks displays two pages, as shown in Figure 15-3.

Once you choose your preferred font and type size (as explained later in this chapter), there is nothing left to do but read. You advance pages by tapping the right side of the window or go backward by tapping the left side of the window.

If you tap and hold the right side, you can pull the page over. This page-turn animation is one of those small touches that Apple is so good at. It is immediately responsive. You can pull the page over as quickly (or slowly) as you want. As you turn the page, the back of the turned page shows an imprint of the text from the preceding page, as if the ink bled through the paper. The overall experience creates the feeling that you are actually reading a printed book.

The reading controls are simple. (If you don't see them, tap the center of the window.) The Library button, in the top-left corner, closes the active book and

FIGURE 15-3

The reading view in iBooks

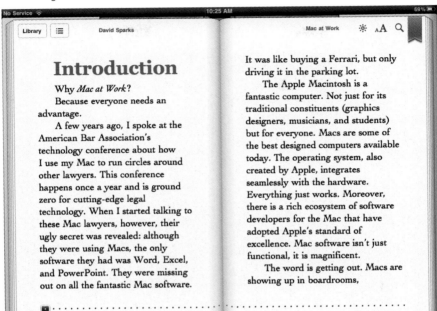

FIGURE 15-4

A table of contents in iBooks

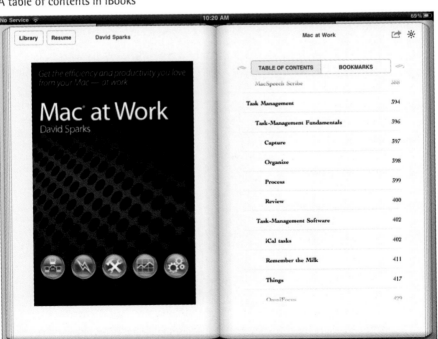

FIGURE 15-5

Searching in iBooks

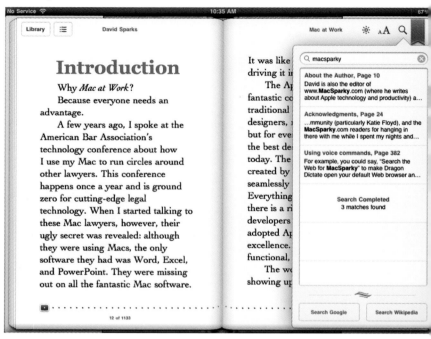

FIGURE 15-6

Highlighting text in iBooks

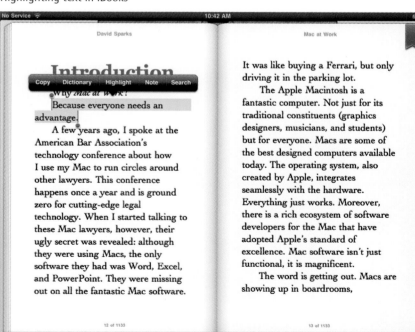

returns iBooks to the bookshelf view. When exiting a book, iBooks remembers where you left off, and the next time you open that book, it returns to the same page.

The Contents icon button (the icon of three lines, each with a dot and dash) opens the current book's table of contents, as shown in Figure 15-4. You can scroll up and down in the table of contents and jump to any entry by tapping it. Alternatively, you can view the active bookmarks in the current book. (I cover bookmarks later in this chapter.)

Because PDF files do not have the same data as ePub files, PDFs do not have the same table of contents view. Tapping the Table of Contents button in a PDF file opens a grid (3×3 in portrait and 4×2 in landscape) showing multiple pages of the PDF file. Likewise, although you can bookmark individual pages, iBooks does not provide a list of bookmarks in the PDF's table of contents as it does with ePub books. Instead, bookmarks appear on the displayed PDF images.

At the top right of the table of contents is the Sharing icon button (the curved arrow icon), which may (or may not) work depending on the digital rights management in the current book. Use the Brightness icon button (the light icon) to set the brightness when reading in a dark room.

While reading a book, there are a few additional icon buttons, shown at the top-right portion of Figure 15-3. Tap the Typeface icon button (the AA symbol) to open the Typeface popover where you can set the typeface, font size, and background

FIGURE 15-7

iBooks' dictionary view

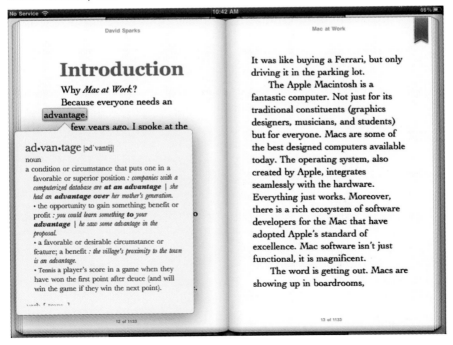

READING PERIODICALS WITH NEWSSTAND

Since the iPad is great for reading books, what about periodicals? It should be easy on the iPad, right? With the release of iOS 5, Apple has added the Newsstand.

The Newsstand is a unique creature on the iPad. First, the Newsstand is not so much an app as it is a smart folder. It holds various periodicals' apps so all your periodical materials are in one place.

Moreover, Newsstand apps are granted a unique superpower by Apple: background downloading. That means while you sleep, the most recent edition of, say, The *New Yorker* automatically downloads into your Newsstand. No other category of app has this ability on the iPad. When you wake up in the morning, you can enjoy the latest news with your breakfast on your iPad. For automatic downloads to work, the iPad must be plugged into a power source and on a Wi-Fi network. (Apple doesn't want Newsstand to use up your battery or bandwidth caps.)

color (white or sepia). One of my favorite iBooks features is its rich assortment of typefaces.

Use the Search icon button (the magnifying glass) to search the text. When iBooks performs a search, it opens a popover with links to the searched phrase and its surrounding text, as shown in Figure 15-5. iBooks can also search your choice of Google and Wikipedia for your search phrase.

Finally, the Bookmark icon button (the ribbon) at the top right of the window bookmarks your current page so you may view it in the table of contents (covered earlier). Tap the Bookmark button and a red bookmark slides down, as shown in Figure 15-3. In the table of contents, tapping the Bookmarks button displays a list of all bookmarks and their creation dates for your current book.

The bottom of the window includes a series of dots indicating the entire length of the book along with a rectangular icon indicating your current position in it. Tap and hold the rectangle and drag it left or right to "scrub" through the book. As you scroll back and forth, a small indicator opens, showing the current subject and page number.

To highlight a word or phrase in iBooks, tap and hold on a single word. The iC selection handles then appear so you can expand the selection. A contextual menu also opens with options to highlight the selected word, as shown in Figure 15-6. Use the Note button for typing notes related to the highlighted text. The menu also has options to copy text (depending on the book's copy protection), search for other instances of the same text in the current book, and define the selected word. The dictionary implementation, shown in Figure 15-7, is attractive.

There are additional settings available only from the Settings application on your iPad. In Settings, scroll down the left pane and tap iBooks to get a pane with options that include the ability to turn off full justification (I prefer ragged right) and auto-hyphenation. If you want iBooks to advance pages when you tap the left margin (helpful when holding the iPad in just your left hand), tap the Tap Left

Margin setting. Finally, you can choose whether to send bookmarks and collections to other iOS devices.

iBooks' limitations

iBooks is a great app. It's classically Apple, so it does not have a lot of extra features, but the ones it includes are implemented exceptionally well. The typography is beautiful and the animations are amazing. iBooks also includes support for hyperlinking so you may tap a link in an ePub e-book and jump to a different location in the book or to a website in the Safari browser. iBooks is my favorite application to read books on the iPad. It has, however, some limitations.

To begin, iBooks is exclusively an iOS application. There is no version for other mobile devices. There also is no version for Microsoft Windows and, remarkably, there isn't even a version for Mac OS X. As a result, any book you buy from the Apple iBookstore can be read only on your iOS devices (iPad, iPhone, and iPod Touch).

Also, sometimes the books you want simply are not available in the iBookstore. Finally, quite often books in the iBookstore are more expensive than the same book in the Amazon Kindle Store (covered later in this chapter) — sometimes the price difference is significant.

Nevertheless, unless the price difference is prohibitive, when a book is available in the iBookstore, I buy it there. The shopping experience is so easy and iBooks' great typography wins me over every time.

Amazon Kindle for iPad

Before Apple unleashed the iPad on the world, Amazon.com was already hard at work developing its own e-book store around its e-book platform, the Kindle. Although the Kindle started out as a dedicated hardware device, Amazon expanded its Kindle products to include reader applications for most mobile platforms, including the iPad. Kindle for iPad (free), shown in Figure 15-8, offers another great way to read e-books on your iPad.

Getting books in Kindle for iPad

Getting books into the Kindle app is slightly more difficult than using iBooks. There is no way to browse the Kindle Store from directly inside the app. Instead, you browse the Kindle Store in the Safari browser or in a third-party browser such as Atomic Web, both of which are covered in Chapter 4, and purchase books from your Amazon account directly on your iPad. After buying an e-book, the next time you launch the Kindle app on your iPad, the book is available for download from the Kindle app's Archived Items button, covered later in this chapter. Although not as seamless as purchasing in the iBookstore, the process is not difficult.

The iBookstore offers convenience; the Amazon bookstore offers selection and price. Generally, the Kindle Store has a larger selection. Amazon has been selling

FIGURE 15-8

Kindle for iPad's library view

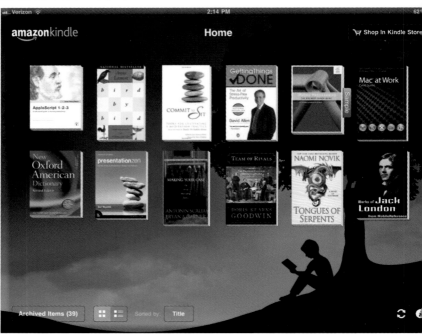

FIGURE 15-9

Reading with the Kindle Reader

David is also the editor of www.MacSparky.com (where he writes about Apple technology and productivity) and a co-host of the popular "Mac Power Users" podcast (www.macpowerusers.com).

David speaks and writes often about Apple technology. David is a frequent speaker at the annual Macworld Conference and Expo and a regular faculty member for the American Bar Association's TechShow, the premier legal technology conference, where he speaks on the Mac, iPhone, iPad, and productivity.

Introduction

Why *Mac at Work*?

Because everyone needs an advantage.

A few years ago, I spoke at the American Bar Association's technology conference about how I use my Mac to run circles around other lawyers. This conference happens once a year and is ground zero for cutting-edge legal technology. When I started talking to these Mac lawyers, however, their ugly secret was revealed: although they were using Macs, the only software they had was Word, Excel, and PowerPoint. They were missing out on all the fantastic Mac software. It was

   Aa

1% Location 45 of 5717

books a lot longer than Apple and so has more publisher deals in place. Moreover, books available in both stores are quite often cheaper in the Amazon store.

A challenge with the Kindle Reader is that it only reads books in Amazon's proprietary Kindle format (also called Mobi). The Kindle app does not read ePub files or PDF files, for example. There are, however, applications available to convert ePub files to the Kindle format (see the sidebar "Create Your Own E-Books").

Once you have a book in the Kindle format, you can add it to the Kindle app in iTunes under the Apps pane, as covered in Chapter 1.

You manage books with the Kindle app through its library window, shown in Figure 15-8. Tapping the Archived Items button in the lower-left corner displays purchased books that have not been downloaded to your iPad. The Sort button provides options to sort your books by title, author, or most recently opened. The Sync icon button in the lower-right corner syncs your last-read page with the Amazon Whispersync service, Amazon's online database that keeps track of where you are in all your e-books. This way, when you open the same book on other Kindle devices, you may continue reading where you left off. The Information icon button in the lower-right corner opens the Information popover, where you can enter your Amazon account information. Without knowing your Amazon account information, the Kindle Store can't download purchased books from your Amazon account to your iPad. The Information popover also includes settings to turn on (or off) basic

FIGURE 15-10

The Kindle Reader's table of contents

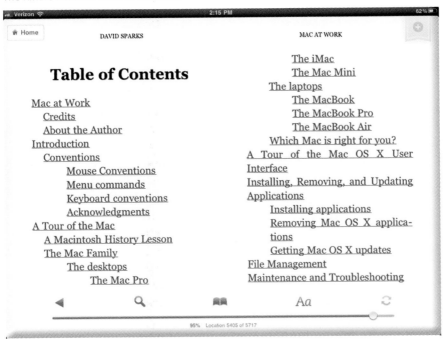

reading mode (which removes the app's animations), popular highlights (covered later in this chapter), and annotations backup.

Reading with the Kindle for iPad app

Open a book in the Kindle app by tapping it in the library view. The reading view in the Kindle app is shown in Figure 15-9. The Kindle app defaults to two columns in landscape mode and one column in portrait mode. The application tools, shown at the bottom of Figure 15-9, disappear shortly after you open the reading view but reappear if you tap in the center of the window.

The first tool on the left, the Back icon button (a left-facing triangle), returns you to the prior view. The Search icon button (the magnifying glass) searches the open book. The Search popover also includes options to run the search phrase in Google or Wikipedia, like iBooks does.

The Go To icon button (an open book), opens the Go To popover allowing yc to jump to the cover, table of contents, or specific location in your book.

Figure 15-10 shows a book's table of contents. If the book you are reading includes any special e-book features, you will find them in the table of contents.

A feature unique to the Kindle Reader app is popular highlights. Tapping the Popular Highlights button shows you a list of locations in the book highlighted by other Amazon Kindle readers.

The Typography popover, accessed with the Typeface tool icon button (the Aa symbol), lets you set the font size, background, brightness, and column view. (The Kindle app does not include options for different font selections as iBooks does.)

Finally, the Sync icon button syncs your current page with the Amazon Whispersync service, so other devices on your account "know" your last-read page.

Overall, I have few complaints with the Kindle's reading experience. The Kindl reader does not offer the fancy page-turn animation and typography you get with

CREATE YOUR OWN E-BOOKS

So now that you're sold on carrying your reference materials on your iPad, what about producing your own e-books? Calibre (donation requested; www.calibre-e-book.com) is a powerful application for Mac OS X, Windows, and Unix to manage and convert e-book formats. Using Calibre, you can manage and convert text to e-books in both ePub and Amazon's proprietary Kindle (Mobi) format for use on your iPad. Note that although it is easy to convert ePub books to the Kindle format (as long as the digital rights management permits it), it is much more difficult to convert Kindle-formatted books to ePub for use in other readers. It is, without tremendous and legally dubious effort, a one-way street.

You can also create ePub files on Mac OS X using Apple's Pages word-processing app. There is also a Google project, Sigil (free; http://code.google.com/p/sigil), that provides advanced ePub creation tools.

MY READING WORKFLOW

I bought a Kindle Reader long before the iPad was released, and over the years I have purchased several books from the Kindle Store. Because those e-books are all in the proprietary Kindle format, I read them in the Amazon Kindle app on my iPad.

However, lately I purchase my books, when available, from the iBookstore. iBooks sits on my iPad home screen and I use it all the time. I prefer the typography and the fit and finish of iBooks over those of the Amazon Kindle app. I realize this precludes me from reading purchased books on other platforms, but because I love my iPhone and iPad, I don't mind. Moreover, because the purchases are in the ePub format, I'm confident I could read them with another device if Apple suddenly disappeared from the face of the earth.

In addition to ePub files, I use iBooks' PDF functionality to read books and other reference materials that do not require PDF annotation and organizational tools available with the dedicated PDF apps covered in Chapter 14. I also use Calibre on my Mac to convert large documents to ePub format so I can read them on my iPad.

iBooks, but the Kindle does work as you would expect: Tap the right side of the screen to advance a page and tap the left side of the screen to go back a page.

Like iBooks, you can bookmark a page by tapping the Bookmark icon button in the upper-right corner. Tap and hold over the text to open a contextual menu with options to add a note or highlight text. The definition for the selected word automatically appears at the bottom of the window. When you select multiple words, the definition disappears.

The choice of which e-book store you shop in may come down to availability and price. If the book is only available in the Kindle Store, you're stuck with the Kindle for iPad app. Also, if you want to read your e-books on devices other than those made by Apple, you're better off sticking with the Kindle platform.

Whichever electronic book reader floats your boat, the iPad will change the way you read books. I carry hundreds of pounds of books with me at all time in my iPad. Whenever I have a spare moment, no matter my mood or interest, I have a book for it.

16

Notes and Meetings

A s soon as the iPad was released, users wondered whether the iPad could replace their familiar paper notepad. Long a fixture of the workplace, the pad of paper is useful for many tasks. Can the iPad really replace paper? It can, and this chapter shows you how.

Taking Notes

You can take notes anywhere, whether sitting at your desk, sitting in a restaurant, pacing at a client's waiting room, or even slogging through a long meeting. Here are some of the best note-taking apps on the iPad.

Notes Plus

Notes Plus ($5), shown in Figure 16-1, brings many of the traditional paper metaphors to the iPad.

The Notes Plus interface looks like a pad of paper, right down to the top binding and torn edges. The left pane holds library-selection tools and the right pane holds notes.

To start a new notebook, tap the New Notebook icon button (the + symbol in a circle) at the top-right portion of the left pane. You can have as many notebooks as you like in Notes Plus and create folders to organize them. The Edit button at the bottom of the left pane brings up tools to organize, delete, and lock notebooks.

Opening a new notebook in Notes Plus presents a blank piece of paper, just like a traditional paper pad. You can use your finger or a stylus to start writing. Use the standard iPad pinch gesture to zoom in the screen so you can write comfortably. When done, zoom out using the expand gesture, and the writing automatically scales to fit the page. Also, when writing in landscape mode, zooming in with the pinch gesture removes the left pane, so your notes fill the full screen. Use two fingers to scroll around the page.

Another way to manage writing small is to use the close-up window. Tapping and holding anywhere on a blank page brings up the close-up window, a zoomed portion of the current location. Anything you write in the close-up window is automatically added at the regular window's insertion point, as shown in Figure 16-2. The app even detects when you are approaching the end of the close-up window line and automatically advances. Tapping outside the close-up window returns Notes Plus to the standard view.

When using a stylus, tap and hold and drag the Palm Pad tab, located at the bottom of the window in Figure 16-1, from the bottom of the window and pull it up toward the center of the window. This creates a safe zone for you to rest your palm, making it easier to write with a stylus.

If you prefer to type, tap with two fingers anywhere on the screen to have the onscreen keyboard pop up. Alternatively, you can change the settings so the Typewriter icon button (the letter A) is added to the toolbar. Once you add text, tap on it to change the typeface, size, and color using the Text Options pane in the Tools popover. (The Tools icon button looks like a wrench.)

FIGURE 16-1

The Notes Plus note-taking app

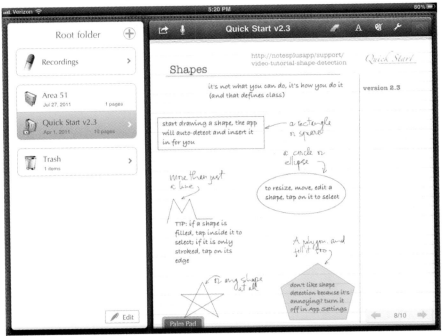

FIGURE 16-2

Using Notes Plus's close-up window

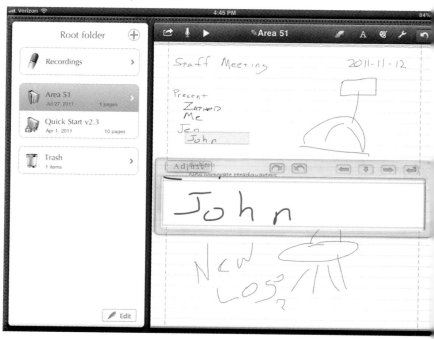

Notes Plus also helps you build shapes in your notes. The automatic shape-detection feature looks at your page and converts roughly drawn squares, circles, triangles, and other shapes into scalable vector images. You can select the vector images and make further adjustments with the Palette popover (click the Palette icon button, which looks like a paint palette), such as changing the stroke, color, and fill. Figure 16-1 shows a note with typed text and with shape detection enabled.

Reorganizing the page is also easy. Select handwriting, typed text, or a shape by drawing a circle around it. Once you've selected an object, you can move it (by dragging it) or resize it (using the pinch and expand gestures). Deleting is also easy: Just "scratch" back and forth horizontally over the unwanted object at least twice to have Notes Plus present a contextual menu from which you can delete it.

Notes Plus also can make an audio recording. Tap the Record icon button (the microphone) in the toolbar to begin recording audio. Tap the Record icon button again to stop the recording. Any page that includes a recording adds the Play icon button (a right-facing triangle) next to the Record icon button. Tapping the Play icon button plays back the recorded audio. Although this feature is a nice addition to Notes Plus, there are better apps for recording audio in a meeting, covered later in this chapter.

Once your notes are complete, tap the Share icon button (the rectangle with an arrow) to export them as an image or PDF file. The Share menu includes options to share a note via export, e-mail, and Google Docs. Moreover, as this book went to press, the developer was working to add Dropbox sync.

The Tools popover includes several options to customize Notes Plus. You can set the thickness, stroke opacity, and color of the Notes Plus pen strokes in the Pen Options pane. Go to the Text Options pane to adjust text, as covered earlier. The Paper Options pane lets you set the background paper (including the traditional yellow pad look), and the App Settings pane has switches to turn off features, such as automatic shape detection.

Notes Plus does a good job of digitally re-creating the analog interface of the traditional notepad. But can Notes Plus replace a paper pad? Most certainly. Is it for everyone? Probably not. For many people, it is hard to give up the paper and pen. (Even being a certifiable nerd, I carry a small notebook and pen in my pocket.) For those willing to take digital notes, however, Notes Plus adds useful features not available with paper and a pen, such as reorganizing the page and recording notes that take advantage of the iPad technologies.

Penultimate

Penultimate ($2), shown in Figure 16-3, provides a different approach to iPad note taking. Penultimate lacks all the fancy bells and whistles found in Notes Plus and instead gives you a virtual piece of paper and room to scribble. Penultimate provides a dead-simple way to take quick notes with your finger.

FIGURE 16-3

Penultimate for iPad

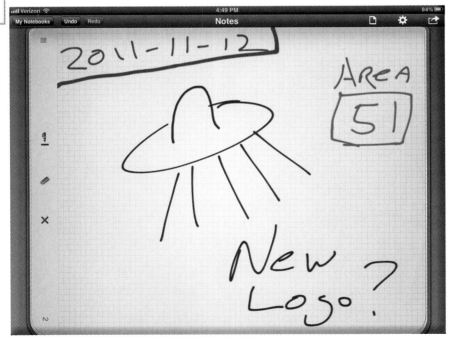

One of Penultimate's best features is the fluid way it inks the page with your finger or stylus. The developer explains it is a gel ink, which makes you smirk when you first read it, but it does actually feel like gel ink. There are six colors and three pen thicknesses, all accessed from the Pen icon button.

There isn't a lot to Penultimate. The icon buttons (on the left side of the window in landscape view and the top of the window in portrait view) change the pen type, erase, and delete the page. The toolbar includes buttons to return to the Notebooks page (where you create new notebooks), undo, and redo.

The Paper icon button (it looks like a piece of paper) opens a popover where you can change the background paper from graph, lined, or plain. You can also purchase additional papers through in-app purchase. There are several paper packs available (each costs $1), including task lists, music notation, design paper, and games (like tic-tac-toe).

The Setting icon button (the gear icon) opens options to turn on or off wrist protection (letting you rest your wrist on the iPad as you write) and adjust the toolbar location.

Finally, the Sharing icon button (the rectangle with an arrow emerging) lets you send your notebooks and pages by e-mail, save to the iPad photo library, or print using the standard iOS 5 Printer popover.

What makes Penultimate remarkable is its lack of features and its zero learning curve. I find it most useful when the bullets are flying in a meeting.

Evernote

Evernote (free) is a multiplatform virtual notebook application. Evernote syncs text notes, images, and audio files. Evernote is best for iPad users who work on multiple platforms. Figure 16-4 displays the Evernote's home window.

This window displays thumbnails of all your notes and images with filters (across the top of the window) to show all notes, specific notebooks, tags, places, and searches.

The lower toolbar includes the Sync icon button (the satellite dish), which brings up a popover to share your data with the Evernote servers. The Evernote Trunk icon button (the + symbol in a circle) opens a window that features additional Evernote related products and technologies.

Tap the New Note button (in the lower-left corner) to open a new note, shown in Figure 16-5.

Evernote embraces several search technologies. Each new note gets a title and can be placed in a notebook. Notebooks are collections of notes. Moreover, Evernote also includes support for tagging, which adds short descriptive terms for a note. For example, if you create a new note every time you talk with someone on the phone,

BEYOND THE NOTEPAD

What if you want to do more than replace a simple notepad? How about replacing a spiral-bound notebook? We all had them at one point in our life. The three-ring binder full of tabs, sticky notes, and the rest of our digital detritus. There's an app for that. Notebook ($30), shown below, creates a digital version of that three-ring binder. It includes powerful text entry, outlining, and diagramming tools. You can easily add attachments or record audio. You can insert PDF files and annotate them and the whole thing is compatible with the Mac OS X Notebook application so you can share it with your Mac.

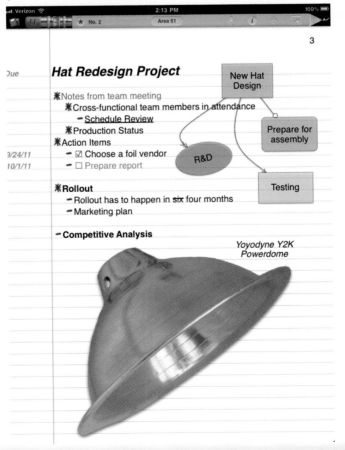

FIGURE 16-4

Evernote's home window

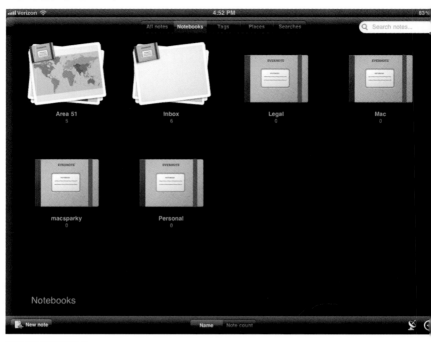

FIGURE 16-5

Creating a new note in Evernote

you could have a tag named "phone call." You could search for all your notes with that tag and get a list of all phone call notes.

You can add media to your note using the icon buttons located across the top of the new note window. The Recording icon button (the microphone) adds a recording to your note. The Album icon button (two photos) adds photos from your existing iPad images and the Camera icon button (the camera) lets you add a picture from the iPad 2's camera.

All your notes are then synced to the Evernote Internet servers and shared with other computers and mobile devices associated to your Evernote account. There are Evernote clients for all major computing platforms, including Mac OS X, Windows, iOS, Android, Windows Phone, and BlackBerry. Using Evernote, you can take notes in a meeting with your iPad and return to your office to access those notes on your desktop PC.

An added benefit of cloud-based data storage is that the Evernote servers can work on your data for you. With the free account, Evernote runs a text-recognition algorithm that extracts the text from uploaded images. With a paid account ($45 per year), Evernote recognizes text in PDF files. For example, you can take a picture of a client's business card with Evernote and, while you drive back to the office, the Evernote servers extract the text so you can search your Evernote database for the client's name by the time you are back in the office.

You can view, append, and modify your Evernote data from any device. Some companies run their entire business through the Evernote database.

Take a Meeting

Even as an admitted nerd, I was initially skeptical about the iPad's utility in a meeting. I wondered if the iPad would become more of a distraction than a tool. A busy meeting, I thought, was one place where the trusty yellow pad still reigned supreme. I was wrong. There are several apps that make the iPad useful in a meeting including simplifying the creation and sharing of agendas, taking notes, and sharing ideas.

Setting the agenda

Agendas ($10) lets you create and share digital agendas. As a presenter, you can create an agenda in advance including text, images, graphs, and even set the estimated time. You can optionally set a security code to keep the agenda private.

Once you have completed the agenda, Agenda shares it with other iPads on the network. You can also send it via e-mail (as a PDF file) or print it.

After you begin the meeting, all attendees with iPads can follow along. The presenter can choose areas of emphasis and even make changes to the agenda during the meeting, which immediately broadcast to all other iPad attendees.

A blue bar stretches across the top of the window and slowly disappears as the meeting proceeds. Once the meeting has exceeded its projected time, the blue bar disappears. This is a great way for everyone in the meeting to know how much time is left and, hopefully, keep matters on track.

There are several additional tools for attendees including the ability to take personal notes on their iPads (that are not shared with the group) and ask questions which are broadcast to the entire group. The presenter can then promote a question and address it during the meeting. Alternatively, all attendees can vote on the questions and the most relevant questions will move to the top.

Working in an office with a lot of iPads, Agendas provides a digital replacement to the traditional paper agenda.

Recording a meeting

Notability ($1) is a great meeting tool for recording and syncing notes. Shown in Figure 16-6, Notability combines an outliner with a recorder. Notes Plus, covered earlier in this chapter, can also record while you take notes. The difference is that Notability indexes the recording to the notes.

There are two primary windows for Notability, the library window and meeting window. Figure 16-6 shows the library window.

In the library window, Notability displays a list of recorded meetings organized by category. Categories act as folders in which you can organize your meeting notes and recordings. Add new categories by tapping the New Category icon button (the + symbol in the upper-right corner of the left pane). You can go back and listen to

FIGURE 16-6

Notability's library window

FIGURE 16-7

Notability for iPad's meeting window

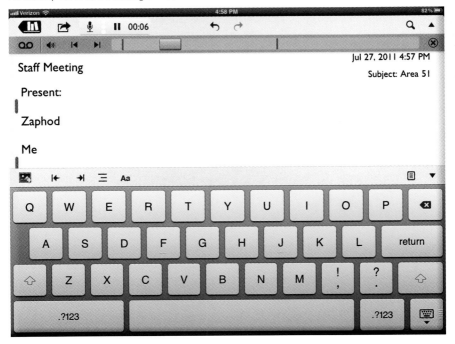

or reference existing meetings from the library window. To start a new meeting, tap the New Meeting icon button (the paper and pencil) in the upper-right corner of t right pane. Figure 16-7 shows the meeting window.

Tap the Record icon button (it looks like a microphone) to start recording. When recording, the Record icon button turns red, and the audio levels are display with the set of three dots next to it. Notability continues to record as you work. Yo can even exit the application and do something else with your iPad (for example, check the calendar or review a PDF file) and the app continues to record. Returnin to Notability, you can type notes and use simple diagramming tools to add notes and diagrams to the recording. When you are done, tap the Record icon button aga so the app stops recording.

Notability remembers what it recorded when you added notes. Later, you can go back to the notes and listen to the recording by tapping the Play icon button (a right-facing triangle). Notability then plays the recording while you view the notes Notability also inserts a series of red vertical lines down the left margin in this mo Tap any of those red lines to have Notability play the recording from the point tha line represents. For example, if during your meeting you type the note "pizza and beer budget," later tapping the red vertical line next to that entry causes Notability begin playing the recording from that part of the meeting.

I use Notability all the time. It makes it easy to take sparse notes during a meeting and easily access the full recording later. One of my common practices is

FIGURE 16-8

Share Board for iPad

MY NOTE-TAKING WORKFLOW

Despite my initial skepticism, I can't imagine attending a meeting without my iPad. I've worked with all the apps covered in this chapter. For taking notes outside of meetings, I often use a simple text editor. In a meeting, I use a combination of the apps from this chapter, depending on the circumstances.

just type the number and title of each agenda item as it comes up during a meeting and let Notability do the rest as I engage in the meeting.

Tap the Sharing icon button (the rectangle with an arrow) in the top-left corner to share your meeting notes and recording. Notability supports sharing via e-mail, iTunes, Dropbox, iDisk, WebDAV, and a local wirelessly connected printer. Moreover, you can choose the export format to be PDF, Rich Text Format, or the Notability format for sharing with other iPad Notability users. You can also choose whether to attach the recording.

Sharing ideas

Have you ever sat in a meeting where everyone is simultaneously trying to explain what to put on the whiteboard? It is always a time-waster and whoever gets his or her hands on the dry erase marker rarely gets it right. What if, instead, everyone could work on the same whiteboard simultaneously? That is the function of Share Board ($8).

Shown in Figure 16-8, Share Board lets you link up to four iPads using Wi-Fi or Bluetooth connections allowing everyone to share the same virtual whiteboard.

The application includes a basic set of drawing and editing tools. You can also import and annotate pictures and graphics with the built-in drawing tools, virtual pens, markers, and highlighters. There are multiple pen colors so each person can use a different color. Share Board also includes several icons you can drop in to additionally annotate diagrams. Although there certainly are superior diagramming tools (covered at length in Chapter 21), Share Board scratches a different itch. It provides a tool for meeting attendees to collaboratively share and develop ideas. Share Board supports Bluetooth, letting you set up a connection even if there is no Wi-Fi network.

The application also includes video-out support so you can mirror the diagram to a projector or external display via a VGA or HDMI cable, even using a first-generation iPad. Moreover, with iOS 5's AirPlay Mirroring feature, you can wirelessly project it to an Apple TV-connected monitor.

17

Brainstorming

Perhaps as a result of its tactile interface, or just because you can use it away from your desk, the iPad is a great tool for developing ideas and concepts. Whether you think linearly and use outlines or more abstractly and use mind maps, brainstorming is effortless on the iPad.

Outlining

OmniOutliner ($20) is the best outlining tool on the iPad. Although based on the popular Mac OS X application, OmniOutliner (shown in Figure 17-1) takes full advantage of the iPad's touch interface.

Creating an outline

Creating outlines with OmniOutliner is a snap. Just start typing in a blank field and use the ← and → icon buttons located in the Edit bar at the bottom of the window to promote or demote entries. For fast outlining, that is it. There is no secret invocation or multiple button taps required. Type the words. Set the level. Move on.

To add rows, tap the New Row icon button (the + symbol) on the right side of the Edit bar at the bottom of the window. Tap and hold the New Row icon button to get more row options, shown in Figure 17-2, including parent and children rows above and below the current row.

Edit a row by double-tapping it. OmniOutliner inserts the cursor at the end of the row and the iPad onscreen keyboard jumps to life. Once you're done editing, tap the row handle to the left of the row to have OmniOutliner

exit edit mode. The row handles also indicate the type of row: Rows without children appear with a dot; rows with children appear with a disclosure triangle. Tapping the triangle collapses and expands the child entries below it.

OmniOutliner can add notes below individual rows. This feature is also in the Mac OS X version of OmniOutliner and the Omni Group's other iPad app, OmniFocus (covered in Chapter 19). The utility of a note field in an outlining app is obvious. You can add extensive, collapsible notes that stay attached to the row. To add a note, tap the Note icon button (a sheet of paper with three lines and the + symbol) in the Edit bar. Press and hold the Note icon button to display or hide all notes.

To move a row, press and drag the row handle to its new locations. To edit groups of rows, tap the Edit button in the toolbar at the top of the window. The toolbar then disappears and a series of edit tools materialize at the bottom of the window. In edit mode, selection bubbles appear at the right side of each row. Tap the selection bubbles for the rows you want to alter and use the Delete, Group, and Move buttons at the bottom of the window to perform edits. When you group a set of rows, the rows get demoted and a parent gets inserted above them.

Using columns

One of Mac OS X OmniOutliner's most popular features is columns. Thankfully, this feature made it to the iPad. OmniOutliner includes options to add columns with several formats, including text, numbers, date, duration, pop-up lists, and check boxes.

To add a column, tap the Tools icon button (the wrench icon) in the toolbar. This opens the Tools popover, which includes the Columns, Styles, and View panes. Tap the Columns pane to have the popover display the columns in the current outline. Tap the New Column button to open the popover, shown in Figure 17-3, to choose a column name and style as well as the data format for the new column.

One of the more useful column types is the check box. I use this for examination and deposition outlines, checking off points as they are covered.

You can further customize OmniOutliner using the Detail icon button (a blue circle around a right-facing arrow) next to the data types, shown in Figure 17-3. For example, you can display a date as 12/18/11 or as December 18, 2011.

The summaries feature allows OmniOutliner to double as a primitive spreadsheet. OmniOutliner can perform several math functions, including totals, averages, minimum, and maximum values. The calculations appear automatically in the parent columns, as shown in Figure 17-1.

Tap and hold the column title to open a popover with the Edit, Sort, Hide, and Delete buttons. To adjust the column width, tap and hold the two vertical parallel lines in the column title and drag to resize.

Using columns expands OmniOutliner's utility. For example, I use OmniOutliner to create chronologies of important events in legal cases. I include five columns: Date, Description, Witnesses, Documents, and a check box column called Key Fact. OmniOutliner sorts the events by the date column, so anywhere I go, I have quick access to the complete chronology.

FIGURE 17-1

OmniOutliner on the iPad

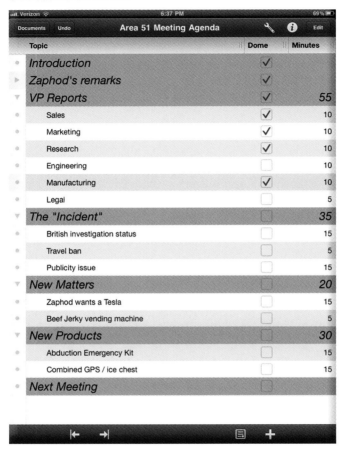

The remaining tools in the toolbar include the Documents button, which returns OmniOutliner to the document browser, and the Undo button. Tap and h the Undo button to redo. You can also change the name of your outline by tappir its name in the title.

Customizing outlines

OmniOutliner includes several customization tools. To access these tools, tap the Styles pane in the Tools popover. You can set styles for the entire document or create custom styles to use later for selected portions of the outline. To create a new style, tap the New Style button. A popover opens with options to set the style name, text attributes, typeface and size, text and background color, justification, a numbering. Styles are a great way to give your outline punch.

FIGURE 17-2

The OmniOutliner Edit bar with the New Row tools displayed

OmniOutliner uses the same color picker as OmniGraffle (covered in Chapter 21), which is my favorite color picker on the iPad. There are several custom palettes, and they all look great when applied to your outlines.

The View pane in the Tools popover includes additional setting for the outline's background color, display magnification, and setting a color for alternating rows.

You can apply styles to individual words, rows, groups of rows, and the entire outline. To apply styles to existing portions of your outline, tap the Info icon button and use the Info popover to add formatting. Spending just a few minutes tweaking the colors and typefaces can make working with your outline more enjoyable.

Managing outlines

OmniOutliner's document browser displays a nearly full size image of each outline. You flick between documents and tap one to open it. There are also options

FIGURE 17-3

Adding columns to OmniOutliner

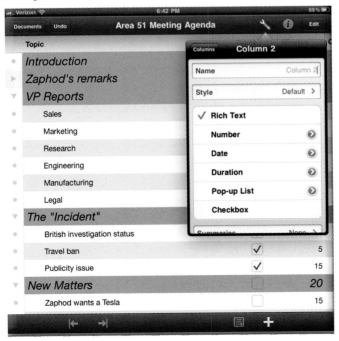

to open documents from iDisk or a WebDAV server. There is no Dropbox support, but you can use DropDAV (covered in Chapter 5) to access Dropbox. You can also export outlines to iDisk, WebDAV, and iTunes or send them as an e-mail attachme Finally, OmniOutliner supports Apple's own iCloud file-syncing service (also covered in Chapter 5). Export options include the OmniOutliner format (which works great with OmniOutliner on the Mac), HTML (both simple and dynamic), plain text, and OPML. (OPML is covered later in this chapter.)

When the iPad was initially announced, OmniOutliner was one of the first apps I thought would be perfect for the iPad. And the Omni Group really delivered. Combining OmniOutliner's simple capture and outlining tools with the considerable formatting and styles options makes it a productivity powerhouse for your iPad.

Mind-Mapping

Mind-mapping is a visual way to develop ideas and thoughts. The first mind maps were nothing more than a piece of paper with an idea or concept written in the middle. From that central idea is attached a series of ideas, sometimes called *nodes*. The nodes themselves then often sprout their own ideas and additional nodes. Before long, the page is full of ideas, all growing out from that central idea concept. When I first learned of mind-mapping, it sounded like hippy nonsense. Bu it's not.

Although starting with analog paper-based roots, computer programmers quickly grasped the idea and began building applications to automate the process of creating mind maps. I used them with some success on my Mac. However, for me, mind-mapping makes more sense on the iPad, and it wasn't until I started mind-mapping with my iPad that it became a regular part of my planning and brainstorming routines.

Mind-mapping on the iPad is a completely different experience than mind-mapping on a computer. Using just my fingers, I can explore, develop, and adjust ideas in a way that is not possible with the mouse and keyboard. My favorite iPad mind-mapping application is iThoughtsHD.

iThoughtsHD ($10) is one of the premier mind-mapping applications on any platform. Shown in Figure 17-4, the basic interface is a blank canvas upon which you begin building your mind maps.

Building a mind map

To create a new mind map in iThoughtsHD, tap the New Map icon button in the toolbar to open the popover in which you type in your filename, then tap Save. new mind map is created and saved.

A newly minted mind map has the filename in the center of the window. You can add child nodes by double-tapping anywhere on the background or tapping th Child icon button in the toolbar. (The iThoughtsHD toolbar is shown at the bottor

FIGURE 17-4

Top: Mind-mapping with iThoughtsHD. Bottom: iThoughtsHD's icon buttons.

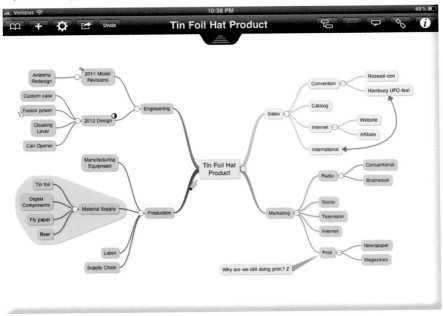

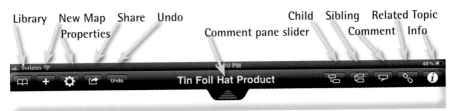

of Figure 17-5.) Tapping and holding the Child icon button provides options for creating parent, sibling, and child nodes.

To edit the text in an existing node, double-tap it. The iPad's onscreen keyboard pops up to perform the edit. iThoughtsHD also works with TextExpander Touch snippets (explained in Chapter 2).

iThoughtsHD lets you create additional nodes while typing. Once you finish typing a node, tap Return on the iPad's onscreen keyboard three times to create a sibling node. Tapping the space bar three times opens a child node. These onscreen keyboard shortcuts work at the end or in the middle of a node. If you use the shortcuts in the middle of a node, it acts as a breaking point, moving the text to the right of the cursor to the new node. For example, tapping Return three times when the cursor is between the words "research" and "development" results in two sibling nodes, one labeled "research" and the other "development." Tapping Delete three times in any empty node deletes the node and returns the cursor to its parent. Using these keyboard shortcuts, you can quickly create a mind map in iThoughtsHD.

To select a node, single-tap it to display a pointing finger. Dragging the pointing finger vertically adjusts the font size while dragging horizontally adjusts the maximum node width before the text is wrapped.

Selecting a node also opens a contextual menu with options to cut, copy, delete or align the selected node. Alignment moves the selected node to the top or bottom of its current siblings. Cutting or copying a node puts the selected node and its children in the paste buffer. Then tapping on a different node opens the option to paste the buffered nodes as a child. Using this workflow you can add template style nodes and quickly build a complex mind map. Tapping a blank area of the window with nodes stored in the paste buffer provides an option to paste the node as a floating node that is not attached to the existing nodes and instead exists separately on the canvas.

Tapping and holding briefly on a node lifts it from its current location. You can then drag the node to a different node or pull it to a blank area of the canvas to delete it.

Use the pinch gesture to zoom in and out of the map. Tapping on the mind map's title in the toolbar centers the map on the currently selected node. Double-tapping the mind map title centers the map on the root node.

The easiest way to move nodes is to tap and hold the node and drag it to its new location. If the map gets too messy, turn on the Keep Organised option (iThoughtsHD uses British spellings) from the Properties icon button's popover (the button looks like a gear) to have iThoughtsHD automatically clean up the organization of your nodes. I always leave the Keep Organised option turned on as I create and move nodes.

As your mind map starts coming together, you may want to temporarily hide children of a specified node. Tapping the Collapse/Expand button (a – in a circle) collapses all child nodes; the – changes to a +. Tapping the Collapse/Expand button again expands the child nodes. If you are giving a presentation and only want to open the child nodes one level at a time, double-tap the Collapse/Expand button.

Sometimes two nodes are related even though they are not siblings or even in the same mind map. iThoughtsHD can connect related topics with the Related Topic icon button (it looks like a chain). To relate two nodes, select the first one, tap the Related Topic icon button, and then tap the related node. iThoughtsHD creates a red line between the two nodes, as shown connecting the International and Hamburg UFO-fest nodes in Figure 17-5.

The Callout icon button (it looks like a cartoon speech bubble) adds a separate node that points at the selected node. To highlight a particular node, use the Callout icon button. For example, notice the Print node in Figure 17-5.

iThoughtsHD also can add detailed notes to a node. To do so, first select the node by tapping it. Drag down the Comment pane's slider (under the mind map's name in the toolbar), exposing the Comment field. Tapping inside the Comment

FIGURE 17-5

Adding comments to an iThoughtsHD mind map

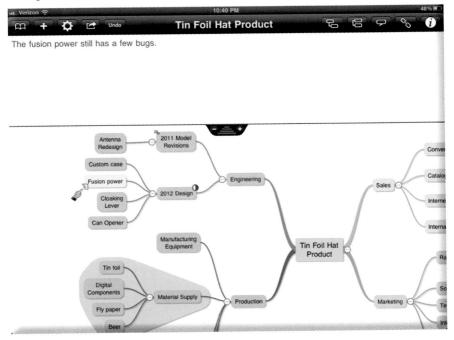

field brings up the iPad's onscreen keyboard. Once you finish typing your comments, push the Comment Pane slider back up to the top. Nodes with comments attached include an indicator icon (a small notepad with pencil), like the Fusion power node in Figure 17-5.

Formatting a mind map

Tapping the Info icon button with a node selected opens the Info popover whose Image pane includes a series of icons and images that can be added to the selected node. You can also add images from the iPad's Photos library; with an iPad 2, you can use the built-in camera to take a picture and add it to a node.

The Colour pane includes options to change the color of a selected node. iThoughtsHD ships with eight primary colors and eight additional blank customizable color buttons. Setting up your own color schemes in iThoughtsHD can be tedious, especially compared to OmniOutliner (covered earlier in this chapter). Selected colors may be restricted to the currently selected node or applied to children, siblings, or both.

The Shapes pane includes options to change the shape of individual nodes or groups of nodes. This pane also includes switches to declare the selected node a callout (also covered earlier) or add a boundary. Boundaries create a perimeter around the selected node and all its children. They are useful for highlighting selected portions of the mind map. (Figure 17-5 has a boundary around the Mater Supply series of nodes.)

The Text pane includes options to change the text emphasis (italic and bold), along with justification buttons. The formatting can be applied to just the selected node or to its siblings and children.

The Task pane includes a progress slider. Dragging this slider to the right adds a progress icon to the selected node that displays the completion in 25-percent increments, as shown on the 2012 Design node in Figure 17-5. You can quickly set a progress value of 0 percent for a task by tapping on the word Progress to the left of the slider. You can also add start dates and due dates from this pane.

Finally, the Link pane lets you link the selected node to a website, e-mail address, or other mind map. Linking to a different mind map works great on large projects where individual project nodes can require separate maps. When you set a link, the node displays a small blue arrow in a corner, as shown in the 2011 Model Revisions node of Figure 17-5. When you jump to a separate mind map with a link, iThoughtsHD adds the Back icon button (a left-facing solid triangle) to the toolbar. Tapping the Back icon button returns iThoughtsHD to the original source mind map

iThoughtsHD includes undo support: Tap the Undo button to undo; tap and hold the Undo button to redo.

The Properties icon button includes several additional options for your mind maps. You can change the window background to gray, black, lined, and grid paper There are also settings for children to inherit color and shape from their parents. Y can add drop shadows to the mind map's nodes, which looks great. The Rainbow setting automatically applies a rainbow spectrum of colors to the mind map's node as shown in Figure 17-5.

Saving and archiving

After creating the mind map, there is no need to further save them. iThoughtsHD saves automatically every 30 seconds and every time the app is close iThoughtsHD also works with the iCloud service, backing up your data to your iCloud storage.

Moreover, every day the app is used, iThoughtsHD compresses all the mind maps into a Zip archive that you can copy to your Mac or PC through iTunes sharing or by e-mailing it from the Transfer icon button's popover. In the event of data loss or a failed iTunes backup, the Zip file can be restored, returning your mind maps to iThoughtsHD. To restore the files, copy the Zip file to iThoughtsHD in iTunes, as explained in Chapter 1, and tap the Copy from iTunes button in the Transfer popove

iThoughtsHD works with other popular mind-mapping applications and file types. It imports and exports the Freemind, Freeplane, XMind, Novamind, MindManager, MindView, Concept Draw, Mindmap, MindGenius, and iMindMap formats. It also supports OPML (covered next in this chapter), so you can send a mind map directly to OmniOutliner as an outline. Finally, iThoughtsHD exports to PDF and PNG formats.

MY BRAINSTORMING WORKFLOW

Ideas come to me at the strangest times. When inspiration strikes, I immediately start building a mind map in iThoughtsHD. My best planning is done away from my desk with the iPad. Sometimes I'll take my iPad to lunch and sit on a park bench or fiddle with it at my standing desk. The trick is to not "schedule" it. Just let your mind roll. Often, I will spend a week going back and working with the mind map. I normally have 15 or 20 half-baked mind maps on my iPad. Because iThoughtsHD exports to OPML, I can also tinker with them using OmniOutliner on my iPad and Mac.

For smaller projects, once I have the idea fully baked, I look at the outline or mind map on my iPad and start dictating it into my Mac using Dragon Dictate. For bigger projects, I import the final OPML file in Scrivener and start writing. By then, I've lived with the ideas for some time and have a good idea of where I'm going. As a result, I rarely encounter writer's block. I just start cranking through the Scrivener binder. If something doesn't feel quite right, I move to the next subject and come back later.

Pasting a copied branch into an e-mail adds an indented text outline to the body of the e-mail. Conversely, copying lines of text from an e-mail body and pasting it in iThoughtsHD node creates a series of child nodes from the lines of copied text.

The Advantage of OPML

Both OmniOutliner and iThoughtsHD can open and save OPML files. Why should you care? Because it lets you easily jump between both applications with your data. OPML, which stands for Outline Processor Markup Language, is an XML format for outlines. Over the past few years, it has become the digital intermediary for getting your planning and outlining ideas from one app to another. It is enjoying wide adoption from Mac OS X and iOS developers, which makes it particularly useful to writers and others who prefer to sort those jumbled ideas knocking about in their brains.

Because most mind-mapping and outlining applications speak OPML, you are not tied to just one app. You can start a project as a mind map, save it to OPML and then open it in OmniOutliner for more refinement. You can also send the OPML file to your Mac or PC and open it in your favorite mind-mapping or outlining app that supports OPML (my favorites on the Mac are OmniOutliner Pro and MindNode Pro) and then round-trip it back to your iPad.

Once your outline/mind map is complete, you can also open the OPML file with the Scrivener writing app on the Mac to build your outline and get down to the business of writing. Indeed, that is exactly how I went about writing this book.

18

Presentations

O ften, the only reason to pack your laptop for a business trip is to make a presentation. So does the iPad have enough muscle to power your presentation? Quite possibly yes. This chapter covers the tools necessary to present with your iPad.

Keynote

Apple's Keynote ($10) is the premier presentation tool on the iPad. Released at the original iPad launch (along with the other iWork apps), Keynote sets the bar high for touch-based presentation apps.

Creating a presentation

When you first open Keynote, it displays the presentations view, shown in Figure 18-1. This view shows all your existing Keynote presentations. You can sort the presentations by date or name by tapping the corresponding buttons at the top-center of the window. (If you do not see the Date and Name buttons in the window, tap and hold anywhere on the window and drag down.) To open an existing presentation, tap it.

To create a new presentation, tap the New Presentation icon button in the upper-left corner (a + symbol). This opens a popover, shown in Figure 18-1, with options to create a new presentation from scratch or copy a presentation to Keynote from iTunes, iDisk, or WebDAV. If you tap Create Presentation, Keynote displays a window with 16 templates to choose from.

If you are importing an existing presentation, note Apple's description in the popover shown in Figure 18-1. You are *copying* a presentation from iTunes, iDisk, or WebDAV — not opening the presentation. Once you copy a presentation to your iPad, the original file at its source destination remains untouched. Although iTunes backs up the new copy on your iPad, any changes you make are not automatically updated to the source file on iTunes, iDisk, or WebDAV. This could be a nasty surprise on presentation day if you assume your changes have been updated. To get your iPad modified presentation back to iTunes, iDisk, or WebDAV, you need to export it (covered later in this chapter).

You can also organize your presentations into folders in the presentations view. To do so, tap the Edit button and then tap and hold a presentation until it appears to lift off the screen. Then drag it on top of another presentation; Keynote creates a folder. (This is similar to how you move app icons on the iOS home screens, as covered in Chapter 1.)

In edit mode, you can also duplicate a presentation by tapping the Duplicate icon button (two overlapping pages with a + symbol on the top page). When you open a presentation in Keynote, all changes are automatically saved. There is no turning back after you start making modifications. So, if you want to keep the presentation's original state (for example, if you are using a presentation as a template from which to build similar presentations), duplicate the presentation first and then work from the copy, leaving the untouched original available for future use.

FIGURE 18-1

Keynote's presentations view

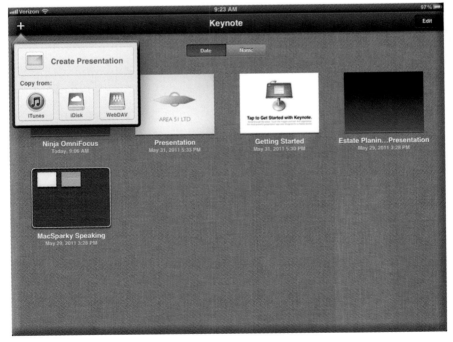

To delete a presentation, tap the Delete Presentation icon button (the trash can

Editing a presentation

When you open a presentation, Keynote displays the slide-editing view, show in Figure 18-2. The left side of the window includes the Slide Navigator, and the toolbar is at the top of the window. The rest of the display shows the current slide.

The Slide Navigator

You can scroll through the slides by dragging a finger up and down inside the Slide Navigator. To move a slide, tap and hold it. After a moment, the slide breaks free of the Slide Navigator and slowly pulses under you finger. Drag your finger to the new destination in the Slide Navigator and lift your finger. The slide drops bac into the Navigator at its new location.

Tapping on a slide in the Navigator opens a contextual menu with several options (shown in Figure 18-2), including Cut, Copy, Delete, and Skip. The Skip option lets you temporarily deactivate the selected slide so it does not appear in you presentation. If you think you may have future use for a slide that doesn't fit in your current presentation, skip it. If you ever need to bring the slide back, tap the slide in the Slide Navigator again and then tap the Don't Skip option to return it to your presentation. You can also add a slide by tapping the New Slide icon button (the + symbol) at the bottom of the Slide Navigator.

FIGURE 18-2

Keynote's slide-editing view

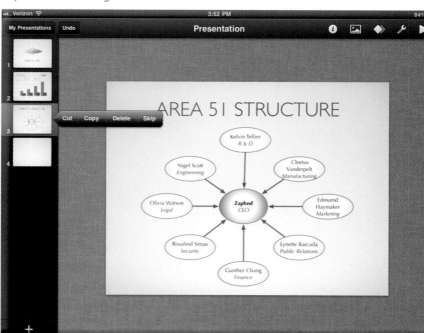

The toolbar

The Keynote toolbar stretches across the top of the window, as shown in Figure 18-2. The left side of the toolbar includes the Presentations button (which returns Keynote to the presentations view) and the Undo button. There is no save button; Keynote saves (both locally and to iCloud) automatically while you work. If you exit the app or your iPad battery runs down, Keynote picks up where you left off the next time you load the presentation.

The right side of the toolbar includes five icon buttons.

Info: The Info icon button opens a popover with customization options for the selected object. When a graphics object is selected, the popover includes Style and Arrange panes.

The Style pane offers border options for the selected object, including lines, shadows, and curls, as shown in Figure 18-3. The Style Options button at the bottom of this pane opens additional options, including line color, width, line styles, shadows, reflections, and opacity.

The Arrange pane includes options to flip, mask, and move an object forward and backward. If you want a flying saucer image to appear behind your text, move it backward in this popover.

FIGURE 18-3

The Style Info popover

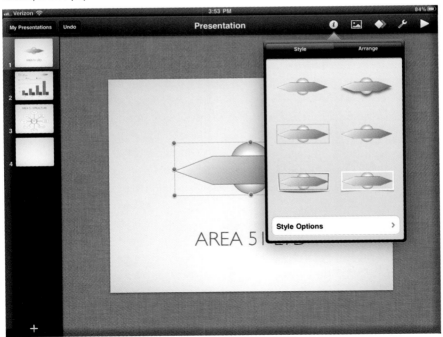

When you select text and tap the Info icon button, a third pane appears, calle Text, where you can set text styles such as title or bullets and text effects including bold, italic, underline, and strikethrough.

The Text Options button, located at the bottom of the Text pane, includes tex settings for size, color, font, alignment, and margin. iPad Keynote has a "you take what you get" attitude about fonts. There are more than 50 available fonts, but yo cannot add your own. If you import an existing Keynote or PowerPoint presentatic Keynote makes its best guess at font substitutions.

 Insert: The Insert icon button opens a popover with four panes: Media, Table Charts, and Shapes. Shown in Figure 18-4, you add objects to your slides using thi popover.

The Media pane displays the photos on your iPad for easy insertion into your Keynote presentation. Think ahead and load your iPad with pictures for your presentation. You can also add pictures on the fly. To do so, tap and hold on an image attached to an e-mail or in the Safari browser until the Save Image contextu menu appears. The image is then available in Keynote's Media pane in the Camera Roll library.

The Tables and Charts panes each include several pages of attractive tables an charts for inclusion in your presentation. To insert a table or chart, tap and hold t desired object and drag it on to the slide. Once you add a table or chart, double-ta it to edit the data, as shown in Figure 18-5.

You can choose from six sets of graphic elements in the Shapes pane and dro them in your presentation. Keynote includes a range of shapes and colors. If you need something special, try OmniGraffle for iPad (covered in Chapter 21). You car copy graphics straight out of OmniGraffle and paste them on your Keynote slide. (built the flying saucer in Figure 18-3 this way.)

Once your shapes are in the presentation, you can use gestures to manipulate them. Tap and hold an object to drag it around the slide. Once you select an objec you can resize the shape by dragging the blue selection handles. To rotate an objec tap and hold the object with two fingers and use the rotation gesture. As you rotat an object, Keynote even shows you the degree of rotation and snaps to angles at 45-degree increments as you near them. To add text to a shape, double-tap it.

Single-tapping a shape opens a contextual menu with options to cut, copy, delete, and replace. Copying the shape is useful when you have a shape set up "jus right" and want to use it again. After copying it, tap on any blank space on the slid to paste it.

To add a text box to your slide, drag the large T icon, shown in Figure 18-4, onto your slide. Once you've added a text box, tap inside it to bring up the onscree keyboard. You can make adjustments to the text using the Info tool, covered earlie

Keynote automatically detects hyperlinks when you type in a website URL or e-mail address. You can adjust hyperlinked text by tapping it; a series of contextual menu buttons appear. These buttons include options to open or copy the link. You can also edit the displayed text or hyperlink destination. For example, you could

FIGURE 18-4

Keynote's Insert popover

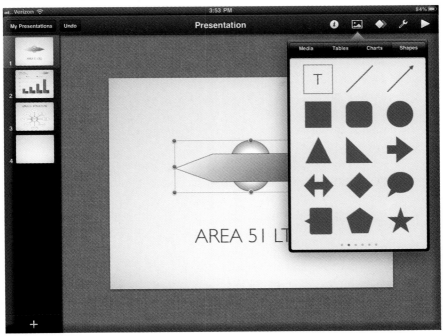

make the text "MacSparky" point to www.macsparky.com. Finally, Keynote provides an option to remove the hyperlink.

In iPad Keynote, hyperlinks work only for website URL addresses or e-mail addresses. There is no option to hyperlink to other slides in your presentation. If, for example, you want to embed a hyperlink at Slide 1 that jumps to Slide 7, you're out of luck. Indeed, if you import a presentation from your Mac or PC (importing presentations is covered later in this chapter) that includes hyperlinks between slides, iPad Keynote removes them during import.

 Animation: Tapping the Animation icon button with an object selected opens a popover with options to add build-in and build-out animations. Keynote includes 15 animations. From this popover, you can also set the animation options, delivery, and order. Adding and modifying animations on the iPad is more intuitive than on the Mac or PC.

Tapping the Animation icon button with no objects selected opens the animation view. The toolbar turns blue and the Animation popover opens when you tap on any object. This is the most efficient way to set animations for several objects.

You can also set slide animations while in Animation view. To do so, tap any slide in the Slide Navigator to open the Transitions popover that provides slide-animation options. There are 23 possible transitions, ranging from the understated fade to the expressive twirl. Each transition has its own options, set with the Options button in the Transitions popover.

FIGURE 18-5

Editing chart data in Keynote

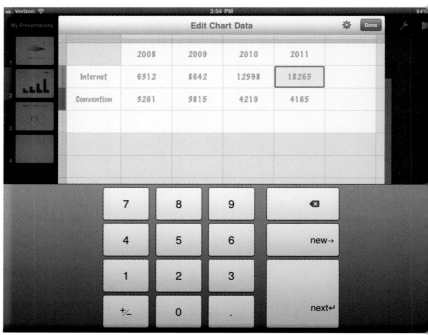

Keynote also brings over the Magic Move transition from the Mac OS X version. If you have never tried Magic Move before, play with it. Magic Move looks at all the objects in the first slide and all the objects in the slide immediately following it. If any object remains in both slides, Magic Move magically moves the object from its position in the first slide to the its position in the second slide, setting the animation path and object resize automatically. I remember spending hours setting animation paths to get this effect in years past. Now you just tap a button. To turn on Magic Move, tap the Magic Move button in the Transitions popover for the first slide of the Magic Move.

Once your animations are set, tap the Done button at the far right of the toolbar to exit the animation view.

 Tools: The Tools icon button opens the Tools popover. This is a collection of the tools that don't fit anywhere else.

The Share and Print button opens a popover with a Print button to print your presentation using the standard iOS print controls. The Share and Print popover also includes several sharing options, covered later in this chapter.

The Find button opens a popover with the find and replace tools. The Settings button (the gear icon) to the left of the Search bar in the Find popover provides options to match case or whole words with your search.

The Presenter Notes button opens a yellow pad where you can make notes concerning specific slides. (I cover presenter notes later in this chapter.)

The Settings button opens several options concerning spelling, slide numbers, and guides. The guides are helpful when using graphic elements in your presentation. They snap the objects to the slide so everything looks crisp as you transition between slides.

The Settings button also includes the Remote button. Tapping this lets you link your iPad to an iPhone or iPod Touch using the Keynote Remote app. Using this feature, you can remotely control your presentation using an iPhone or iPod Touch. (You can also control a Mac running Keynote from an iPhone, iPad, or iPod Touch.) If your conference room has an Apple TV-attached projector, you can also use the iOS 5's AirPlay Mirroring feature to play your presentation wirelessly from your iPad. Walking the room with my iPad in hand while my presentation plays through the Apple TV is my favorite way to present. Although you can remotely advance slides with an iPhone or iPod Touch or wirelessly send your presentation using AirPlay mirroring, there is no way to use iPad Keynote with a third-party remote control.

The Go to Help button opens the iPad Keynote support documentation in the Safari browser.

Play: The Play icon button starts your presentation from the selected slide. In addition to starting slide shows, it is a great way to test the graphics and animations you've built with the other tools. To start a presentation from the beginning, flick to the top in the Slide Navigator and tap the Play icon button.

Presenting with Keynote

Whether you built your presentation directly on your iPad or imported a Keynote or PowerPoint presentation from you Mac or PC, the iPad is an excellent device with which to give your presentation.

Presentation controls

The controls in Keynote while presenting are, thankfully, simple. To advance to the next slide or animation, tap anywhere on the screen. You do not need to look down at the screen to advance.

TABLE 18-1

Keynote Presenter Controls	
Action	**Gesture**
Advance to the next slide	Tap anywhere or swipe left
Go back to the previous slide (or first build of the current slide)	Swipe right
Move to a specific slide	Open the Slide Navigator and tap the directed slide.
Use the virtual laser pointer	Tap and hold the screen
Exit the presentation	Double-tap the screen

Alternatively, you can swipe left to advance or swipe right to go back a slide (return to the first build of the current slide). To exit the presentation, double-tap the screen. To jump to a particular slide, tap and hold on the left side the window (where the Slide Navigator is normally) and swipe toward the center. The Slide Navigator appears, and you can tap a slide to jump to it. If your iPad is connected an external display and you are using the presenter display view, the Slide Navigat appears on your iPad, but not on the external display.

Finally, when you want a pointer to appear on the screen, tap and hold on the screen and, after a moment, a virtual laser pointer appears at your finger location; you can move this pointer around the screen. When you lift your finger, the laser pointer goes away.

That is it; there are no further controls available for giving a presentation with iPad Keynote. Table 18-1 summarizes the presenter controls.

Keynote works with projectors, monitors, and televisions using VGA or HDMI cable connectors (covered in Chapter 1) or Apple TV using the new AirPlay Mirroring feature in iOS 5. If you're using an adapter, just plug your adapter cable into the projector, TV, or monitor. Keynote automatically detects the connection and sends the presentation to the external display. This feature works with both th original iPad and the iPad 2.

When you're showing a presentation, Keynote gives you more detail about your presentation on the iPad screen, such as your slide notes, while showing the audience only the slides, in what Keynote calls the *presenter display view*. Shown in Figure 18-6, the toolbar's lineup in presenter display view changes and provides k data while you're giving a presentation.

The left side of the presenter display view's toolbar displays the current slide number and the total number of slides in the presentation. Next is a status indicat that displays either green or red. If the status indicator is red, the current slide buil is not complete. This signals the presenter that Keynote is not ready to continue. When the light is red, tap to advance at your own peril. If you do so, it is very likely the slide will jump to the next transition immediately upon completion of the current one. Instead, accept the red light as a warning to keep your hands off your iPad and engage your audience while your slide finishes building. Once the status indicator turns green, you are free to tap and move on to the next transition animation, or slide.

The center of the presenter display view's toolbar shows a presentation timer. The timer starts running as soon as you activate the laser pointer or advance the fir slide of your presentation. Alternatively, if you tap the timer, it switches to a clock showing the current time. (The presenter display view is in clock mode in Figure 18-6.) Tapping again switches back to the timer.

The Layout icon button opens a popover with options for the presentation view's layout. You can see the current slide, the next slide, both the current and the next slide, or the current slide with your presenter notes. (You can change among these views while giving your presentation.)

FIGURE 18-6

Keynote in presenter display view

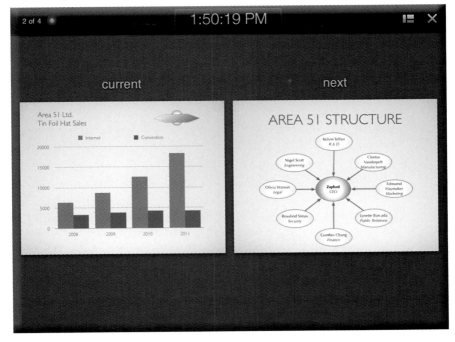

No matter which display you select for your presenter display view, Keynote sends only the current slide to the external display. Although Keynote in Mac OS X provides more options for the presenter display, the iPad's options are usually enough.

For example, if a slide contains a detailed diagram, change the layout to just show the current slide and use the laser pointer to explain pieces of the diagram to your audience. When the slide has speaker notes, switch to the current slide with presenter notes display. Otherwise, keep both the current and next slides on the presenter display view so you can see what is coming next and make smooth transitions.

Presentation day

When you get to presentation day, the kit list for presenting with your iPad is small. Make sure to pack the following:

▶ Your iPad
▶ A HDMI or VGA dongle (or both)
▶ An extra length of VGA or HDMI cable
▶ The iPad's AC power adapter and 30-pin-to-USB charging cable
▶ An Apple TV with the necessary power and connector cords if you intend to use AirPlay Mirroring.

The HDMI adapter allows you to connect both the power cable and HDMI cable to your iPad at the same time, whereas the VGA adapter allows only the VGA cable to be connected. Thus, if you are projecting through VGA, you cannot supply power the iPad. So make sure to charge your iPad ahead of time.

Get to the room early so you can make a dry run before the audience shows up Also, make sure to turn off all notifications in the Settings app. Unless my presentat relies on Internet access, I put the iPad in airplane mode, also via the Settings app. The last thing you want in the middle of your presentation is for your audience to se a notification that your friend just played "flatulence" for 40 points in Words with Friends. Finally, set your presentation to the title slide using the Slide Navigator, and go get a cup of tea and sit tight until you begin.

Presenting to small audiences

Another use for iPad Keynote is the small presentation setting. When you're in a room with just a few people, don't bother with a projector. Instead, sit down nex to them and run your Keynote presentation on your iPad. This provides a degree c intimacy not normally possible when presenting from a large screen.

Moreover, when you're done, hand your iPad to your audience. The controls easy enough that even a neophyte can figure them out from watching you. Then si back and observe. Seeing your audience flick through your presentation, gives you lot of feedback about what they think is important. It also empowers your audienc and gives them a sense of ownership in the presentation. It's a win-win, and a trick I've used many times to my benefit.

Sharing presentation files

Keynote offers several options for importing and exporting your presentation fi

Importing presentations

In addition to building presentations on your iPad, you can import presentations created on your Mac or Windows PC. To import via USB cable, conn your iPad to your computer and copy the presentation into Keynote's data storage in the Apps pane for your iPad in iTunes, as covered in Chapter 1. After syncing, th presentation appears in iPad Keynote.

Any presentations in your iCloud storage automatically appear in Keynote and sync among your Mac, iPhone, and iPad. You can also transfer presentations to your iPad wirelessly using the MobileMe iDisk service or a WebDAV server. If you're a Dropbox user, consider using the DropDAV service, covered in Chapter 5, to get acce to your presentation files in your Dropbox storage. Box.net has a similar service.

To access iDisk and WebDAV storage, return to presentations view, shown in Figure 18-1, and tap the appropriate Copy From button in the New Presentation popover. Keynote also opens presentations from e-mail attachments. Tap and hold the presentation in the e-mail message and use the Open In menu to open it in Keynote.

Keynote imports both Mac OS X Keynote and PowerPoint files. Upon import, if the presentation uses any unsupported fonts or features, iPad Keynote makes any necessary changes and provides a notification of what changed. For example, if your presentation includes hyperlinks between slides, iPad Keynote removes those hyperlinks. Keynote also converts three-dimensional Mac OS X Keynote graphs to two dimensions.

Exporting presentations

Similarly, Keynote can export your presentation. To do so, tap the Share and Print button in the Tools popover in the slide-editing view, shown in Figure 18-2. You can export presentations through iTunes sync, iDisk, and WebDAV, all as mentioned earlier. You can also send the presentation via e-mail.

When you export an iPad Keynote presentation, Keynote provides the option to export it as a Keynote, PowerPoint, or PDF files.

Keynote has the additional ability to share your presentation through iWork. com, Apple's online collaboration site for iWork documents. Once uploaded to iWork.com, you can send a link to your co-workers where they can view, annotate, and download the presentation, depending on the permissions and settings you choose.

Keynote's limitations

Keynote sets the standard for presentation applications on the iPad. Using Keynote to create and display presentations is easy (and fun). It does, however, have limitations. When using a laptop-based presentation application, such as PowerPoint or Keynote for the Mac, you have more control over your presentation than on the iPad. There simply are more options for transitions, animations, and fonts.

Nevertheless, as the iPad hardware improves, I suspect iPad Keynote will catch up. In the meantime, if you can live with iPad Keynote's limitations, walking in to a meeting with nothing but your iPad and giving a killer presentation is liberating.

Displaying PowerPoint Files

The easiest way to display a PowerPoint presentation is to import it into Keynote and take advantage of all Keynote's presentation, animation, and transition tools. Alternatively you can open a PowerPoint presentation in GoodReader (covered in Chapter 14) but the slides display only as static images.

Another option is to use Quickoffice Pro HD's PowerPoint support. Quickoffice ($15) has controls for adding shapes and adjusting objects in the presentation. There is, however, no support for building animations or transitions.

Documents to Go ($17) also has support for displaying and editing PowerPoint presentations.

Neither of these apps, however, stand up to the tools and features in Keynote.

Keynote Alternatives

As fine a presentation application as Keynote is, it is not the only way to prese
on the iPad. Several developers have come up with their own innovative solutions.

Picture Link

Picture Link ($3) is a different type of presentation app. Shown in Figure
18-7, Picture Link is not about flashy transitions and text effects but instead about
hyperlinking. In fact, Picture Link is *all* about hyperlinking.

Using Picture Link, you can set up a series of images and create hidden links
on each page, letting you jump to any predesignated slide. For example, you could
have an index slide with hyperlinks pointing to five separate slides. When you are
interacting with your audience, tapping one corner could lead to slide 10 whereas
tapping the opposite corner would jump to slide 20. In essence, this app capitalize
on Keynote's inability to hyperlink slides.

Picture Link does not provide tools for generating the slides; you need to creat
the images in another app. One potential workflow is to build slides in Keynote
and take screenshots of them. (Press both the Home button and On/Off button
simultaneously to take screen shots, which appear in the Photos app's Camera
Roll album.) You then add the screenshots to Picture Link to build a hyperlinked

FIGURE 18-7

Hyperlinking images with Picture Link

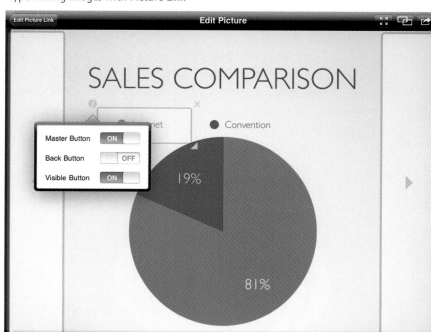

presentation (without all Keynote's fancy transitions and animations, of course). For interactive presentations, Picture Link scratches the itch.

Prezi

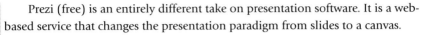

Prezi (free) is an entirely different take on presentation software. It is a web-based service that changes the presentation paradigm from slides to a canvas.

The Prezi app displays presentations created online at www.prezi.com. Start with Prezi by creating an online canvas at www.prezi.com using a Mac or Windows PC. From your computer's browser, add graphics and text. You can even import PowerPoint and Keynote slides as a starting point for a Prezi presentation. Once the canvas is complete, set the navigation points; Prezi creates animations, jumping through the presentation to the predesignated points.

The way Prezi zooms in and out of the canvas as it transitions is striking. Screenshots don't do it justice; you have to see Prezi in action to fully appreciate it: The audience watches the presentation jump around on a large canvas spinning and twirling from one navigation point to the next.

Although you cannot create Prezi presentations on the iPad, you can view presentations created at Prezi.com using the Prezi app, and they look great both on the iPad and projected to an external display. If your Keynote presentations are getting stale, I suggest you try Prezi. Prezi also gives you another way to get around the hyperlinking limitations with Keynote: Using Prezi, you can zoom out to show the entire canvas and use your finger to tap on the areas of emphasis.

To use Prezi, you need a membership. A free account includes 100MB of space on the Prezi server. The "enjoy" account costs $60 per year and includes 500MB of storage and the ability to make your content private and add your logo instead of Prezi's to the presentation. Finally, a Pro account costs $160 per year and includes 2GB of space and the ability to create Prezi presentations offline.

Use the iPad as a Teleprompter

If you are not interested in using the iPad as a presentation device but are giving a prepared speech, consider using Teleprompt+ for iPad ($15). This app turns your iPad into a teleprompter, displaying your speech and scrolling it up the screen as you speak.

You can type the speech directly in Teleprompt+ or paste it in from a text editor. There are fine controls over the scrolling speed and support for a Bluetooth keyboard or foot pedals to set the speed manually. Teleprompt+ works with an external display, and can invert the text so it can be reflected off a mirror.

App-Based Presentations

Sometimes, you don't need a presentation app for a presentation. For example, if you need to explain quarterly results, open Numbers (covered in Chapter 20) or share a mind map from iThoughtsHD (covered in Chapter 17). These apps might be all you need for some presentations.

The iPad 2 can mirror any iPad app's screen to an external display. Moreover many iPad apps include the ability to send output to an external display even on a original iPad. The Photos app, for example can display pictures from your iPad to external projector. Similarly GoodReader (covered in Chapter 14) also has built-in support for an external display.

Using the iPad as a Kiosk

Another type of presentation is one without a presenter. The kiosk-type presentation is common at trade shows and points of sale. So why not use an iPad for such kiosk-style presentations?

Sure enough, there is an app for that: AVD Browse ($8) is a crippled web browser perfect for turning your iPad into a kiosk device. It turns off the address bar, search field, bookmarks, and every switch, dial, and lever a user could activate to escape the kiosk presentation. AVD Browse even turns off the iPad sleep mode s it keeps going throughout your conference. The app can access a website from the Internet or use local storage for its presentation.

Presentation Mojo

No matter how you go about presenting with your iPad, don't put your audience to sleep with endless slides full of tiny text and more bullets than a milit supply dump.

A presentation fundamentally serves to enhance your speech, not replace it. Don't insult your audience with slides that repeat your words. Instead, enhance yo words with slides that hammer home your points.

With the presentation apps in this chapter, you can combine verbal and visual learning for maximum impact on your audience. But to do so, you need to stop using slides as giant shared cue cards. This is not easy.

It starts with you breaking down each presentation into its key components. A presentation is a story. It needs a beginning, middle, and an end. It needs to be emotional and involve your audience.

I plan presentations carefully using brainstorming tools like those covered in Chapter 17. In addition to outlining the general chronology of my presentation, I also give thought to the ebb and flow of the points and how they fit together. Any presentation has high and low points. Spend time thinking about how best to fit them together.

This initial planning takes time. In my case, it usually takes hours (sometimes days). When a young lawyer, I was told once that if I couldn't summarize any case in two sentences, I didn't know the case well enough. This advice applies equally to planning presentations. You need to spend lots of time looking at each component and distilling it down to its simplest form for your presentation. Your audience is not interested in doing the hard work of figuring out your product, plan, or case. Y have to do it for them, in advance.

MY PRESENTATION WORKFLOW

Keynote is my presentation software of choice. I use it both on my Mac and my iPad. Since first getting my iPad, I have grown to appreciate Keynote even more.

Building presentations on iPad Keynote is simple and intuitive. Although there aren't quite as many bells and whistles as you get with the Mac OS X version of Keynote, there are enough. Using my iPad, I have prepared Keynote presentations on an airplane and given them hours later in a conference room. I do not find giving Keynote presentations with my iPad distracting or difficult. Overall, Apple did a fantastic job bringing presentation software to the touch interface.

Although I have yet to give a Prezi presentation in the heat of battle, exploring it for this book piqued my curiosity and now it is only a matter of time.

Once you have those simple pieces laid out, begin making slides. Pick the most important points and reinforce them with slides. The slides shouldn't be filled with bullets and words but instead with visual representations of your most important points. Pictures, analogies, and simplified data and graph slides are a great way to reinforce your points without losing your audience.

Once you've prepared a polished slide deck start practicing with it. The sad truth is there is no magic formula to giving a good presentation. Instead, it comes down to spending an obscene amount of time practicing. When I give a big presentation, I practice it endlessly. I script it in my mind as I prepare the slides. I say the presentation out loud as I revise the slides. I give it in the mirror. I give the presentation to patient family members. I even talk through the presentation as I sit in traffic. There is no substitute for the process of getting the words from your mind to your lips many times. Until you are comfortable speaking your presentation, you are not ready.

After all that hard work, when presentation day finally arrives, you will be full of confidence that only comes from practice and you will be brilliant.

19

Task Management

A s life gets faster and faster, there seems to be more stuff to do than we can possibly keep track of in our heads. Nothing is easy anymore and there are few iPad workers that can get away with having their task list on the back of a napkin. Because of its portability and connectivity, the iPad offers a unique opportunity to effectively manage your task list. App developers did not miss this point. The App Store is bursting at the seams with task management applications.

Some iPad task management apps are no more than a simple list whereas others offer powerful (and complex) tools to manage the most demanding users. This chapter covers several of the best iPad task management tools.

When choosing a task management app, go with the easiest solution you can get away with. If your task management app is more complex than it needs to be, you will waste time fiddling with it and later give up on it. However, if a lighter task management app doesn't cut it, do not shy away from a more powerful task management app. All the apps covered in this chapter are great tools to help you manage (and complete) your task list.

Reminders

Reminders (free) is Apple's task management app that started shipping as part of iOS 5. When the iPhone was first released, everybody was shocked that Apple didn't include a task management app. When Apple opened the iOS operating system to third-party developers, there was a flood of task management apps. (The winners of that fight are covered in this chapter.) About the time everyone accepted that Apple wasn't going to release its own task app, it surprised us all and did. At least most of us were surprised: The existing task manager developers had a different emotion about the release of Reminders.

Shown in Figure 19-1, Reminders uses a two-pane format. The right pane holds your task list and the left pane can display either a calendar (as shown in Figure 19-1) or a choice of task lists (shown in Figure 19-2).

Creating tasks with Reminders

Task creation with Reminders is easy. Just tap a blank line in the right pane (or tap the New Reminder icon button, the plus (+) symbol, in the top-right of the window) and start typing. If your task is more than one line, as shown in Figure 19-1, Reminders automatically adjusts the line spacing to fit. When you are done, you'll have an easy to read list of your tasks ready to check off with a tap of your finger. If your task management needs are simple, you now have everything you need.

Tap a task item to open the Details popover, where you can edit the task text. This popover also has the Remind Me button to set notifications for your task (covered later in this chapter). Tapping the Show More button opens the popover with even more options, as shown in Figure 19-2.

FIGURE 19-1

Apple's Reminders app

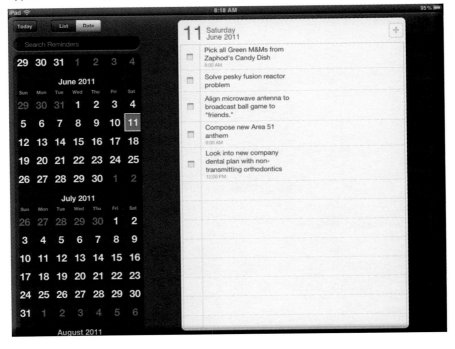

WHAT ABOUT USING MULTIPLE TASK APPS?

There are several good solutions in the chapter. Some iPad workers keep separate task lists for different areas of their lives. For example, you may use OmniFocus for your work tasks but use Apple's Reminders for your personal tasks. While it is easy to say that multiple systems can wreak havoc, there's really nothing wrong with multiple apps if it works for you. However, if you do, pay particular attention to whether or not anything is getting dropped. If you find the complexity of having two different task apps results in broken commitments, pick just one and make it work.

The expanded Details popover adds options to set a due date, schedule repeating tasks, set a priority level, and assign the current task to a different list (li are covered later).

To set a due date, tap Due in the Details popover; Reminders presents a new popover and date picker. From this popover you can also turn the due date on or Furthermore, you can assign a specific due date and time or make the task due all day. Once a task has a due date, Reminders notifies you when the due date arrives.

Tap Repeat on the Details popover to open a popover where you can set the t to repeat every day, week, two weeks, month, or year. There is no option for setting a task to repeat on just weekdays. Instead, you need to make a separate task for ead day (Monday through Friday) and have each one repeat weekly.

The Priority popover (accessed from the Details popover) provides an option set a task priority to low, medium, high, or none. At this point, adding priorities to tasks in Reminders is an empty gesture. The Reminders app doesn't do anything w the task priorities. You cannot change the sort order of your tasks or filter tasks bas on priorities.

Tap Lists in the Details popover to move a task to a different list. Lists give you a way to separate task lists based on area of responsibility. To work with lists, tap tl List button at the top of the left column to open the list view, shown in Figure 19-2.

By default, you have one list, called Tasks. Ad more lists by tapping the Edit button at the top-left portion of the window. This lets you delete, reorder, and creat new lists. You can make lists for different work and personal projects an

A REMINDERS ALTERNATIVE: BUSYTODO

If you want iCal task list integration but Reminders doesn't do it for you, look no further than BusyToDo ($10). Developed by the same people who created BusyCal on Mac OS X, BusyToDo provides immediate and flawless task list syncing with iCal on the Mac.

FIGURE 19-2

Reminders' Details popover

assign tasks to the individual lists. You can filter the list view to show just the tasks assigned to a specific list by tapping on it.

Each new task gets a check box, and tapping the check box marks the task as done. Completed tasks get moved to the Completed task list.

There is a Search bar at the top of the left pane in both list and date views. Reminders searches as you type in your search term. The search is, however, case-sensitive, so pay attention to your case usage in the Search bar.

Reminders notifications

Notifications are Reminders' most innovative feature. To set a notification, tap Remind Me from the Details popover; the Remind Me popover opens. From this popover, you can set a notification for a particular date or time or tie the reminder to a specific location. The location-based notifications are unique among iPad task manager apps. You can set the notification to go off when you arrive or leave a particular location. The app then monitors your location and notifies you accordingly. Want to make sure you get a reminder to pick up oranges when you leave the office? Set a notification for when you leave and, as your iPad senses you leaving the office, it notifies you to go buy oranges.

Reminders shares your tasks with all other iOS devices using the iCloud service. Reminders also syncs your tasks with iCal on your Mac or Microsoft Outlook on your PC if you have Exchange server access set up on your iPad, as covered in Chapter 12.

Reminders is a simple task management app. Although it does not boast all the features of some of the other apps in this chapter, its easy syncing and unique notification system make it a worthy contender for task management duty.

Zenbe Lists

Zenbe Lists ($5), shown in Figure 19-3, is an elegant Internet-based task management tool for iPad users with modest task management needs. Zenbe Lists started life as a web service (www.zenbe.com/lists) and grew into an iOS application. Indeed, you can still use the web service regardless of whether you own an iOS device.

As the name implies, Zenbe Lists is a list-keeping service. Using the app or logging on at the website, users can create multiple lists, including task lists. For example, you could make a list of groceries, or your five-step plan to take over the world ("Acquire Death Ray"? Check.)

Using the Zenbe Lists app on your iPad is simple. The app has two panes, shown in Figure 19-3. The left pane describes each list and the right pane shows e item on the selected lists. Tap the New List button in the upper-left corner of the l pane to start a new list. This brings up the onscreen keyboard (unless your iPad is paired with a Bluetooth keyboard). Because these are just lists, you can get as spec or generic as you need. Some users manage all their tasks on one list while others may use 20.

Adding tasks with Zenbe Lists is not difficult. Tap the relevant task list in the lef pane and the New Item icon button (the + symbol) at the top-left of the right pane. A text entry window appears at the top of the right pane and the onscreen keyboard slides up. You can then type the task name and tap Done on the iPad keyboard. Tapping your new task item opens a popover with options to set a due date and priority status. This popover also includes an option to move the task to a different l

Tap the Sorting icon button (which states "sorted manually" in Figure 19-3) a the bottom of the right pane to change how Zenbe Lists sorts your tasks. Zenbe Li can arrange tasks by due date, priority, alphabetically, or manually. If you manuall sort your list, tap the Edit button in the upper-right corner of the right pane and rearrange your list by tapping and holding the Reorder icon button (the three bars at the right of each task and dragging it to its new location.

You can also delete tasks in the edit view. When you are finished, tap Done (i the upper-right corner) to exit edit view. Zenbe Lists recognizes phone numbers ar addresses in task items, so tapping them opens the address in Google Maps on yo iPad (or dials the selected phone number on an iPhone).

As you add tasks on your iPad, tap the Sync button at the bottom of the left pane to sync your lists with the Zenbe Lists web servers.

Zenbe Lists on the iPad

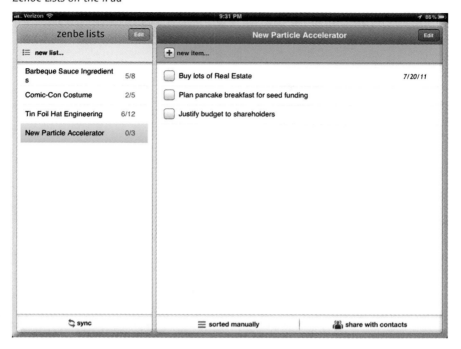

Because the service is web-based, you can also access your Zenbe list from all current web browsers. That means you can edit, modify, and check off tasks from your Mac, Windows PC, and Android device in addition to doing so inside the slick iPad app. This flexibility is one feature that several of the more complex task management apps covered in this chapter can't match.

Another benefit of Zenbe's web roots is easy sharing. Tap the Share with Contacts button at the bottom of the right pane to send an e-mail link for your list. Friends and co-workers can see the lists by logging in to Zenbe's website, whether or not they own an iPad. Any changes they make at the web interface appear automatically on your iPad.

Zenbe Lists is a simple task management application. It is inexpensive and easy to use. Moreover, the web-based syncing makes it ideal for users with uncomplicated task list needs and often work on other computing platforms, particularly Windows.

Toodledo

Toodledo ($3) is an iPad task manager with a web component similar to Zenbe Lists. Toodledo, however, has more task management horsepower. Shown in Figure 19-4, Toodledo features two panes. The left pane tracks your task lists, with sorting criteria that include starred items, folders, due dates, priorities, and the most recently created tasks. The right pane displays individual tasks.

Toodledo task management

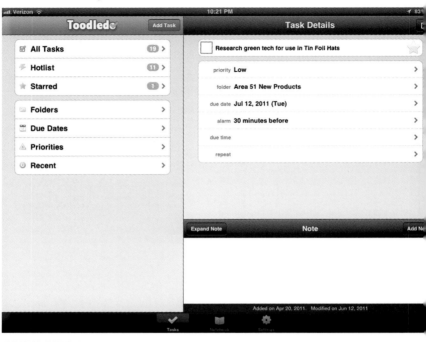

Toodledo's web interface from a desktop browser

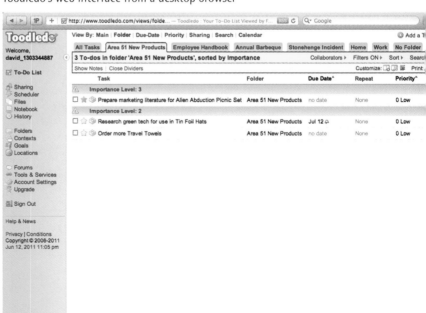

Tapping the items in the left pane expands those items for further inspection. For example, tapping the Folders item brings up a list of all the folders in your to Toodledo database in the left pane. From there you can edit the folders or add new ones. Toodledo works the same for due dates and priorities.

To create a new task, tap the Add Task button at the top-right corner of the left pane. Toodledo then opens a new task item in the right pane. You can set the new task's priority (choosing among five options), folder, due date, alarm, due time, and set the task to automatically repeat. Tapping the star icon at the far right of the task description adds the task to your list of starred items and makes it available with the starred items filter in the left pane.

All Toodledo's data is synced with the web servers and available from the Toodledo's website at www.toodledo.com. You can use your data on any computer that can access the web, including a Mac or Windows PC. Being web-based, Toodledo is great for collaboration. The app includes a permission system providing controls over who reads and edits your tasks. Although the web sync, shown in Figure 19-5, provides feature parity with the iPad app, the interface is not very attractive.

Nevertheless, this app delivers. Toodledo is a solid answer for iPad users looking for a web-based solution and for whom Zenbe Lists is not enough. For Toodledo power users, there are additional features available for a yearly subscription. For $15 per year, you can add statistics, subtasks, and encryption. For $30 per year, you can add all those additional features plus the ability to upload file attachments.

Todo for iPad

Todo ($5) is one of the prettiest task management applications on the iPad. Shown in Figure 19-6, the app looks like a traditional spiral-bound planner. The left side of the page holds a virtual bookmark upon which the application keeps search criteria and task lists. The right side of the page holds the individual task items.

The left pane is a digital facsimile of the plastic bookmark found in most paper-based day planners. The left pane includes two boxes. The top box is a list of filters. Tapping these you can display all tasks, a filtered list, just start items, or the inbox.

The lower box in the left pane includes all the user-created task lists. To create a new list, tap the Edit button at the lower-right portion of the left pane. A popover appears from which you can edit and create new task lists. The list scrolls to accommodate many tasks, but the list also can become unmanageable. OmniFocus, covered later in this chapter, does a better job with numerous projects. Regardless, once you are done creating new lists, tap Done to exit the new list mode.

Tapping on a task lists presents all the associated tasks in the right pane, as shown in Figure 19-6. To add a new task, tap the New Task icon button (the + symbol) at the top-right of the right pane and the new task popover opens.

Todo lets you assign the type of task at the time of creation. For example, if your task is to call a client, you can designate the task as a call and assign contact

FIGURE 19-6

Todo for iPad

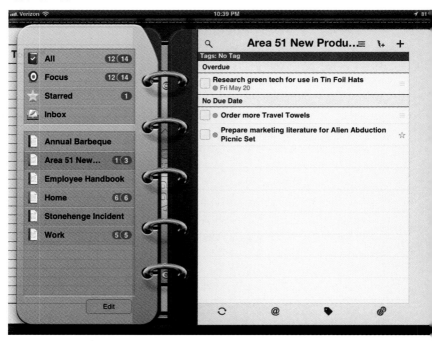

information to the task when you create the task. When the task shows up later, all the necessary information is already attached to the task. It works the same for e-mail, SMS, visiting a location, and visiting a website.

Additionally, you can create a new task as a normal task, project, or checklist. Creating a task as a project task opens a blank task page where you can keep all th related task items to that project together. A checklist task works the same but the new list is a checklist instead of a task list.

For quick entry, tap the Quick Task icon button (the icon is a lighting bolt ne to the + symbol) at the top-right portion of the window in Figure 19-6. This allow you to skip the selection of a specific task type and instead provides a text entry bc

Todo for iPad's tools for creating new tasks are practical and immediately use As shown in Figure 19-6, the net result is an attractive task list you can efficiently work through. For example, tapping on an e-mail task item opens the option to create, compose, and send the e-mail directly from within Todo.

Tapping on an existing task in the right pane opens the Edit Task popover. Fro here you can assign additional information to your tasks including due date, due time, repeat frequency, priority, and other additional data. From this popover you can also move the task to a different list or change its type. For example, you coulc convert a standard task to an e-mail task.

Todo for iPad also supports contexts. Tapping the Context icon button (the @ symbol at the bottom of the right pane) opens the context popover. From here you can view and filter your tasks by context. Tapping the Edit button in this window, you can also add, modify, and delete contexts. Contexts are assigned to tasks in the Edit Task popover.

Likewise, Todo includes support for tagging. Tapping the Tag icon button (it looks like a gift tag) in the lower portion of the right pane opens a popover where you can create and assign tags to your task items. Your imagination is the limit. You can create tags for the duration of the task, necessary people, specific locations, or any criteria that would be helpful for you to narrow and find your tasks.

You can sync your Todo for iPad data with the developer's web-based syncing service or with Toodledo (covered earlier in this chapter). Additional customization settings include sort priority and alert sounds. You can set a passcode lock to keep your data from unwanted eyes. Todo includes TextExpander Touch support (covered in Chapter 2), so you may use your TextExpander snippets when creating new tasks. Finally, you can customize the look of your task binder by choosing the color of the leather, the paper, and other elements of your virtual task planner. The application includes four completed themes, but you can download more, for a fee, from within the app.

Todo for iPad is particularly suited to people who are familiar with traditional spiral-bound day planners. If that is you, you will feel right at home with Todo's digital representation of its interface. The app is attractive and the user interface is intuitive. Overall, Todo is a great experience for keeping and tracking tasks on your iPad.

OmniFocus

There is task management and there is *task management*. Although the tools covered thus far in this chapter are more than adequate for many users, sometimes you need more. Life is complicated. We are expected to produce more and faster in every aspect of our lives from the office to the Girl Scout camp-out. With so many plates being juggled, it is no wonder that we so often find them crashing to the ground.

If you are banging your head into the constraints of the typical task management applications, step up to OmniFocus for iPad. OmniFocus ($40), shown in Figure 19-7, is the 800-pound gorilla of task management on the iPad. Lovingly developed by the Omni Group, OmniFocus provides superb task management tools and keeps up with your needs whether you have a dozen projects or a thousand.

OmniFocus is an app that has both rabid fans and confused detractors. There are a lot of moving parts to OmniFocus. It goes far beyond a simple task list, and that is why people love it so much. That is also why a lot people give up on it, deciding that the barrier to entry is not worth any eventual payoff.

Although OmniFocus works in both portrait and landscape view, landscape works best, presenting the familiar "steering wheel" control scheme with navigation on the left pane and data manipulation on a larger right pane. The left pane includes the New Task icon button; the Inbox icon button (which displays the current inbox count); Project, Context, and Map views; the Forecast view (covered later);

FIGURE 19-7

OmniFocus for iPad

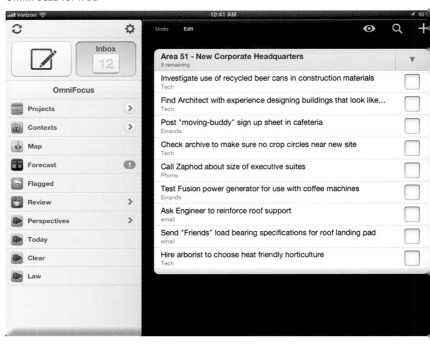

flag status; the Review button (covered later); and custom perspectives. If you use the OmniFocus in portrait mode, you activate the navigation pane by tapping the OmniFocus button in the upper-left corner.

Capturing tasks with OmniFocus

OmniFocus for iPad includes several ways to add new tasks to your list. The easiest is the Quick Entry window accessed with the Quick Entry icon button at the upper-left corner of the left pane. You can also get the Quick Entry window by tapping the New Task icon button (the + symbol) at the top-right of the right pane.

The Quick Entry button allows you to add new tasks without leaving your current context or project. This is great for the little things that occur to you while random synapses are firing but you need to keep on with your work. (Like when you are neck deep in a writing project and suddenly remember you need more spicy carrots.)

No matter how you go about it, when you add an action, OmniFocus displays the Action Editor, shown in Figure 19-8. This is the standard window for editing actions in OmniFocus. It includes four tabbed panes: Info, Dates, Notes, and Attachments.

You can adjust an action's name from any tabbed pane. The Info pane includes context, project, and flag status. By tapping any of these buttons, you can add or adjust the entry. Tapping the gray circled-X icon to the right of any field deletes its

FIGURE 19-8

OmniFocus's Action Editor

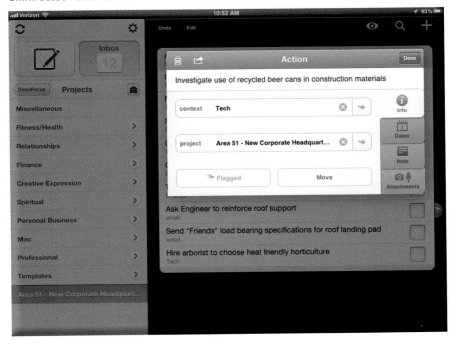

current entry. The app is intelligent about adding contexts and projects. For example, for a MacSparky blog entry project, I can type "mbe" and the app figures it out. If you type in a new project or context for an action, OmniFocus gives you the option to add it.

The Dates pane lets you set start and due dates for new and existing tasks. Tapping the Date field opens the slot machine-style date picker. The Dates pane also has buttons to quickly move a task forward a day, week, or month. Start dates are useful with OmniFocus. Setting future start dates for tasks lets you push those tasks out of view until you need to see them. For example, if you are not going to start a new project until next month, set the start date for next month. Between now and then, the task will not clutter up your list.

Tap Repeat to make an action repeating. OmniFocus lets you set a repeating task on a set schedule, like every five days, or you can set the repeat to trigger on task completion, like five days after completion. This difference is subtle but can be useful. For example, you may only need to wash your car every two weeks after you finish washing it, but you may need to prepare for a staff meeting every seven days regardless of completion.

The Notes pane lets you add notes to a task. OmniFocus gives you the option of opening this window to a full screen text editor. Adding detailed notes to your tasks can be useful. You can also use this field to paste portions of an e-mail or website links you want to reference with the task.

Finally, the Attachments pane lets you add photos and voice notes to you actions.

You don't need to add all this extra data to actions. I often quickly add tasks with just their names and no additional information. Later, when I have more tim I'll open the inbox (at the top of the left pane) and add context, start dates, and related metadata to tasks using the Action Editor.

Organizing tasks with OmniFocus

OmniFocus makes it easy to jump among perspectives, contexts, and projects to organize your day. Using the iPad, you can organize your tasks over tea, in bed, or anywhere you happen to be. The process of tapping on tasks and resetting dates and priorities is intuitive and fast. In all views, you can collapse or expand objects tapping and holding the disclosure triangle.

If you want to focus on a particular project or context, tap and hold its name open the Project popover. This is similar to the Action Editor popover except the I pane has entries for type and status.

Although it has no traditional task-priority system, OmniFocus lets you set fla To do so, tap the Flag button in the Info pane of the Action Editor, covered earlier this chapter and shown in Figure 19-8. To display flagged tasks, tap Flagged in the left pane. Flags are a good way to filter your tasks down to just those critical items that must get done.

FIGURE 19-9

OmniFocus's Map view

OMNIFOCUS WITHOUT A MAC

OmniFocus grows out of the popular OmniFocus for Mac application. Although OmniFocus for Mac is a great product, it is not required to use OmniFocus for iPad. Indeed, as OmniFocus for iPad continues to get better, I find myself using OmniFocus on my Mac less and less frequently. Several of the iPad OmniFocus features (such as the Forecast and Review views) are simply better than in OmniFocus on the Mac.

The only feature missing on OmniFocus for iPad is the ability to set custom views (called perspectives). You can import OmniFocus for Mac perspectives to OmniFocus for iPad. You just can't create them on the iPad as of this writing.

Although iPad OmniFocus was developed as a companion application for OmniFocus on the Mac, iPad OmniFocus most certainly can stand on its own. I often perform all my task management work inside OmniFocus for iPad. OmniFocus includes powerful tools to manage even the most demanding task lists and is an excellent addition to your iPad. OmniFocus is overkill for some, but if you need a sophisticated task management application, you will not go wrong with OmniFocus.

The Map view is similar to the notifications in Apple's Reminders app, covered earlier in this chapter. Using the Map view you can assign locations to contexts. To do so, open the OmniFocus Map view and link a context to a specific location. For example, open OmniFocus at your office and link your Office context to your office location, as shown in Figure 19-9. Then you can have OmniFocus only display tasks that are in the context near your current location.

Processing your tasks in OmniFocus is easy. You can jump between Perspective and Context views, obliterating your task list as you go. Because some of my daily routine involves working on a Windows PC, it is nice have my OmniFocus list on that big iPad screen nearby.

Forecast view

The Forecast view, shown in Figure 19-10, is clever. It breaks down tasks that are starting and due over the next seven days. Tapping on Tomorrow, for example, gives you a list of all tasks that are due or starting tomorrow, along with a time line of your calendar events for the day. You can tap any specific day in the next seven to see what you are up against.

With OmniFocus's Forecast view, you can know at a glance if next Thursday you are going to get crushed with deadlines and thus be able to plan appropriately. Every afternoon I spend time in the forecast for the next few days.

Review view

One of OmniFocus's killer features is its Review view. You can set a review timer for each project. For important projects, that review timer may be a week. For back-burner projects, it may be three months. OmniFocus then gives you a list of projects

Reviewing projects with OmniFocus

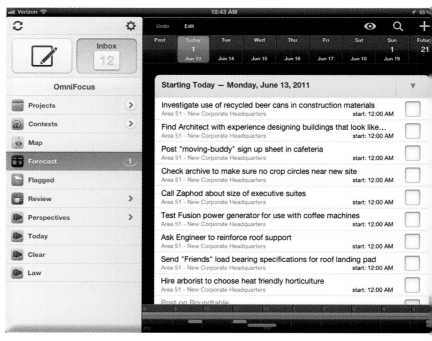

that are due for review. You can go through each project and confirm they are still relevant and on track.

iPad OmniFocus makes review easy. Tap Review in the left pane to see the Review view, shown in Figure 19-10.

In Review view, the left pane shows a list of all projects due for review and the right pane shows a list of all tasks in the selected project. The bottom of the right pan includes buttons to drop a project, mark it as completed, put it on hold, or mark the project as reviewed. Finally, you can view (or change) the review timer by tapping the Last Reviewed button in the lower-left portion of the right pane. If you manage a lot projects, using a Review process makes a huge difference in project management.

You can sync your OmniFocus data via Wi-Fi, WebDAV, or the Omni Group's free syncing service. If you also use OmniFocus on the iPhone or Mac, OmniFocus provides over-the-air syncing so all your devices are always up to date. If you are ju

TEXT LISTS FOR TASK MANAGEMENT

Another simple task management system is to just use text lists. Simplenote (covered in Chapter 13) includes a list mode ideal for this purpose. Simplenote transforms text files into lists with the touch of a button. Remember, the point of choosing a task management app is to get it as complex as you need but no more.

MY TASK MANAGEMENT WORKFLOW

All the tasks management apps covered in this chapter are good solutions. I get things done with OmniFocus. OmniFocus is the digital incarnation of my personal assistant. It warns me of upcoming deadlines and helps me keep on track. Every morning I go through my daily task list on my iPad and spend the rest of the day checking off tasks. In the evening, I take a look at what's left and what's tomorrow. Then I move, edit, and delete tasks as necessary. At least once a week, I wake up early and review my OmniFocus projects on my iPad.

using OmniFocus on your iPad, sync your data to the Omni Group's free syncing service anyway for an extra backup.

20

Calculators and Spreadsheets

Despite all its fancy bells and whistles, the iPad is, at its core, a computer. Computers are really good at calculating numbers, and the iPad is no different. There are two general categories of number crunchers on the iPad: calculators and spreadsheets. This chapter covers some of the best options available for both categories.

Calculators

With its large touchscreen interface and the ability for developers to put interface elements anywhere on the screen, the iPad opened the door for innovative calculators. Because there are so many kinds of calculators, there is no single best calculator on the iPad. There are, however, some very good calculators.

The simple tape calculator: Calcbot

For a simple tape calculator, Calcbot ($2) is one of the best. Shown in Figure 20-1, the app presents a simple gray interface with a paper tape along the right side.

The Calcbot developer sweated all the details, right down to audio with the satisfying clicks and whirls you would expect from a real tape calculator. The layout is clean and the buttons are hard to miss.

Swiping the calculator to the left or tapping the small dot at the bottom-center of Calcbot slides to reveal an additional window of advanced calculator functions.

Tap a calculation on the tape for a popover with options to use the result, copy the result, or attach the calculation to an e-mail.

The Settings icon button in the upper-right corner opens a popover with options to send the entire tape as an e-mail or clear the tape. The Info icon button in the lower-right corner opens a popover with options to turn off sounds (though I think the sounds are one of Calcbot's strong points) and round results for currency.

Although not particularly powerful for day-to-day calculations, Calcbot helps get the job done.

PowerOne Financial Calculator Pro

The PowerOne Financial Calculator Pro ($5), shown in Figure 20-2, is really two apps in one.

First, as shown in Figure 20-2, it is a standard calculator, featuring a tape, calculator history, and memory. The calculator works in both algebraic and Reverse Polish Notation (RPN) modes (see the sidebar "What on Earth Is RPN?"). The standard calculator performs calculations in decimal, scientific, engineering, fraction, or feet-inch format with functions that include powers, logs, and trig.

PowerOne really earns its place on your iPad with its second feature: calculator templates. PowerOne uses templates to perform commonly used complex calculations. These templates are similar to spreadsheet functions. Figure 20-3 shows the TVM (time-value-money) template.

FIGURE 20-1

Calcbot's tape calculator

FIGURE 20-2

PowerOne Financial Calculator Pro in calculator mode

FIGURE 20-3

PowerOne Financial Calculator Pro's TVM template

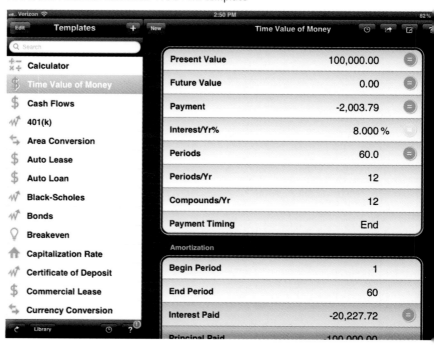

WHAT ON EARTH IS RPN?

Reverse Polish Notation (RPN) is a mathematical notation where the operator follows the operands. Put simply, instead of `(1 + 2)-3`, RPN uses `Enter 2 + 3 -`. Once you wrap your head around RPN, it is pretty useful. Because RPN performs the calculations as you enter the individual operators, there is no ambiguity and no need for parentheses. RPN is fast, requires fewer keystrokes, and provides interim results.

Using a template is easy. Tap the variable you want to enter, such as Present Value in Figure 20-3. A popover opens for you to enter the value and save it to the template. Repeat this step for all the necessary variables. Solvable variables have an orange = symbol next to them. Tap the = for the missing variable and the PowerOne solves for it.

There are hundreds of templates, covering mortgages and real estate, finance and investing, math and science, medical, health, conversions, and construction. Do you want to calculate the exact cost of a commercial lease? There is a template for that. Do you need to convert Celsius to Kelvin? PowerOne has you covered.

The Library button at the bottom of the left pane, shown in Figure 20-3, opens the Library browser where you can download even more templates from PowerOne.

FIGURE 20-4

Sharing a calculation from PowerOne Financial Calculator Pro

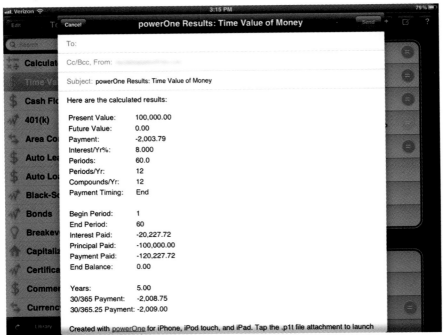

If you still can't find the template you need, there is the PowerOne scripting language for enterprising users to build it themselves. Scripting your own template is, however, no easy task and beyond the scope of this book.

PowerOne remembers past templates and computations. Access them by tapping the History icon button (it looks like a small analog clock set at three o'clock) shown at the top-right portion of Figure 20-3. From the History popover, you can return to prior calculations to change variables, annotate, name, and even share them.

You can also share the active template via e-mail. Tap the Sharing icon button (the rectangle with an arrow emerging) at the top-right of the right pane's toolbar to open an e-mail message with the calculation summary, shown in Figure 20-4. For TVM calculations, it even attaches an amortization schedule. The e-mail also attaches the PowerOne template so colleagues can open the calculation in PowerOne on the iPad or iPhone.

Science and engineering calculator: PCalc

PCalc ($10) started on the Mac, where it is the third-party calculator of choice. So it was only natural for the developer to bring this experience to the iPad. PCalc is aimed at scientists, engineers, students, and programmers.

Shown in Figure 20-5, PCalc features the calculator on the right side of the window with a strip at the left of the window that may act as a paper tape or display a memory stack.

PCalc is the most customizable calculator covered in this chapter. In the application settings (tap the Info icon button in the top-left of the toolbar), you can toggle RPN mode, multiple memories, and the thousands separator. You can also display digits in normal, scientific, and engineering modes. PCalc's ability to perform hexadecimal, octal, and binary calculations make it a favorite among computer programmers.

PCalc also has themes. The app ships with ten themes, ranging from subtle to loud. You can also choose the number of lines to display and from several key layouts in the application settings to add (and remove) functions.

OLD-SCHOOL WITH THE HP 12C

In every trade, some tools become legendary. This is true for the HP 12C financial calculator. A lot of business and financial wizards learned their trade using one of these calculators and naturally want the same calculator on their iPad. Look no further than Calc-12E RPN Financial Calculator ($6) for a faithful re-creation of the classic.

FIGURE 20-5

PCalc displaying the paper-tape view using the Touch of Color theme

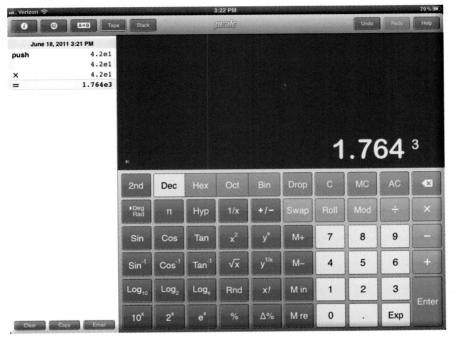

PCalc shares your results via the Email button at the bottom of the left pane, shown in Figure 20-5. The Constants icon button (a circle enclosing the number 42) opens a popover with a series of scientific and mathematical constants that range from the Earth's mass to the Rydberg Constant. Just about every iOS-using programmer or scientist I've met runs PCalc.

Spreadsheets

It didn't take long for traditional computer spreadsheets to find their way to the iPad. Spreadsheets on the iPad, however, are not the same as Mac and PC spreadsheet apps. They are lighter on overhead and features. I once sat in an airport next to a nice fellow who watched me working in Numbers on my iPad. After a few minutes, he asked, "Does it do pivot tables and macros?" I explained it did not, to which he replied, "then it's not a real spreadsheet."

None of the spreadsheet apps in this chapter can boast 100-percent compatibility with Microsoft Excel. There are advanced features in Microsoft Excel that simply don't translate to the current iPad spreadsheet applications. I doubt even Microsoft could create an iPad app that would include full Excel compatibility — even its Mac version of Excel isn't 100-percent compatible with the Windows version. Macros don't work and advanced formulas are not supported.

If you are an Excel power user, there's a good chance — like the guy in the airport — you will find the iPad spreadsheet apps too constraining. For the rest of us mortals, however, these apps bring over the most common features and provid basic compatibility with Microsoft Excel. That makes them "real" to me. There are several good spreadsheet apps for the iPad, starting with Numbers.

Numbers

Numbers ($10), shown in Figure 20-6, is the iPad incarnation of Apple's iWo spreadsheet application, Numbers for Mac OS X. Numbers was the first spreadshe application designed around the iPad and has many innovative touch-based featu

Before getting started with Numbers for iPad, there is something you must accept about this app. It is not Excel. There is no chart at Apple comparing feature of the two apps with eager young engineers racing to catch up. In fact, Numbers is the anti-Excel. The application was conceived and designed with the idea that it would never be used to create complex, macro-driven spreadsheets from which you could engineer the hostile takeover of a Fortune 500 company. Instead, Apple designed Numbers to be more accessible and less powerful. Quickoffice and Documents to Go, covered later in this chapter, provide a more traditional Excel environment.

Opening and creating spreadsheets

Starting iPad Numbers opens the document-selection window, shown in Figu 20-7. This window works similar to the document-selection windows in Pages and Keynote, displaying thumbnail images of as many as 16 spreadsheets. You can organize the spreadsheets by name or date by tapping the appropriate buttons at t top of the window. (If you don't see the Name and Date sort buttons, tap and hole anywhere on the screen and pull down.)

You can stack spreadsheets into folders for better organization. To create a folder, first tap the Edit button in the upper-right corner. Then tap and hold a spreadsheet's thumbnail image until it appears to lift off the screen and drag it on top of another spreadsheet. When you lift your finger, Numbers creates a folder. (This is a lot like making folders on the home screen, as explained in Chapter 1.) While in edit mode, you can duplicate a spreadsheet by tapping the Duplicate icon button (two overlapping pages with the + symbol on the top one) or delete a spreadsheet by tapping the Delete icon button (the trash can), both in the upper-l corner of the window. Once you are finished organizing your spreadsheets, tap the Done button in the upper-right corner to exit edit mode.

There is no Save button because iPad numbers saves automatically as you work. Although auto-save is great, it also creates a problem if you are working from a custom template spreadsheet. If, for example, you have a monthly budget spreadsheet you use as a template, any changes you make are automatically saved. little time, your template ceases being a template. To prevent this from happening,

FIGURE 20-6

Numbers on the iPad

FIGURE 20-7

Numbers' document-selection window

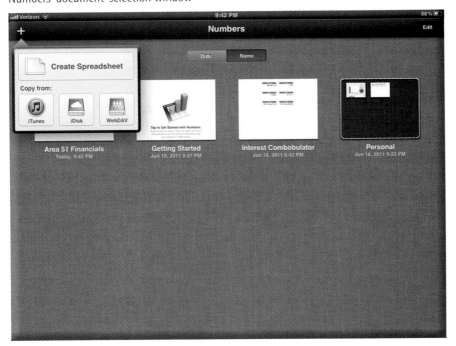

duplicate a custom template spreadsheet in the document-selection window *before* opening it in Numbers.

While in the document-selection window, you can create a new spreadsheet b tapping the Create Spreadsheet icon button (the + symbol) in the upper-left corne of the window. This opens the Create Spreadsheet popover shown in Figure 20-7.

To create a new blank spreadsheet, tap the Create Spreadsheet button and choose from any of the 16 built-in templates. There are several useful templates fo business, including invoicing, expense reports, employee schedules, and checklists These templates, however, are just a jumping off point: You can customize each on

Alternatively, you can import existing Numbers and Excel spreadsheets into Numbers from the Create Spreadsheet popover shown in Figure 20-7. Numbers can import a spreadsheet stored in iTunes, iDisk, or a WebDAV server. Note that th Create Spreadsheet popover says "copy" and not "open." A spreadsheet imported from an external source gets added to the Numbers document library. Although the document then syncs with the iCloud service, it does not sync with its original external source — you're working on an independent copy once it's in Numbers. T push your changes onto the external source, you need to export the spreadsheet to the original's location, overwriting it (as covered later in this chapter).

To import a spreadsheet attached to an e-mail, tap and hold the file in the e-mail until the Open In menu appears. If the spreadsheet is on your Mac or PC, send it to iPad Numbers through iTunes as explained in Chapter 1. You can also send spreadsheets to Numbers from other iPad spreadsheet apps (with their sharir button) or cloud apps, like Dropbox or Box.net, by storing the spreadsheet on the cloud server and using the Open In menu in their iPad apps. Numbers does not natively support Dropbox and Box.net but you can use a DropDAV account, cover in Chapter 5, to access Numbers spreadsheets from your Dropbox; Box.net has a similar WebDAV capability.

When opening Excel files, Numbers does its best to convert the files to the Numbers format. If there is an unsupported feature, Numbers modifies the spreadsheet for the iPad and explains what it changed.

The Numbers interface

With a spreadsheet open, the Numbers spreadsheet interface, shown in Figure 20-8, consists of a toolbar across the top of the window with buttons and tabs.

The tabs are relative to your active spreadsheet. Each tab represents a different sheet. For example, the spreadsheet shown in Figure 20-8 shows six sheets. You ca jump among the sheets by tapping the associated tabs.

The Spreadsheets button at the top-left of the window returns Numbers to the document-selection window. Tap the Undo button to undo. Tap and hold the Und button to redo.

Numbers includes four icon buttons on the right side of the toolbar: Info, Insert, Tools, and Full Screen.

FIGURE 20-8

The Numbers spreadsheet interface, with the Table pane of Numbers' Info popover

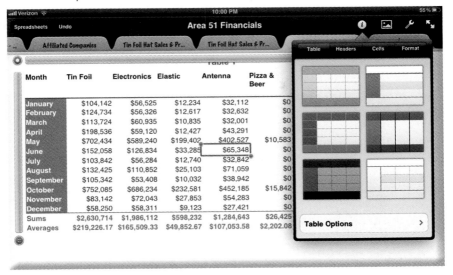

The Info icon button. The Info icon button opens a popover that provides formatting and editing options for objects in your spreadsheet. The Info popover is context-sensitive, so, for example, when a table is selected, the Info popover contains tools to adjust and customize a table. When text is selected, the Info popover includes text tools.

From the Info popover, you can apply alternative table formatting in the Table pane by tapping the previews. The sample table designs look great but can also serve as a jumping-off point for further customization using the other panes.

The Table Options button brings additional customization options, including displaying the table's name, creating a border, and providing alternate row shading. You can also enable grid lines and make adjustments to the table's typeface and size.

The Headers pane includes options to create dedicated rows and columns on the top, bottom, or left side of a table. These rows and columns hold labels and functions. Many veteran spreadsheet users forget about the footer row, but setting the footer row lets you keep a dedicated row at the bottom of your data for sums, averages, and other functions. Using a footer row avoids the practice of keeping extra rows just to preserve your calculations at the bottom of a table.

Numbers does not add rows and columns to the table when adding header rows, columns, and footers. Instead it converts the existing top, bottom, or left rows. If you want to add headers and footers to an existing table that already contains data, add the column or row first. The Headers pane also provides options to freeze rows and columns.

You adjust the look and feel of the spreadsheet with the Cells pane. It includes all the customization tools for your cells except formatting, which are in the Format pane (covered later). In the Cells pane, you can set text formatting (such as bold,

Formatting cells with Numbers

italic, underline, and strikethrough), justification and alignment, colors, and borde
styles. The Cells pane also includes a switch for enabling text wrap in cells.

The text options in the Cells pane are different from the text options available
in the Table pane covered earlier. The Table text options set text for the entire table,
whereas the cell-level text options work only on the selected cells. As an example,
you can increase the typeface size and color for your footer row using this Cell pan
Text Options button.

Finally, the Format pane includes buttons to set the individual cell formatting.
As shown in Figure 20-9, Numbers includes several cell format options including
numbers, currency, percentages, date and time, durations, check boxes, ratings,
and text. You can specify formatting for most cell types. For example, the currency
formatting includes options to set the number of decimal places, use of the comma
separator, and the type of currency (for example, U.S. dollars). You can also specify
how Numbers displaces negative currency amounts (with a different color, a
minus sign, or parentheses). Similar options exist for cells formatted as numbers,
percentages, date and time, and duration. Formats with additional settings have the
Detail Disclosure icon button (a blue circle enclosing a right-facing arrow).

Setting cell formatting is important in Numbers for several reasons.

First, it is just good practice to use correct formatting so the app knows what
kind of data it is working with and what types of calculations it can perform.
Numbers performs math functions on cells formatted as dates, for example,
differently from how it performs math functions on cells formatted as currency.

Second, data entry on the iPad depends on the cell formatting. For example,
when typing in a cell formatted for text, Numbers brings up the standard iPad

FIGURE 20-10

The Date & Times keyboard

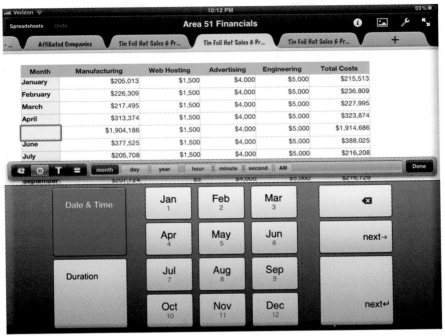

onscreen keyboard. Working with a cell formatted for date and time, however, brings up the Dates & Times keyboard, shown in Figure 20-10.

There is also an onscreen keyboard for entering numbers and formulas. Because the onscreen keyboard is virtual, the software designers can create a custom keyboard for every type of data. These specialized keyboards are one of Numbers' most innovative features.

At the top of the keyboard is the data-entry bar that lets you switch the keyboard's format. The Numbers icon button (the number 42) exposes the Numbers keyboard, the Date & Time icon button (the analog clock) brings up the Dates & Time keyboard, the Standard icon button (the capital T) brings up the standard keyboard, and the Formula icon button (the = symbol) displays the Formula keyboard, covered later in this chapter.

Tap the Info icon button with text selected to see the text tools. The Info popover for text includes panes to change the text style, text formatting, and arrangement.

The Style pane includes options to set a border and line style, fill color, shadow, and opacity for text boxes. Change text emphasis, size, color, justification, and margins with the Text pane. The Arrange pane adjusts the front-to-back order for the selected object.

The Info icon button also provides options for dealing with images, tables, and charts, all covered later in this chapter.

The Insert icon button. Where the Info icon button lets you adjust tables, charts, and text, the Insert icon button is all about letting you create them. Tap the Insert icon button to open a popover, shown in Figure 20-11, with panes to insert media, tables, charts, and shapes in your Numbers spreadsheet.

The Media pane displays the pictures in your iPad photo album (the Photos app). Tap and drag any image to drop it in your spreadsheet.

The Tables pane includes six sheets of preformatted spreadsheet tables, including several options for headers, footers, and check boxes. Again, to add a tal to your spreadsheet, tap and drag it onto the spreadsheet window.

The Charts pane similarly includes six sheets full of charts in various formats and color schemes. The default chart styles in iPad Numbers include horizontal and vertical bar charts, line charts (both filled and unfilled), pie charts, and scatter charts. All the charts in Numbers are two-dimensional — sadly, those attractive 3D charts you create in Numbers on your Mac do not display on the iPad: Upon impo Numbers converts them to two dimensions.

Finally, the Insert popover's Shapes pane includes a selection of lines, arrows, shapes, and text boxes to use in your spreadsheet. The tab includes six sheets of shapes in various colors and formats.

 The Tools icon button. The Tools icon button opens a popover with the settings and tools that don't fit anywhere else. The Share and Print button opens a popover with printing and sharing options. The print function in Numbers is unique: Rather than use the iPad's standard Printer Options popover, Numbers opens a print preview window, shown in Figure 20-12.

FIGURE 20-11

Numbers' Insert popover

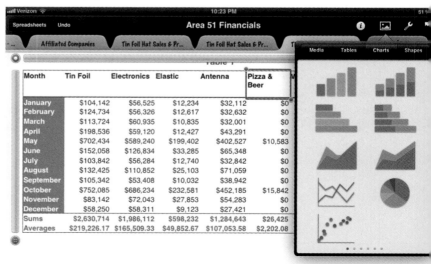

In the print preview window, Numbers displays how your spreadsheet will print on paper. Use the bottom toolbar to make adjustments using the slider bar or simply tell Numbers to make the document auto-fit the page. You can also specify portrait or landscape printing from this view. The Options icon button in the top right of the window lets you specify whether to add page numbers and repeat table headers on each page. Once you have everything just right, tap the Print button in the bottom toolbar, and Numbers displays the standard iPad print dialog box. (I cover Numbers' sharing tools later in this chapter.)

The Tools popover's Find button opens the Search bar.

The Options icon button (the gear icon) to the left of the Search bar opens a popover with options to find and replace and to limit the search to match case or whole words.

The Tools popover's Settings button includes switches to toggle spell-checking and to toggle edge guides.

Finally, tap the Help button to get further help with Numbers from Apple's website.

 The Full Screen icon button. The Full Screen icon button at the top right of the toolbar removes the toolbar and navigation tabs and commits your full screen to the current spreadsheet. Tap the center of the spreadsheet to exit full-screen mode.

Working with sheets and tables

To add a new sheet to your Numbers spreadsheet, tap the New Sheet tab, the far right tab with the + symbol on it. Numbers then opens a popover with options to open a new sheet or new form. (Forms are covered later in this chapter.) When you tap the New Sheet button, a separate sheet opens in your Numbers spreadsheet. Add a table using the Insert icon button (covered earlier); your iPad screen will look similar to Figure 20-13.

Numbers includes several table-adjustment tools. Activate the tools by tapping the table. The table then looks like what is shown in Figure 20-13. Tap and hold the resizing handles (the blue dots) and drag them on the screen to resize the table. The resizing handle at the center of the right vertical line lets you adjust the width of the table without altering the height. The resizing handle at the center of the bottom horizontal line does the opposite: You can adjust the height without altering the width. Finally, the resizing handle at the bottom-right corner lets you adjust both the width and height at the same time. When you use this diagonal resizing tool, Numbers displays a diagonal dashed line so you may choose to keep the resized table in the same proportions as the original.

The circle around a dot at the top-left corner is the table handle. Tap and hold the table handle to move the table around the sheet. The circle at the top right enclosing a 2x2 grid is the column handle. Tapping this adds a column to the table. Tap and hold the column handle to add and remove columns from your table by dragging right or left respectively. The row handle, at the bottom left of the table, works the same way with rows.

FIGURE 20-12

Numbers' print preview window

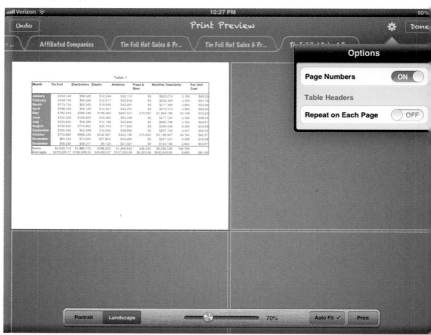

The long bars between the table handle and the respective column and row handles, are the table tabs. Tapping a table tab selects the adjacent row or column. Once selected, you can resize the selected row or column by tapping and holding the two vertical lines that appear. Alternatively, you can move the selected column or row by tapping and holding it anywhere except the two vertical resizing lines and dragging the column or row to its new location. With a table selected, a two-finger tap opens a contextual menu with options to cut, copy, and delete it.

To select a cell, tap it. If you tap and drag, you can select multiple cells. Tapping again on the selected cells opens a contextual menu with options to cut, copy, paste, delete, and fill the selected cells. To move data from one table to another, tap and drag the source data until it is all selected. Then tap the selected data and tap the Copy option from the contextual menu. Finally, tap the destination cell and then tap it once again to display the Paste option, which you then tap to complete the move.

To add data to your table, double-tap a cell to have Numbers open the appropriate keyboard for the selected cell's format, as covered earlier in this chapter.

Double-tapping a cell also provides the data-entry bar, which includes the Formula button (the = symbol). Figure 20-14 shows the Formula keyboard.

You create calculations with iPad Numbers the same way you do on a Mac or PC: Select cells and then select mathematical operators for the desired calculations. Numbers includes more than 250 functions, ranging from sums and averages to yield discounts and Bessel functions.

FIGURE 20-13

Adding a table to Numbers

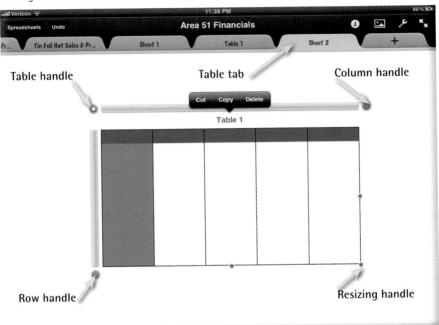

Table handle

Table tab

Column handle

Row handle

Resizing handle

FIGURE 20-14

Numbers' Formula keyboard

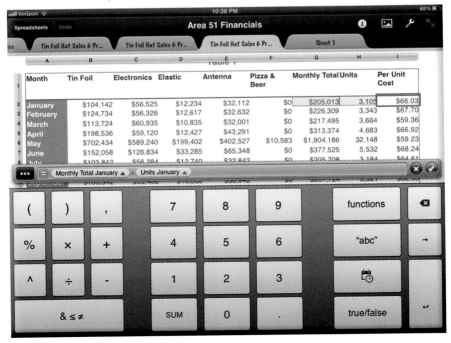

FIGURE 20-15

Adding a chart to a Numbers spreadsheet

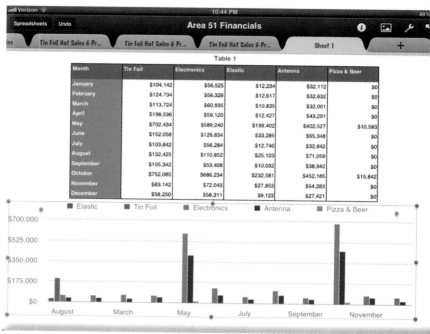

Working with charts

Charts are a great way to bring life to your spreadsheet. Add a chart via the Insert icon button, covered earlier. To add data, double-tap the chart. Numbers then places thin blue line around the chart, as shown in Figure 20-15. Then tap data in a table to have the chart auto-update based on the selected data. The chart is dynamically linked to the selected data, so if you change the data in the table, the chart updates itself.

Single-tapping a chart selects it. Move a selected chart by tapping and holding the center and moving it with your finger. Tap and hold the blue resizing handles to adjust the table size. Tapping the Info icon button with a chart selected opens a popover with additional chart options, including chart type. Numbers provides column, bar, stacked column and bar, area, line, pie, and scatter charts. Depending on which chart type you pick, the popover includes options and switches for legends, typography, separate X and Y axis settings, and a back-to-front arrangement slider.

You can also manually adjust individual components of a chart. For example, tap and hold an individual slice of a pie chart and drag it away from the rest of the chart.

Using forms

Because of the iPad's portability, the Numbers developers added a feature not found on Mac- and PC-based spreadsheets: forms. Shown in Figure 20-16, a form is a separate sheet tab that simplifies data entry for a specified table.

To create a form, tap the New Sheet tab and select New Form from the popover. Numbers provides a list of all tables in the active spreadsheet, organized by sheet. Tap the table you want to use to have Numbers create a form, as shown in Figure 20-16.

Sharing Numbers documents

In the Tools popover, tap the Share and Print button to share your spreadsheet via e-mail, iTunes, iDisk, or WebDAV. Although there is no native Dropbox or Box. net support, you can export your spreadsheet to those services using Dropbox's DropDAV service or Box.net's WebDAV service (covered in Chapter 5). All your spreadsheets are automatically synced via the iCloud service to other iOS devices and Macs using Numbers.

Numbers can export your spreadsheet to Microsoft Excel, PDF, and Numbers formats. Numbers also can export a spreadsheet to the iWork.com service, covered in Chapter 13, for sharing spreadsheets with co-workers and clients.

Numbers has its limitations: It cannot display hidden columns or merged cells. It certainly doesn't have all the features available in a traditional desktop spreadsheet program. Nevertheless, Numbers succeeds as an innovative spreadsheet application that takes advantage of the touch interface. I use it all the time.

FIGURE 20-16

Using forms

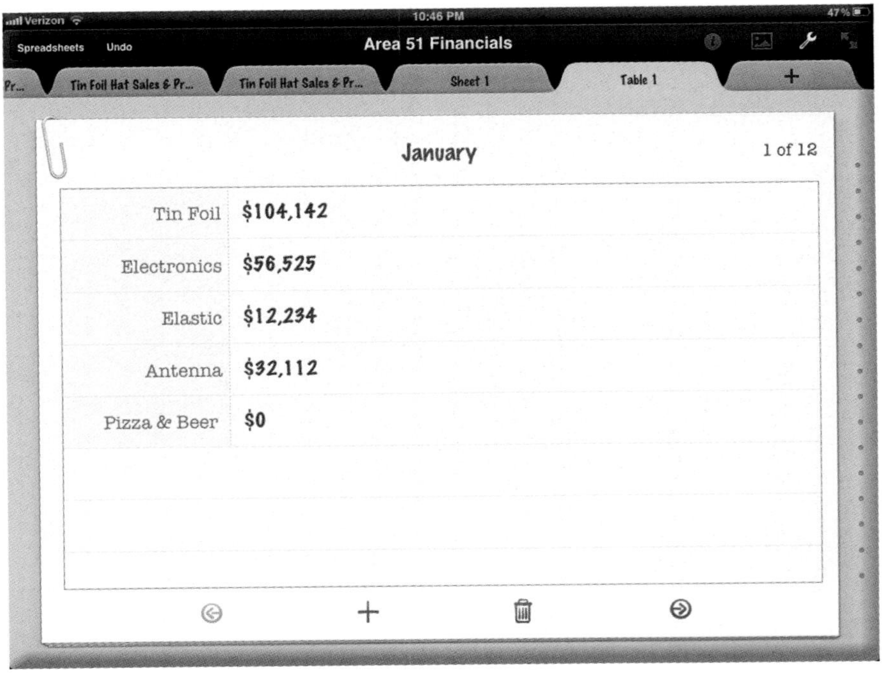

Working with Quickoffice and Documents t Go

Many power users argue, convincingly, that the best spreadsheet application o any platform is Microsoft Excel. Although Microsoft has not created an iPad-friend version, several app developers have released spreadsheet apps that work with Microsoft Excel files (in addition to Numbers).

The two biggest contenders for Excel compatibility on the iPad are the Quickoffice Pro HD ($15) and Documents to Go for Pad ($17) office suites

I cover both apps in detail in Chapter 13, but several points from that chapter apply here as well: The file-management system for both applications is identical; they both use a centralized file system that works for word processing, presentation and spreadsheet documents. Likewise, their word-processing strengths and weaknesses apply equally to spreadsheets: Quickoffice is friendlier, more stable bu includes fewer features, whereas Documents to Go has more features but is a bit more difficult to use.

SUPERCHARGED GRAPHING

There are limits to what you can graph using a spreadsheet application. If you aren't happy with Numbers' graphing capabilities, look at OmniGraphSketcher ($15), shown below, It takes graphing to the next level. In addition to building graphs on spreadsheet data you import from Numbers, you can manually add points of emphasis, fills, labels, and shapes. Graphs built with OmniGraphSketcher just look better (and more convincing) than anything you can do with a traditional spreadsheet app.

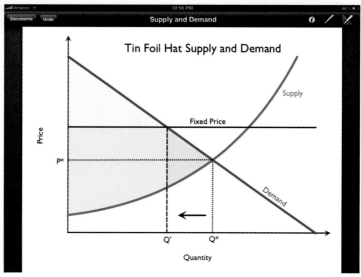

USING GOOGLE SPREADSHEETS

Google Spreadsheets, the online collaborative spreadsheet, is gaining popularity at the workplace. Although Google Spreadsheets doesn't have the extensive toolset that Microsoft Excel and iWork Number do, it nails collaboration. Multiple users can work in the same spreadsheet at the same time.

Unfortunately, running Google Spreadsheets in the iPad Safari browser is possible but not easy. Instead, use one of the native iPad spreadsheets that syncs with Google Docs. Both Quickoffice and Docs to Go sync with Google Docs. Box.net also works with Google Docs.

Quickoffice Pro HD

Figure 20-17 shows Quickoffice Pro HD's spreadsheet view. The left side of the toolbar includes icon buttons to apply bold or italic formatting to the selected cells. The Cell Formatting icon button (the piece of paper with the $ symbol) opens the Cell Formatting popover. There are several supported cell formats, including numbers, currency, accounting, date, time, percentage, scientific, and text.

The right side of the toolbar includes icon buttons to print, insert and delete rows and columns, and undo. Finally, the Settings icon button (the capital A with a gear behind it) opens a popover with panes to set fonts, alignment, color, and borders for selected cells.

The available sheets in the currently active spreadsheet appear with a series of tabs along the bottom of the window. Tapping the New Sheet tab (the + symbol) adds a new sheet.

Add data to Quickoffice by tapping the desired cell and then tapping the data entry bar below the top toolbar. The iPad keyboard then appears, from which you can enter your cell data and calculations. The Formula icon button (to the immediate left of the data-entry bar) includes a series of common, mathematical, statistical, logical, date and time, financial, informational, and reference formulas for use in your spreadsheet.

Documents to Go

Figure 20-18 shows the Documents to Go spreadsheet view. Its interface is slightly more cryptic than Quickoffice's, but it has more tools if you do a little digging.

The top toolbar in Documents to Go includes the Back icon button (the ← symbol) that returns to the document selection window. The right side of the top toolbar has the Undo and Redo icon buttons.

The bottom toolbar includes icon buttons with spreadsheet editing tools. The Save icon button (a page with an arrow pointing up) provides options to save, save as, send, and open the existing spreadsheet in a different application. Using the Open In menu option, you can copy your spreadsheet to Numbers or any application on your iPad that can read an Excel file. (There are a surprising number of them.)

FIGURE 20-17

Quickoffice Pro HD's spreadsheet view

FIGURE 20-18

Working with a spreadsheet in Documents to Go

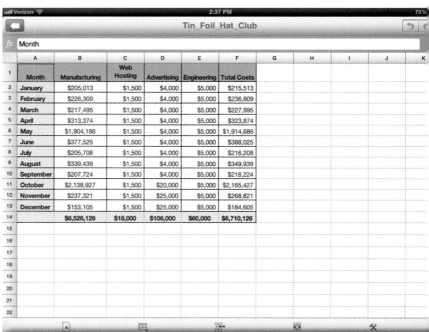

MY NUMBER-CRUNCHING WORKFLOW

Although I keep buying iPad calculators, I find that on a day-to-day basis, I use Calcbot most often. The combination of simple features and a great user interface make it the go-to app for simple calculations. I even keep it on my home screen. When I need something more powerful, I use the PowerOne Financial Calculator to bail me out.

I have spent plenty of time with Documents to Go and Quickoffice (along with several of their competitors), but I keep coming back to Numbers on my iPad when it comes to spreadsheet work. Numbers is the only spreadsheet application designed specifically for the iPad, including features and user interface elements that you would never consider on a Mac or PC.

Although I appreciate there are features in Microsoft Excel on a Mac or PC that simply don't exist in these apps, I'm fortunate in that my spreadsheet needs are tame enough that I don't miss them. Indeed, the iPad's portability lets me use custom spreadsheets in my law practice for settlement conferences and witness presentations that would be difficult with Excel and a laptop. Moreover, I appreciate how I can effortlessly use Numbers spreadsheets on both my Mac and iPad using the iCloud service.

The Format icon button (a 3×2 grid) opens a popover with options to set cell types (numbers, currency, dates, and times), along with text and number formatting tools, such as justification, typeface, and color.

The Insert icon button (an inserting row) includes tools to insert and delete rows and columns.

The Hide icon button opens a popover to hide, unhide, and freeze rows and columns. (Numbers cannot hide columns and rows.)

Finally, the Tools icon button includes an assortment of other useful tools including sorting, finding, clearing cells, and switching to full-screen mode.

Switching between sheets requires tapping the Sheet icon button to the right of the text-entry bar (below the top toolbar). This is not intuitive. By contrast, Numbers and Quickoffice display the sheets with tabs on the window, which is a better approach.

You can edit the data in selected cells using the data-entry bar, below the top toolbar. Like Quickoffice and Numbers, Documents to Go includes a wide assortment of functions for use in your spreadsheets.

Both Documents to Go and Quickoffice are more liberal about syncing with cloud services than Numbers. Documents to Go syncs with Google Docs, Dropbox, Box.net, iDisk, and SugarSync. Quickoffice syncs with all these services plus Huddle.com.

Although Documents to Go includes more features, Quickoffice is more intuitive. If you can get away with using only the included tools in Quickoffice, use it. If you need the extra tools available in Documents to Go, it is still a good application.

21

Business Graphics

Business graphics — those notes, diagrams, and charts we all rely on — are difficult for most workers to create and edit even using a fully loaded Mac or PC with the latest and greatest graphics hardware. Although the iPad doesn't have the same hardware muscle as a desktop computer, it is surprisingly adept at creating business graphics. There are many solid graphics packages for the iPad. Two of the best are OmniGraffle and SketchBook Pro.

Diagrams with OmniGraffle

The Omni Group's OmniGraffle ($50), shown in Figure 21-1, is my favorite diagramming and graphics package for the Mac. When the Omni Group first announced it was bringing this app to the iPad, I was skeptical. It just didn't seem possible to transition such a keyboard and mouse dependent application to the iPad. I was wrong.

iPad OmniGraffle was one of my first "wow" experiences on the iPad. Rather than just port over the Mac app, the developers started over and designed the interface around the iPad. This app does, however, come with a word of warning: OmniGraffle uses a lot of unique touch controls, probably more than any other app covered in this book. Using OmniGraffle is a bit more like playing a musical instrument than using a computer. Nevertheless, everything is intuitive and, with a little practice, you can make stunning diagrams on your iPad.

You create a new diagram in OmniGraffle by tapping the New Diagram button in the diagram view when you first start the app. This opens a blank window, called a *canvas*, upon which you build your diagram.

Using stencils

One of OmniGraffle's best features is stencils. The Stencil icon button (the four-shapes box), on the right side of the Canvas toolbar, opens the popover shown in Figure 21-1 that contains a series of categorized, preformatted vector images, which OmniGraffle calls *stencils*. The built-in stencils include basic shapes, connections, wireframes, and flowchart tools. To insert a stencil, select a category and tap and hold the desired stencil. Then drag the stencil on to the OmniGraffle canvas. On your canvas, resize and otherwise manipulate the stencil as covered later in this chapter.

In addition to the included stencils, the Stencil popover also includes the images in your iPad's photo album (the Photos app). You can drag an image on your canvas just as you would a stencil. There is a website called Graffletopia (www. graffletopia.com) that includes hundreds of user-created stencils for download, ranging from diagramming electronic circuit boards to coaching basketball. Several of the downloadable stencil sets are useful for presentation work, including the BlockHeads stick figures shown in Figure 21-2. The Omni Group built Graffletopia support into the Stencil popover. To download new stencils, type your search term in the Search bar at the top of the Stencil popover to have OmniGraffle return the

FIGURE 21-1

Using OmniGraffle stencils

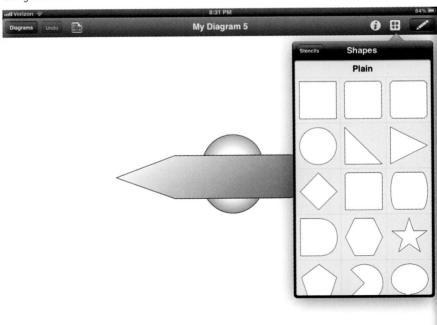

Installing a Graffletopia stencil set

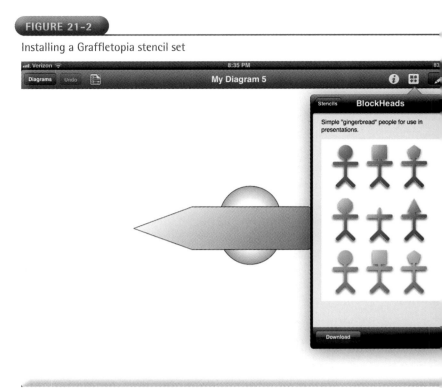

matching results. Tap the Graffletopia stencil set you want and download it direct to your OmniGraffle stencil library on the iPad, as shown in Figure 21-2.

Without digging any further in OmniGraffle, you can make compelling diagrams just using the stencils. But of course, there is a lot more to OmniGraffle.

Adding objects in draw mode

To go beyond the stencils, tap the Draw Mode icon button (it looks like a pencil) in the upper-right corner. OmniGraffle exits canvas mode and enters draw mode, which replaces the standard toolbar with a burgundy one populated with object-creation tools.

Draw mode is all about getting objects onto the canvas. There are several icon buttons for various object types, including shapes, freehand lines, straight lines, and text. While in draw mode, one of these icon buttons is always selected. The only other icon buttons in draw mode are the Undo button, the Info icon button (explained later), and the Done button to exit draw mode and return to canvas mode.

Tap the Shape icon button (the rectangle) to add shapes. Tap and hold the Shape icon button to access a small popover with five shapes to choose from. One you've selected a shape, tap and drag to create it on the canvas.

The Freehand icon button (the icon of a hand-drawn circle with a + symbol) lets you create custom shapes. Tap it once and begin drawing with your finger or stylus. Tap and hold the Freehand icon button to change the fill type.

Create lines the same way: Tap the Lines icon button and then draw a line on your canvas. Tap and hold the Lines icon button to get a popover with an assortment of lines and arrows types.

In addition to drawing lines on the canvas, you can also use this tool to connect objects. To do so, tap the Line icon button (the icon of an arrow with the + symbol) and then tap and drag a line between two shapes. Once connected, the line remains attached to the two objects, even as they are moved around the canvas.

To add text, tap the Text icon button (the Aa icon) and then tap anywhere on the canvas. The onscreen keyboard appears (unless the iPad is paired with a Bluetooth keyboard) so you can add text. To label an object, just double-tap it. To select a different typeface, tap and hold the Text icon button.

For additional options with any of the draw mode tools selected, tap the Info icon button. For example, with the Shapes icon button active, tapping the Info icon button opens a popover, shown in Figure 21-3, with options to change the shape type beyond just the five options available from the Shapes icon button. The Shapes Info popover also includes customization options for the pen stroke, fill, and shadow.

Tapping the Info icon button with the Text icon button selected in draw mode brings up even more options for additional typefaces, point sizes, and text formatting. Take the time to look through the options available with the draw mode's Info icon button.

Although there is also an Info icon button in OmniGraffle's canvas mode, the two buttons behave differently in the two modes. In draw mode, the Info icon button sets properties before creating objects. For example, to make a dashed line, tap the Line icon button and then the Info icon button and set the dashed line parameters exactly how you want them. You then tap anywhere outside the Info popover to dismiss it and draw your line; the new line has all the properties you set in the Info popover. You cannot, however, make further adjustments to that line's properties after creating it in draw mode. Instead, return to canvas mode and use the canvas mode's Info icon button to make adjustments to existing objects.

When you are done adding objects, return to the canvas mode by tapping the Done button. The toolbar's color returns to teal and the icon buttons revert to those shown in Figure 21-1.

Manipulating objects in canvas mode

After returning to the canvas mode, you can refine your diagram. Adjusting objects on the Mac takes a mouse and the keyboard's arrow keys. The iPad, however, has neither of those input methods, so iPad OmniGraffle relies on sophisticated gestures.

To select an object, tap it. To select multiple objects, tap and hold the first obj and, without letting go, tap the additional shapes you want to select. You can also select multiple objects with a tap and drag gesture. To deselect an object (or group objects), tap elsewhere on the canvas.

To move an object first tap and hold, then drag with your finger. By default, OmniGraffle snaps the object to a grid. (You set grids with the canvas mode's Info icon button, covered later.) To move an object without snapping to the grid, tap an hold the shape and, while dragging the shape to its new location, tap and hold a second finger.

You can add text by double-tapping any blank area of the canvas. To add text an object, double-tap it.

To resize the canvas, use the pinch gesture. To automatically fit the canvas to t iPad screen, double-tap the canvas with two fingers. To resize an object (or group objects) so it fills the iPad screen, double-tap it with two fingers.

Tapping a selected object in canvas mode opens a contextual menu with options to cut, copy, select, and delete the object. After copying or cutting an objec paste it by tapping a blank area of the canvas with three fingers. To resize an objec tap it once in canvas mode, and then tap and drag the selection handles. Using OmniGraffle's gestures, you can create sophisticated diagrams in a short amount o time on your iPad.

FIGURE 21-3

The draw mode's Info popover

In canvas mode, the Info icon button's popover includes options to customize both the canvas and any objects. Several of the Info popover tools are similar to those available in draw mode. For example, the Fill button opens a popover with options to choose the fill type (including solid fill, linear blend, linear double blend, radial blend, and radial double blend) and an intuitive color picker for the fill colors.

The Shape popover includes the option to change the selected object into a new shape. These shapes are separate from the stencils, covered earlier, but are similarly useful to quickly get the right look on the canvas. The adjustable shapes have handles that you can drag to change their appearance. The Shape popover also includes tools to set the corner radius for sharp or rounded corners.

The Info icon button's Geometry popover does not exist in draw mode. It includes tools to set the precise location, height, and width of the selected object. There are also buttons to rotate the object left or right or to flip an object horizontally or vertically. These are all powerful tools that you would not expect to find on an iPad.

One thing OmniGraffle really gets right is color selection. OmniGraffle offers several color palettes selected by some design-savvy people at the Omni Group. If you want to choose your own colors, OmniGraffle includes all the tools needed to do so. However, the included color schemes are much better than anything I could cook up.

There are also tools in the Info popover for line stroke, shape, image, text position, and font. Working in canvas mode, you can quickly modify and arrange your diagram.

With no objects selected, the Info popover shows just the canvas-related options. The Canvas Size button lets you set the canvas height and width. The Background button includes options to set solid color and gradient fills on the canvas background. The Units & Scale button opens a popover to set the screen units and scale. You add grids and adjust grid spacing to the active canvas with the Grid button in the Info popover. The Diagram Layout button opens the Diagram Layout popover, shown in Figure 21-4. The Diagram Layout tool in the Diagram Layout popover examines all objects on your canvas and makes its best guess at the hierarchical relationships between the boxes based on how they are connected. (OmniGraffle usually gets it right.) You can then change the diagram layout between vertical and horizontal by tapping the appropriate popover button. You can also adjust the spacing between objects in this popover, shown in Figure 21-4.

The Contents tools

 The Contents icon button (the mini-diagram icon) is located next to the Undo button in canvas mode and includes tools and information about the canvases, layers, and objects in the current drawing.

OmniGraffle can include multiple canvases in a single diagram. When presenting with OmniGraffle, you can jump between diagrams without loading a separate file.

The Canvas pane in the Contents popover shows all active canvases in the current diagram. Tap on a canvas to see it. To create a new canvas, tap the New Canvas icon

FIGURE 21-4

OmniGraffle's Diagram Layout popover

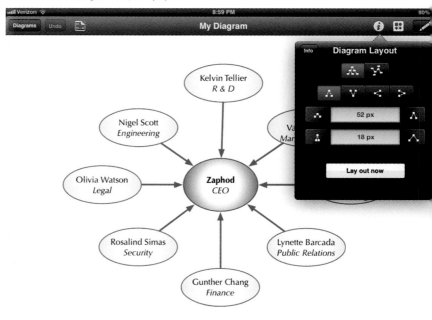

FIGURE 21-5

The Layers pane in OmniGraffle

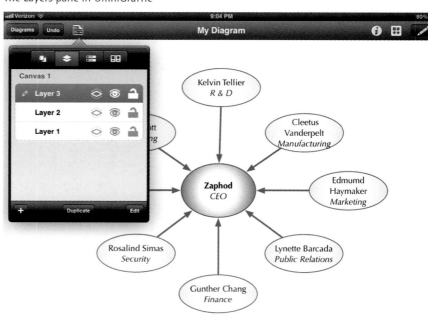

GETTING YOUR DIAGRAM IN KEYNOTE

So you're at about 35,000 feet, winging your way to an important meeting, when suddenly it occurs to you that your Keynote presentation needs just one more diagram. It's not a problem if you have your iPad. Prepare the diagram in OmniGraffle and select all the objects you want to import into your Keynote slide. Next, copy the selected objects in OmniGraffle. (To perform the copy, select all the objects and then tap them once again to open the copy-and-paste contextual menu.)

Then switch to Keynote on your iPad. Create a blank slide where you want the diagram to appear, tap the slide canvas, and tap the Paste button. Keynote pastes the OmniGraffle diagram, and you are good to go. The added benefit of doing it with copy and paste (rather than exporting the image from OmniGraffle and importing it to Keynote) is that the background gets removed from the copied OmniGraffle diagram, so your slide background remains visible, as shown below.

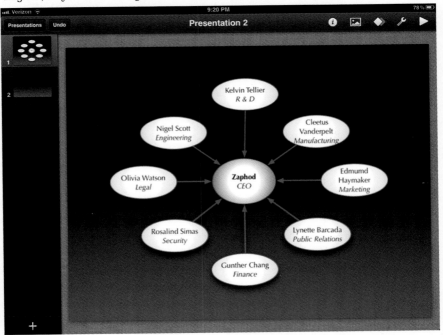

button (the + symbol). The Canvas pane also includes buttons to duplicate and edit the canvas's name and display order.

Just as a single diagram may have multiple canvases, a single canvas may have multiple layers. The Layers pane of the Contents popover, shown in Figure 21-5, lets you add and duplicate layers. You can then turn the individual layers off (or on) from this popover. Layers are useful in OmniGraffle when working with complex diagrams. Using layers, you can start with the most basic components and then gradually adding complexity with each additional layer. Later, when presenting the diagram to co-workers or clients, you can break the diagram down to its individual components by selecting and deselecting specific layers. To turn a layer on or off, t the Layer Visibility button, which looks like an eye.

Although layers are designed in an individual canvas, you can share a layer across multiple canvases by tapping the Shared Layer icon button, which looks like three stacked diamonds. When active, the shared layer appears in all canvases in th individual diagram. Finally, tap the Lock icon button to lock the layer, preventing further modification.

The Object List pane shows all the objects in the current diagram. From here, you can rearrange, delete, and edit individual objects or groups of objects on the canvas. To edit multiple objects, tap each object in this popover and then tap the Info icon button. Any changes you make from the Info popover are applied to all t selected objects.

The Object Filter pane works the same way except rather than displaying all th objects in the canvas, it groups them by object type. If, for example, you want to ad a shadow to all the circles in the diagram, select them in this view with one tap an then tap the Info icon button to add a shadow to them all.

OmniGraffle file management

OmniGraffle manages files in the diagram view. The left side of the toolbar includes the New Diagram button and the Import icon button (the icon of a tray and a down-pointing arrow).

Tapping the Import icon button opens a popover with options to import OmniGraffle documents from the MobileMe iDisk service or from a WebDAV serve There is no Dropbox or Box.net sync. You can, however, access these services using the DropDAV service (covered in Chapter 5). OmniGraffle also shares all your diagrams via the iCloud service. The Omni button at the top-right of the toolbar opens a popover with options to get help, contact Omni, and view release notes.

There are also the Export, New Document, and Trash icon buttons at the bottom of the diagram-selection window. In addition to the OmniGraffle format, OmniGraffle exports to PNG and PDF formats.

At $50, OmniGraffle is one of the more expensive apps covered in this book, but if you want to create sophisticated diagrams on your iPad, there is nothing better.

Sketch with SketchBook Pro

You can also use a more traditional art tool on your iPad for creating graphics. One of the best is SketchBook Pro for iPad ($5). Shown in Figure 21-6, SketchBook Pro is intended as an artist's tool to draw pictures on your iPad. It includes a sophisticated set of drawing tools such as brushes, layers, and fonts. In addition to using it to draw the next Mona Lisa, you can also use SketchBook Pro for quick diagrams and as an electronic whiteboard.

Tap the SketchBook Pro canvas with three fingers to bring up the toolbar and display the Radius/Opacity puck. The puck is an innovative tool to quickly set the radius (dragging left and right) and opacity (dragging up and down) of your brush.

Like OmniGraffle, SketchBook Pro also includes innovative gestures. Swiping left or right with three fingers invokes undo or redo. Swiping down with three fingers opens the brush editor. And swiping up with three fingers opens the layer editor.

SketchBook Pro also includes palettes for your canvas that let you quickly choose colors and tools when drawing. Tap and hold a palette tool to open a popover that lets you change the tool (or color) for that palette location.

The Gallery button in the toolbar exits the canvas window and returns SketchBook Pro to the drawing-selection window. The additional toolbar icons buttons are as follows:

The New Sketch icon button opens a new, blank canvas ready for you to start work on.

The Information icon button displays the properties of the selected object and app preferences.

The Undo and Redo icon buttons offer the standard undo and redo behaviors.

The Brush Editor icon button opens a popover where you can select the brush type (such as pencil, marker, or paintbrush) and the radius and opacity of the stroke. It also includes controls for choosing the brush's color.

FIGURE 21-6

SketchBook Pro for iPad

VECTOR DRAWING

What about vector images? Vector images use points, lines, curves, and other shapes to create scalable images you can shrink or expand to use in your presentations and documents. Contrasted with bitmap images, which become pixelated and blocky when enlarged, vector images keep their integrity and look great when enlarged.

To create vector images for your presentations and documents, look no further than Inkpad ($5). Shown below, Inkpad's tool set is similar to that found in SketchBook Pro, though it's not as extensive. However, Inkpad does include vector-specific tools such as Bézier paths and compound paths, masks, and groups.

Vector images created in Inkpad may be exported via e-mail or Dropbox sync in JPEG, PNG, SVG, PDF, and Inkpad formats.

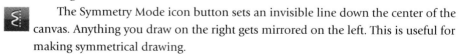

The Draw Style icon button lets you switch between lines, shapes, and painting on your canvas. This is particularly useful when using SketchBook Pro during a meeting.

The Symmetry Mode icon button sets an invisible line down the center of the canvas. Anything you draw on the right gets mirrored on the left. This is useful for making symmetrical drawing.

Using the Text icon button, you can add and modify text.

The Free Transform icon button lets you move, rotate, and scale objects in the active layer.

The Layer icon button includes tools to create new and modify existing layers in your sketch. Although in some respects, these layer tools are more powerful than those found in OmniGraffle, I find OmniGraffle's layers more useful for business

MY GRAPHICS WORKFLOW

I squeeze every penny out of my $50 investment in OmniGraffle. Using it, I can prepare professional-looking diagrams with just my fingers on my iPad. Several times, I've prepared diagrams while interviewing a client or witness that I later used as legal exhibits with very little modification. Moreover, the ability to share my OmniGraffle library with my Mac using iCloud makes OmniGraffle even more useful. Although I don't use SketchBook Pro as often, it does scratch a unique itch (making quick diagrams) when the need arises.

application. (Perhaps it is my lack of artistic ability, but I can get OmniGraffle's grid-based diagrams to line up better in layers than the more freeform objects I create with SketchBook Pro.) Nevertheless, you can use layers in SketchBook Pro exactly as explained earlier with OmniGraffle: You build separate pieces of a drawing and then turn them on and off using the layers function to illustrate your point.

SketchBook Pro imports pictures from the Photos library, Dropbox, iTunes, or (on the iPad 2) the built-in camera. Often a photograph can be a nice starting point for a drawing. As a real-world example, I once took a picture of a floor plan with my iPad and then traced over the dimensions with my finger using SketchBook Pro. I made the sketch in a separate layer so later, when I turned off the layer with the image, I had a passable diagram to scale.

SketchBook Pro's Gallery mode lets you save your pictures to the iPad Photos app's library, as well as send them to iTunes, Flickr, Facebook, Dropbox, or e-mail. SketchBook Pro exports your drawing as an unalterable (flattened) image or a layered Photoshop (PSD) file. You can also export an image as a PDF file.

Where OmniGraffle excels at building diagrams, SketchBook Pro excels at drawing diagrams. Although this point is subtle, it is important. Unless you are a talented artist, you probably are not going to get a lot of pictures out of SketchBook Pro for use in your presentations or documents. However, it is very useful when in a meeting while the bullets are flying and you need to demonstrate your point with a quick drawing.

22

Databases

Databases store those bits of data that every business needs. Whether you are tracking customer orders or counting the number of hamster wheels in the warehouse, chances are a database application is holding your data. Managing lists is one of the things computers are uniquely suited for, and database applications were some of the first programs made for this purpose. Today, databases are easier to use and more powerful than ever. The iPad's portability makes it a natural for database applications.

Bento

Bento ($5), shown in Figure 22-1, is an easy-to-use, customizable database app for the iPad. Developed by FileMaker, the same Apple subsidiary that publishes FileMaker Pro (covered later in this chapter), Bento favors simplicity over advanced features. There are Bento versions for the Mac, iPad, and iPhone.

The Bento file system works differently from a traditional database app. Bento does not keep a separate data file for each database. Instead, Bento uses a single data file that includes all your databases (called *libraries*). Opening Bento opens all your libraries at once. Each library contains a group of database records. A record is one thing, whether it is a contact, an inventory item, or your favorite tea. In turn, each Bento record contains several fields. A field holds a single piece of information relevant to the record. It could be a contact's phone number, the quantity of a specific inventory item, or the name of the store where you bought that perfect oolong tea.

So as a context for Bento in this chapter, you need to understand that Bento has a single data file that holds a collection of libraries, each of which contains a series of records, each of which includes several fields. As this book goes to press, FileMaker is evaluating whether it can sync the Bento libraries using iCloud.

Opening a Bento library

To open an existing Bento library, tap the Libraries button in the toolbar. This opens the Libraries popover, shown in Figure 22-1. This is a list of all libraries in your Bento file. To open a library, tap it.

Some libraries include multiple collections. (Collections are subgroups of records in a single library; I cover them later.) When you have multiple collections, the number of collections appears next to the library name. If a library has multiple collections, tap the Collections icon button to open a specific library collection instead of the entire library.

To open a new library, tap the New Library icon button (the + symbol) at the top left of the Library popover. This opens the New Library popover shown in Figure 22-2.

Bento ships with several library templates, many of which are business-friendly, including projects, contacts, to-do items, events, inventory, time billing, expenses, customers, and issue tracking. You can also create a new library.

FIGURE 22-1

Bento's main window

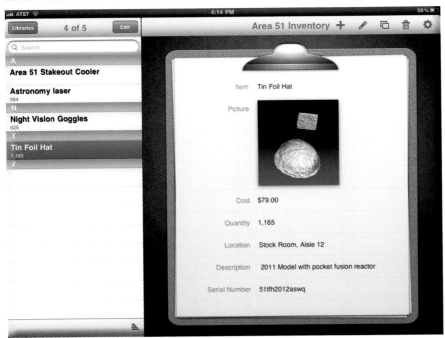

Bento's New Library popover

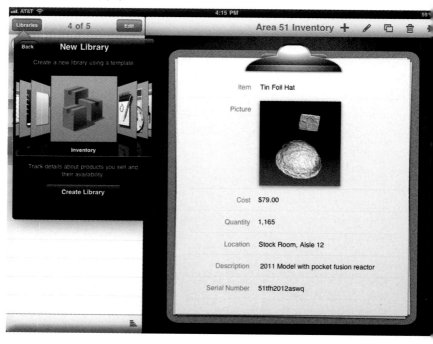

Working in a Bento library

Figure 22-3 depicts an open library on Bento for iPad. To navigate between records in portrait orientation, tap the Back and Forward icon buttons (the left- and right-facing triangle icons, respectively) in the toolbar or double-tap the left or right side of the current record to move backward or forward, respectively. In landscape orientation, use the records list on the left side of the window or swipe right or left on the current record to move forward or backward, respectively.

To rename the library, tap its name in the main Bento view while the library is open. A popover appears with an option to rename the library.

Bento also lets you reorder the libraries in the Libraries popover. To do so, tap the Edit button and then tap and hold the Reorder handle (the icon with three horizontal lines) next to the desired library and drag it up or down in the library list.

If you sync Bento to a Mac, PDF files in the Mac's Bento library sync to the iPad. To view an embedded PDF file, tap the View icon button (the icon of a human eye) in the media field that contains the PDF file. (Bento has a built-in PDF viewer.) Once open, you can share the PDF file with other PDF apps on your iPad using the Sharing icon button (the rectangle with an arrow emerging).

Using Bento collections

In addition to libraries, records, and fields, Bento collections are a subgroup of an existing library. For example, the Address Book library may have collections for employees, customers, and vendors. Using Bento collections, you can get to your database records even faster.

To create a collection, open a Bento library and tap the Collections icon button (the two overlapping rectangles) in the toolbar. This opens the popover shown in Figure 22-4.

Type in the collection name and then tap the Done button. Bento adds your new collection to the active library. To add a record to the new collection, tap the record and then tap the Collections icon button in the toolbar. That opens the Collections popover with a list of the existing collections. Tap the destination for the selected record and Bento adds the record to the collection. Bento for the Mac also includes smart collections, which are collections based on a specified set of criteria. For example, you can create a smart collection from your contacts database that includes all people who live in your city.

FIGURE 22-3

Working with a Bento library

FIGURE 22-4

Creating a collection with Bento

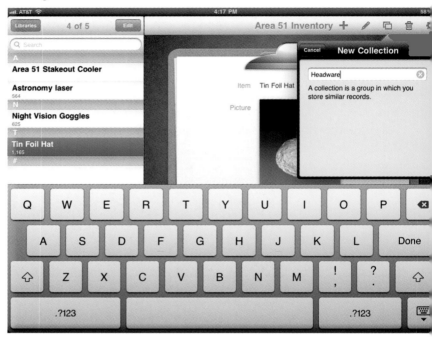

Adding records

To add a new record to a library, open the library and tap the New Record ico button (the + symbol) in the toolbar. A new blank record appears. Tap the empty fields to fill them in. You don't need to fill in all the fields or press a Save button. Indeed, there is no Save button. Just flip to a different view or create a new record; Bento saves automatically as you work. To delete a record, tap the Delete icon butt (the trash can) in the toolbar.

To search your library, type a word or phrase in the Search bar at the top of th left pane. Bento uses live search technology, so as you type each letter, the search results narrow. (In portrait orientation, you must first tap the Search icon button, whose icon is a magnifying glass, to open the Search bar.)

To sort the records of an individual library or collection, tap the View Settings icon button (the icon of four stacked lines) in the lower-right corner of the left pa This opens the View Settings popover, shown in Figure 22-5, where you may set th displayed fields, the sort field (such as last name or company), and the sort order (ascending or descending).

Customizing record layout

Although Bento's included library templates are all useful, half the fun of usir Bento is customizing the record layout. You can add or delete fields from the activ record template using the Customization icon button (the pencil icon). To add a field, tap the New Field icon button (the + symbol) or drag the New Field button onto the record.

This opens the New Field popover, where you select the field type. Bento includes several field types for use in your libraries, as summarized in Table 22-1.

Using Bento themes

Bento includes several prepared graphics and color schemes, called themes, that you can apply to your database. All the included themes are attractive and useful. To change the theme for your library, tap the Customization icon button (the pencil icon) in the toolbar and then tap the Change Theme button. This opens a popover

TABLE 22-1

Bento Field Types

Field	Function
Text	A text field is a catch-all for holding letters, numbers, symbols, and anything else you can squeeze out of the iPad keyboard. Text fields can be sorted alphabetically, so take this into account as you set up and create records with text fields.
Number	A number field stores integers and decimal numbers.
Choice	A choice field lets you set predesignated options, from which you may pick one. For example, a tea database may include a choice field with options for green, white, and oolong.
Check box	A check box field is a simple yes-or-no field. Check boxes are remarkably useful in databases. For example, you can add a holiday card check box field to your contact database and then easily sort by that field to get a quick list of your holiday card list.
Media	A media field holds pictures, movies, and sound files. Bento imports the existing media with a database from a Mac OS X Bento library or you can add media directly from your iPad. Bento also recognizes the iPad 2 cameras, so you can add pictures to your library directly from your iPad 2 camera.
Time	A time field stores the time of day, including hours and minutes.
Date	A date field holds the month, day, and year. You can also optionally add a time value to a date field.
Duration	A duration field stores an amount of time in weeks, days, hours, minutes, and seconds. The notation is easy. For 2 weeks, type 2w. For 3 weeks, 2 days, and 4 hours, type 3w 2d 4h.
Currency	A currency field stores an amount of money, such as $42.08.
Rating	A rating field lets you rate a record between one and five stars. This seemingly consumer-oriented feature is quite useful for work. Use it to rate sales leads, vendor quality, or any value judgments you bump into at work.
Related Data	A related data field connects data from one library to another.

FIGURE 22-5

Bento's View Settings popover

FIGURE 22-6

Changing a library theme in Bento

you can print your database straight from your iPad if you have a compatible printer. FileMaker Go also uses secured logins.

FileMaker Go displays FileMaker Pro charts on your iPad. If your iPad is connected with FileMaker Server, the charts update automatically as the data does on your server. Another mobile-friendly feature in FileMaker Go is digital signatures. This lets you capture a client's signature with your iPad at the client's office immediately upon closing the sale. FileMaker Go exports signed documents or uploads them to a FileMaker Server hosted database.

There are, however, limitations:

▶ You cannot create a new database or modify the underlying database schema of an existing database on the iPad. For example, you can't change tables, fields, relationships, data sources, or privileges.

▶ Nor can you change the database structure, layouts, or custom menus.

▶ Some of the higher-end FileMaker Pro sharing features are also turned off, including sending records to Excel and the use of snapshot links (a way to share selected pieces of the database with co-workers).

▶ Plug-ins and web publishing are also disabled on the iPad.

Although this appears to be a big list, it really isn't. All these features are architectural in nature and don't lend themselves to being done on the iPad.

FileMaker Go is by no means a replacement for FileMaker Pro but instead is an easy way to access and modify your data while mobile. There are many potential uses for access to a powerful database application on the iPad, including conducting inventory from a warehouse, preparing customer orders at the customer's place of business, and updating a project's status while on the road. Any place where access to your data is a good thing and fumbling with a laptop is a bad thing, FileMaker Go fits the bill.

HanDBase

Another iPad database worthy of mention is HanDBase ($10). HanDBase, shown in Figure 22-8, walks a middle path between Bento and FileMaker Go. It is a full-featured database and follows more traditional paradigms then Bento but doesn't stray into the stratosphere of database superfeatures that you get with FileMaker Pro.

You can create a new database on HanDBase for the iPad. To do so, tap the New DB icon button (the + symbol) at the lower-left portion of the left pane. When you create a new HanDBase database, the app prompts you for database properties before building the new database.

HanDBase supports several data field types, including text values, integers, popups, and time. With little effort, you can have a functional database working on your iPad. HanDBase has more than 2,000 database templates available for download, ranging from business to genealogy.

FIGURE 22-8

Creating a new database with HanDBase

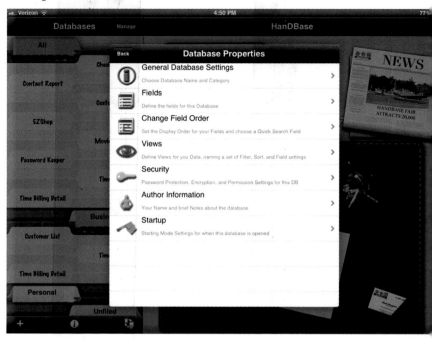

HanDBase also includes several sharing features. E-mail your HanDBase database to a co-worker. When the co-worker opens the database, changes are sync to his or her iPad. HanDBase also can sync via Wi-Fi to a Mac or PC and export its data as a comma-separated value (CSV) file, the lingua franca of database file types.

Unlike Bento, which just works on the Mac and iOS, HanDBase is truly multiplatform, with compatible apps on Palm OS, Android, and BlackBerry. There are also Mac and Windows PC companion apps available from HanDBase, starting at $25.

I'm not sold on HanDBase's user interface. Although the app gets the fundamentals right (everything works), the interface's attempt to appear like a

MY DATABASE WORKFLOW

Having worked with all the database apps in this chapter (and several more that didn't make the cut), I still find Bento is the best solution for my database needs. I have multiple databases ranging from inventories to tea tastings, and for this Bento is perfect. Nevertheless, I was impressed with HanDBase and would recommend it, especially if you are working with multiple platforms. Furthermore, if I needed a sledgehammer database app, there is no question I'd use FileMaker Server and access all my data from my iPad with FileMaker Go

real file folder strikes me as awkward and a waste of space. But you may find that HanDBase's interface works for you better than Bento's.

23

Project Management

Despite its small size, the iPad can manage complex projects with multiple dependent tasks and team members. There are several project management apps for the iPad. This chapter covers one of the best (SG Project Pro) and a simpler, iPad-friendly, web-based tool (Tom's Planner). Chapter 19 explains task management for your individual tasks. This chapter focuses on project management.

SG Project Pro

SG Project Pro ($40) is a powerful project management tool built just for the iPad.

Using SG Project Pro

Figure 23-1 shows the SG Project Pro startup window. The Main Menu icon button (a gear icon) in the top-left corner opens the main menu, shown in Figure 23-1. From here you can select one of seven windows for project management. Start by tapping Portfolio Home.

Portfolio Home window

The Portfolio Home window presents an overview of all current projects and available people, along with a summary of the selected project and its time line.

The Projects section provides a list of all active projects. Tap on a project to select it. Use the Rearrange handle (the icon with three horizontal lines) to rearrange the projects. Tap the Import button to import projects from a Microsoft Project XML file or an SG Project Profile file. The New Project button opens the window shown in Figure 23-2.

New project settings include the project name and description. You can choose whether the calendar display includes all days or just weekdays and choose a start date. Tap the Done button to have the window return to the Portfolio Home window. Tap the Detail Disclosure icon button (a blue circle with a right-facing arrow) next to the new project for options to duplicate the project if you intend to use it as a template.

The People section of the Portfolio Home window lists the current team members. You can add new people by tapping the New Person button or rearrange the list using the Rearrange handle.

The middle section of the Portfolio Home window shows a summary of the selected project, including the project details, financing, and tasks during the next and prior 90-day periods. Tap the Task Plan button to view and edit the tasks for the selected project.

The lower portion of the window displays a Gantt chart for the selected project. In addition to displaying the time period for specific tasks, this view also displays the percentage completion for each task with the progress line inside each time period.

FIGURE 23-1

SG Project Pro's main menu (at left)

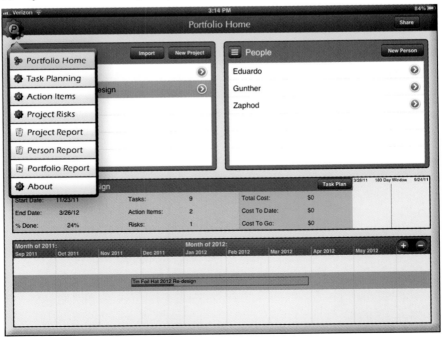

SG Project Pro's New Project window

The Portfolio Home provides an overview of your project data. The remaining windows accessed from the main menu provide more precise details over your projects.

Task Planning window

Tap Task Planning in the main menu to enter SG Project Pro's Task Planning window, shown in Figure 23-3.

The Task Planning toolbar includes the name of the active project. Tap the Project button to import, select, and edit projects. The Share button opens a popov with options to preview, e-mail, export, or send the project's display to a projector (if you have a VGA or HDMI adapter for your iPad). Export formats include PDF, Microsoft Project XML, and SG Project Pro. There is also built-in Dropbox support. (I cover sharing later.)

The remainder of the Task Planning window displays the specific tasks associated with the selected project. In this view, you can see the task name, duration, start and end dates, percentage complete, responsible person, and any dependencies. Additionally, you tap on the End Date button to toggle between displaying the end date and task cost. To add a new task, tap the New Task icon button (the + symbol inside a circle) that appears under the last task.

FIGURE 23-3

SG Project Pro's Task Planning window

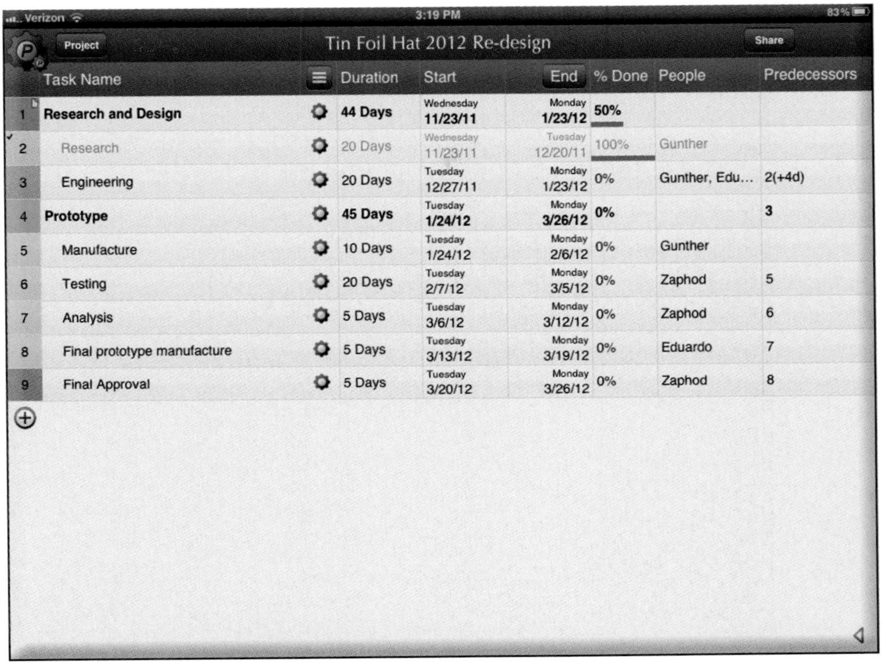

	Task Name	Duration	Start	End	% Done	People	Predecessors
1	Research and Design	44 Days	Wednesday 11/23/11	Monday 1/23/12	50%		
2	Research	20 Days	Wednesday 11/23/11	Tuesday 12/20/11	100%	Gunther	
3	Engineering	20 Days	Tuesday 12/27/11	Monday 1/23/12	0%	Gunther, Edu...	2(+4d)
4	Prototype	45 Days	Tuesday 1/24/12	Monday 3/26/12	0%		3
5	Manufacture	10 Days	Tuesday 1/24/12	Monday 2/6/12	0%	Gunther	
6	Testing	20 Days	Tuesday 2/7/12	Monday 3/5/12	0%	Zaphod	5
7	Analysis	5 Days	Tuesday 3/6/12	Monday 3/12/12	0%	Zaphod	6
8	Final prototype manufacture	5 Days	Tuesday 3/13/12	Monday 3/19/12	0%	Eduardo	7
9	Final Approval	5 Days	Tuesday 3/20/12	Monday 3/26/12	0%	Zaphod	8

Use the Rearrange handles to rearrange the order of the tasks. If there is a small check mark in the upper-left corner, the task is 100-percent complete. The Order column additionally displays the task color from the Gantt view.

The Options icon button (the gear icon) on the right side of the Task Name column opens a popover with additional options. From this popover, you can indent and outdent tasks, insert and delete tasks, and set their cost, owners, and color. There are several other task settings available from the buttons on the left side of the popover, including start dates, durations, warnings, notes, deliverables, risks, and action items. As you can see, SG Project Pro offers a lot of detail in setting up tasks.

The Predecessors field is important. Often, a task depends on the completion of a predecessor task. For example, you can't start buying death-ray components until after you complete the death-ray design. As such, completing the design is a predecessor task to the materials purchase. To create a predecessor, tap the Set button next to the Predecessors field. SG Project Pro displays predecessor relationships graphically in Gantt chart view.

Tap the Arrow Splitter icon button (the left-facing triangle) in the lower-right corner of the Task Planning window to open the Gantt chart view shown in Figure 23-4.

Gantt charts usually include a list of key tasks and milestones next to a time line with a bar placed below the time line for each task, representing its start and end date. The bars are called *time periods*. Gantt charts show each component of a

FIGURE 23-4

SG Project Pro's Gantt chart view

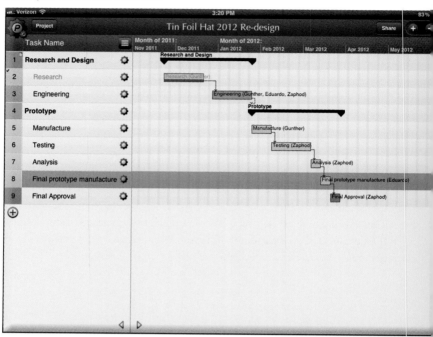

project on any given day and the dependencies among tasks. You can't, for example, start building death rays until you first acquire the necessary parts. Gantt charts really came into their own with the arrival of computers, which automate the labor intensive process of laying out Gantt charts and making adjustments when the inevitable delay occurs.

SG Project Pro brings Gantt charts to the iPad. The time line stretches across the top of the chart. Tap and hold the calendar bar and slide your finger left or right to move the chart forward or backward. Use the Zoom icon buttons (the + and – symbols) in the upper-right portion of the Gantt chart view to move among daily, weekly, monthly, quarterly, and yearly views. Figure 23-4 displays the calendar in monthly view. A red vertical line indicates the current day. A black line points from one task to another where there is a predecessor relationship. For example, the Research task is a predecessor to the Engineering task in Figure 23-4.

To change a task period's color, tap and hold it until the Color Palette popover opens. To move a task period on the time line, tap and hold the task period and drag the time period along the time line. SG Project Pro prevents you from moving a predecessor task. If, for example, the "Buy death-ray components" task depends on the "Complete death-ray design" task, SG Project Pro keeps the affiliated tasks connected.

By default, the Gantt chart view leaves the Task Name column along with the Options icon button on the left side of the window so you may continue to refine the task details. Using the Arrow Splitter icon buttons (the left- and right-facing triangle icons) at the bottom of the window, you can return to the table view or remove the table altogether and turn the entire iPad screen over to the Gantt chart.

Action Items window

SG Project Pro lets you associate both tasks and action items with a specific project. Tasks are time-line-critical items that often include dependencies in which one task cannot begin until the prior task completes. By contrast, action items in SG Project Pro do not affect the project schedule; they exist independently of the time line but are still critical to the ultimate success or failure of the project.

To add action items to your project, tap the Action Items button in the main menu. This displays the Action Items window, shown in Figure 23-5. Tap the New Action icon button (the + symbol) below the last task to add a new action item.

Each task displays its description, priority, status, group, and responsible person. There is a large notes section where you can keep a progress diary. The task also lists the date created and due date. (If the task is past due, its date displays in red.) You can also link actions to specific tasks with the Link to Task button.

FIGURE 23-5

SG Project Pro's Action window

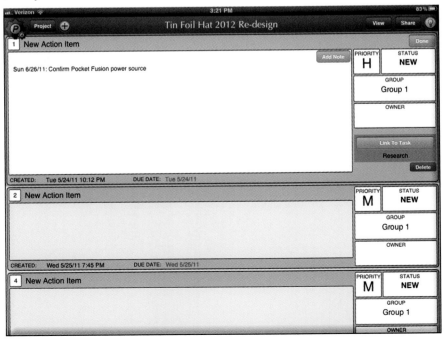

SG Project Pro's Project Report view

Project Risks window

Similar to action items, SG Project Pro also lets you create risk items, to track areas of concern. The Project Risks window shows each risk.

In the Project Risks window are several filters, including the likelihood of risk, severity, rating, coping strategy, and responsible person. Again, as with action items you can diary the risk and assign a due date. One of my favorite touches is how the Likely and Severity filters start out gray at level 0 and work their way to solid red at level 5. Risks can also be linked to specific tasks.

Reports windows

The remaining selections in the main menu are all report types. The reporting views are not for adding and modifying project details but for summarizing them easy viewing and sharing. SG Project Pro displays reports based on project, person, or portfolio (groups of projects). Figure 23-6 displays a project report.

By default, the Project Report view shows a summary of key project dates, task action items, risks, and costs. It also includes a graph showing the amount of work in the 180-day window surrounding the current date. This view places all the tasks action items, risks, and people surrounding the project in one view. Tap the View button in the Project Report toolbar to turn on or off various components of the display.

SG Project Pro works similarly with reports based on person or portfolio. Use the pinch gesture to zoom in and out of the reports and use the Share button in the toolbar to share the report.

Sharing projects

In addition to building projects from the ground up, SG Project Pro can import and export XML files for use with Microsoft Project. There are limits on Microsoft Project integration: SG Project Pro recognizes only the features it supports. Also, there is no way to work collaboratively on a single project with multiple iPads. If you want multiple team members working on the project file at once, you need to use the Mac and PC project management apps.

You can also export your SG Project Pro project as a PDF image. Although PDF recipients cannot make edits or changes to your project (which in some cases is a good thing), they can see the full project time line in any PDF viewer.

So how far can you push SG Project Pro? With the first-generation iPad, the app starts to bog down with around 200 tasks. But I was unable to bog down the iPad 2. However, I suspect that because the iPad 2 is about twice as fast as its predecessor, you would run into trouble at about 400 tasks.

Tom's Planner

Tom's Planner is an Internet-based, no-nonsense, Gantt-chart project management tool. It is free if you have one project. For $9 a month, you can have as many as 20 projects, and for $19 a month, you can have an unlimited number of projects.

Shown in Figure 23-7, Tom's Planner fully supports the iPad. It doesn't use a native app but instead works through (and looks great on) the Safari web browser (so you need an active Internet connection). To use it on your iPad, create an account and log in with Safari.

Tom's Planner tracks project tasks, resources, and status in the left portion of the Gantt chart. To edit a field, tap it; the iPad's onscreen keyboard appears. You can then fill in the Activity, Resource, and Status fields.

To create new rows, columns, and groups, tap and hold on the screen (for a second or two) until the contextual menu appears. Tap the desired menu option to insert and remove rows, groups, and columns. You can also use this contextual view to copy and paste groups and rows.

Once you have a list of all the tasks and resources, begin inserting calendar-time estimates in the Tom's Planner calendar. To create a time period, tap and hold the calendar on the start date until a contextual menu appears. Tap the Insert New Period option. Once you select a color, the new time period appears in the Gantt chart.

Tap and hold the beginning or end of the time period to move the start or finish date. Tap and hold the center of the time period to move it as a unit. These gestures

Tom's Planner on the iPad

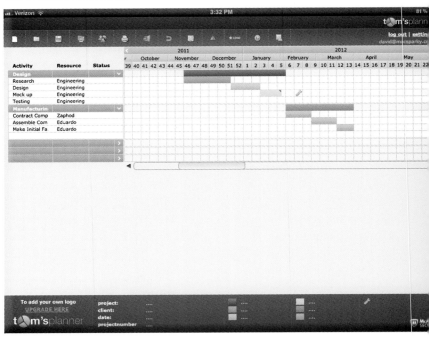

Modifying a time period with Tom's Planner

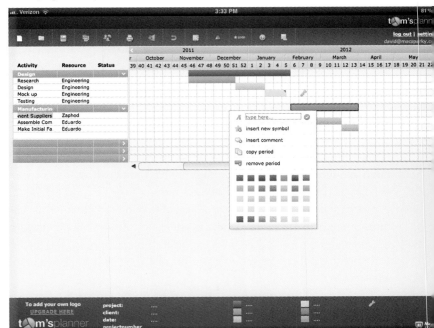

MY PROJECT MANAGEMENT WORKFLOW

I do not routinely work with large teams. However, I have a Tom's Planner account and often use it for quickly laying out Gantt charts. For organizing more complex projects with the iPad, I prefer SG Project Pro because SG Project Pro's modular nature makes it easy to start with a simple Gantt chart and add features, as I need them.

move the time period forward and backward on a specified line or move it to a separate task line altogether.

There is no way to set dependencies between tasks in Tom's Planner. If dependencies exist, you need to move the time periods manually, though this isn't as difficult as it would first seem. By dragging across the calendar, you can select multiple time periods at once. You can then move the selected time periods as a group by tapping and holding, and then dragging the selection to the new location.

Tap and hold on the time period to open the contextual menu shown in Figure 23-8. From its options, you can insert a name, symbol, or comment on the time period. You can also copy the time period for pasting it to another task, as well as delete it. Tom's Planner also imports Microsoft Excel files and builds the Gantt chart from them.

The toolbar, which appears above the Gantt chart, includes options to create a new schedule, open an existing one, and save the current schedule locally or to the web.

The Settings button (the icon of a white sheet of paper with a yellow pencil) lets you set the time period on the Gantt chart as short as five minutes and as long as a month. (The screen images of Tom's Planner in this chapter display one week per box.)

With a paid account, you can share your schedule with others and work collaboratively via the web. A paid account also includes several additional options, including printing to a local printer, exporting as an image, and exporting in Microsoft Project format. With a paid account, you can also upload company logos to customize the look of your schedule.

Although it doesn't boast the rich feature set offered by SG Project Pro, Tom's Planner provides a quick way to create Gantt charts, and it takes about five minutes to learn. Tom's Planner works on Macs and PCs, but the experience is even more intuitive on the iPad. Regardless, it is nice to know you can always log in on your Mac and PC and continue working from there. If you are just getting started with project planning and Gantt charts, start with Tom's Planner. You may find it is all you need.

24

Billing and Finance

I n addition to helping you get your work done, the iPad can help you get
paid. Where financial management software used to require expensive
computer hardware, we are in the midst of a transition where businesses
and workers are switching to more agile apps and Internet-based tools. Of
course, the iPad is at the vanguard of this move.

Billing and Invoicing

Time Master + Billings ($10) is my favorite time-and-billing iPad app.
Shown in Figure 24-1, Time Master combines ease of use with several
powerful features not found in most iPad time-and-billing apps. Time Master
tracks both time and expenses, and offers several reporting and invoicing
options. You can also purchase additional modules inside the app for
syncing among multiple devices, working with QuickBooks, and invoicing
clients directly from your iPad.

The main Time Master window, shown in Figure 24-1, displays the
billing data with icon buttons along the bottom toolbar for Time Entries,
Expenses, Reporting, Modules, and Setup, respectively. All the key functions
are tied to these icon buttons.

Time and expenses

To create a new time entry, tap the Time Entries icon button (the clock
icon) on the bottom toolbar and tap the New Entry icon button (the +
symbol) in the top-right corner. That opens the Add Entry form shown in

Figure 24-2. The General Information fields include Client, Project, Task, and Payroll Item. Client is the only required field but the Project, Task, and Payroll fields provide the option to add further details. If you do more than one project for a client, each should have its own category so they can be billed separately. The Task field lets you categorize the work performed. For example, you can have client meetings and design work as separate categories.

Use the Date and Time fields to record when you work on a task. You can set durations by choosing a start and end time or by choosing a start time and setting a duration with the duration field or tapping the duration buttons at the bottom of the Date and Time fields. The Rate and Attributes fields let you set billing rates and attributes, such as rounding and taxable settings, for the billing entries. Although it takes time to get set up, most of these fields repeat, and before long you can add billing entries quickly by tapping in the billing event and selecting from existing options from the remaining fields.

The Expense icon button at the bottom of the window opens a similar form for expense entry. Several of the expense fields mirror those from the time-billing window except instead of time and duration, the Expense form includes fields for amount, quantity, cost, and attributes (including reimbursable, receipt, taxable, and reported). Using the Time Entries and Expenses forms, capturing time and expenses with Time Master is quick and efficient.

FIGURE 24-1

Time Master + Billings for iPad

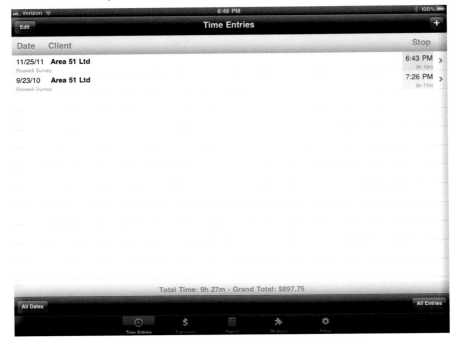

Reports

Once you've dutifully entered your time and expenses in Time Master, tap the Reports icon button to enter reporting mode. Time Master ships with several preconfigured report types: time, expense, time and expenses, and time sheet. (I cover the time sheet report later.) When everything is correct, tap the Generate button to have Time Master prepare the report. Figure 24-3 displays the report.

In addition to displaying a report onscreen, Time Master can also e-mail reports and display them in HTML format (used by web browsers and most e-mail programs). To share a report, tap the Sharing icon button (the pencil-and-paper icon) in the top-right corner of the window. An HTML e-mail report is shown in Figure 24-4.

On your Mac or Windows PC, you can copy and paste the report data to a spreadsheet (such as Numbers or Excel). Time Master can also export tables as a comma-separated value (CSV) file that can be imported to any modern spreadsheet or database application. You set the details of the report in the Settings pane (tap the Setup icon button, which looks like a gear, at the bottom of the window), where you can specify the CSV and HTML formatting.

The time-sheet report breaks up entries by client and project by the week. Each day of the week includes subtotals for each client, as well as a grand total.

FIGURE 24-2

Adding a time entry with Time Master

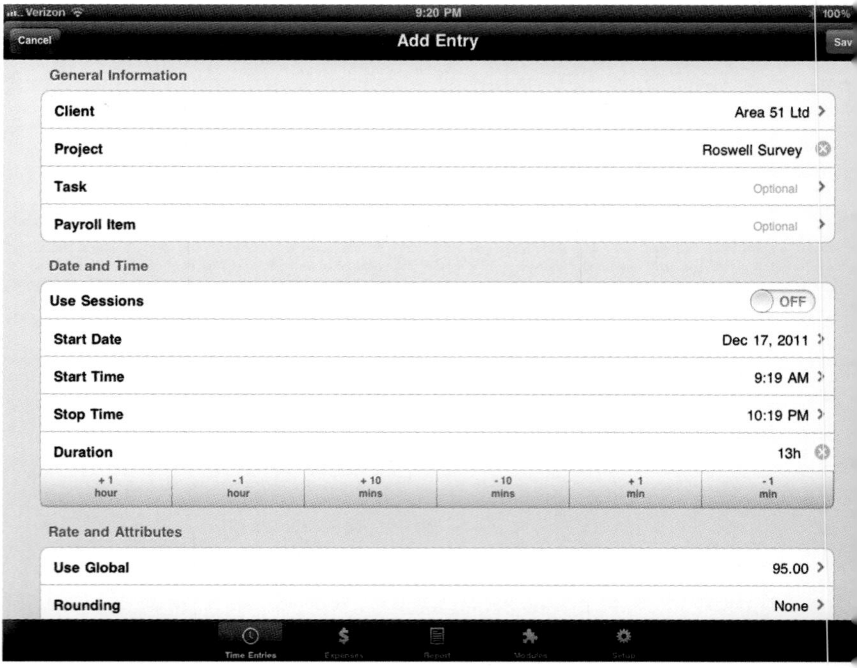

Modules

Time Master includes several enhanced features that can be purchased from within the app. The modules include options to sync among multiple devices, work with QuickBooks, and invoice directly from your iPad.

Invoicing

The invoicing module ($10) lets you generate invoices from your Time Master data. The mere fact that you can run a full time-and-billing app and generate invoices from the iPad is remarkable. Even more so because Time Master pulls it off so well.

Using the Invoicing module, you can specify the company making the billing (Time Master includes support for multiple companies) and the amount of detail for the time-and-expense entries.

The app also gives you control over the look of the invoice, including typeface, font size, margins, and headers (which can be text or an image). You can enable or disable columns for amount, quantity, and taxable. Unchecking an item hides it on the final invoice.

Finally, choose a paper size and you are done. Time Master generates PDF invoices. You can optionally enter your PayPal e-mail address to have Time Master insert a clickable PayPal button on the invoice. When your client clicks the PayPal

FIGURE 24-3

Configuring a Time Master time-and-expense report

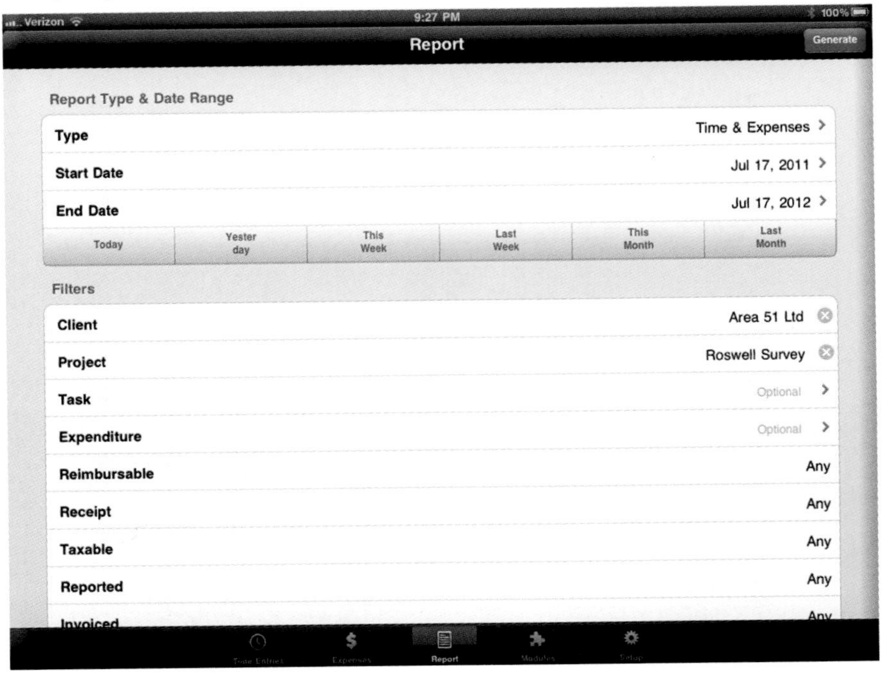

FIGURE 24-4

A Time Master e-mail report

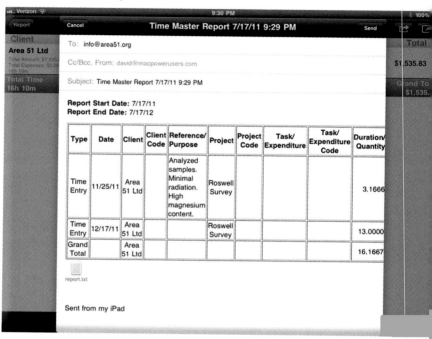

button in the PDF invoice, it launches a web browser and fills in the payment detail for easy processing. Time Master can also automatically send the invoices to your clients via e-mail or, alternatively, you may send them with your own cover e-mail o print them to paper, lick a stamp, and send them the old-fashioned way. Figure 24- shows a Time Master invoice.

Syncing

The Synchronize module ($7) is also an in-app purchase. The Synchronize module lets you sync two or more devices via Wi-Fi or Bluetooth. The synchronization module is not selective; you can only sync the data. If you want to perform a limited sync — for example, not sharing all data with an employee — thi is not the sync method you are looking for. The ideal usage for the Synchronize module is a single user who wants to share his or her data between an iPad and iPhone.

Syncing is hard. The easiest way to cause data corruption is through a bad sync. So before venturing into syncing data, make sure to back up everything. Time Maste has several built-in backup protocols (covered later in this chapter).

QuickBooks export

The QuickBooks Export module ($6) exports your Time Entries into QuickBooks as time activity items. The sync is limited to just time entries; Time

Master does not export expenses to QuickBooks as of this writing, though such export is planned for a future release.

The QuickBooks export works with QuickBooks Pro for Windows 2007 or later. It also works with Mac OS X QuickBooks 2010 or later using the developer's TimeBridge software for Mac (`www.on-core.com/timemaster/tm_quickbooks.php`).

Time Master does a credible job of getting your data into QuickBooks. When you import field variables that don't exist in QuickBooks (such as an employee name or account), QuickBooks creates an entry upon import. Although this is useful, it also means you need to get the entries on your iPad exactly as you have them in QuickBooks or you will create new entries. For example, if you list an employee as `L. Barcada` in QuickBooks but list the same employee as just `Barcada` in Time Master, upon import, QuickBooks will think there are two employees, L. Barcada and Barcada.

This module does not sync with QuickBooks. Instead, it is a one-way export, from Time Master to QuickBooks; you cannot sync back to your iPad. Moreover, QuickBooks does not keep track of the import data, so if you export the same entries again, you will end up with duplicate entries. Moving time and billing data is difficult, so always make sure to back up your QuickBooks data before attempting it.

Sharing data between two software packages is usually hard, and it is even more difficult with complicated billing and invoicing data. For these reasons, I find the QuickBooks Export the least useful of the Time Master modules. If working with

FIGURE 24-5

A Time Master time-and-expense invoice

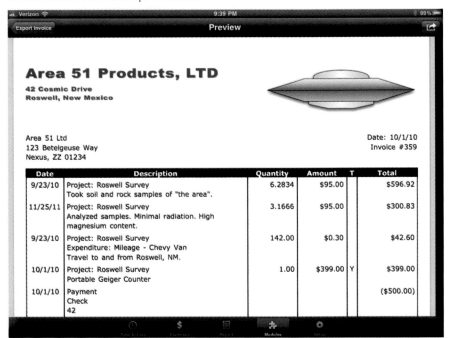

ACCESSING FINANCIAL DATA

There are many iPad apps offering financial information reporting. One of the first (and still one of the best) is Bloomberg for iPad (free). Shown below, Bloomberg for iPad provides news, company descriptions, stock quotes, trends, and analysis for most companies traded on the world's biggest financial markets. Bloomberg does a great job of updating this app. Navigation is easy and load times are fast.

QuickBooks is critical, there are other options available on the iPad covered later in this chapter.

Settings

The Setup icon button (at the bottom of the window) opens the Setup window where you can perform database maintenance and add, modify, and delete clients, projects, tasks, and expenses. You can also purge time-and-expense entries. (Make sure to back up first, as covered later in this chapter.) The General menu includes a mishmash of settings, including rates, subtitles, audible notifications, and rounding.

There are several backup options for your Time Master data. The developer has an app for Mac OS X and Windows, called Time Master Central (www.on-core. com/timemaster/index.php#tmc), for saving database snapshots via Wi-Fi to your computer. You can also back up your data using iTunes file sharing (covered in Chapter 1). Finally, Time Master supports Dropbox, so you can back up your database straight to your Dropbox account.

What about QuickBooks?

QuickBooks is the 800-pound gorilla of business finance software. Unfortunately, it doesn't exist for the iPad. QuickBooks' developer, Intuit, has been silent on whether it will release an iPad version of QuickBooks. Intuit's poor track record with its Mac versions of QuickBooks does not inspire faith for an iPad version any time soon. There are, however, options.

QuickBooks Connect

QuickBooks Connect is a monthly service available to QuickBooks for Windows 2011. (There is no QuickBooks Connect service for QuickBooks for Mac as of this writing.) For QuickBooks Connect users, Intuit has a free iPhone app, QuickBooks Connect. QuickBooks Connect populates your iPhone or iPad with your QuickBooks data and includes tools to add and view customer information and manage outstanding balances. From your iOS device, you can create and view estimates, invoices, and sales receipts. This is not the same complete feature package as having QuickBooks on your iPad, but if you are a QuickBooks Connect subscriber, using this app is a no-brainer.

QuickBooks Online

Intuit also has a web-based version of QuickBooks, called QuickBooks Online (`http://search.quickbooksonline.com`). For a monthly fee, you get a web-hosted version of QuickBooks where you can easily share your data among platforms and people. This is a good solution, for example, where your accountant is offsite and needs online access to the books and records. Although Intuit goes to lengths to describe its security for this service, always remember that using a web-based service requires keeping your data on servers somewhere on the Internet, beyond your control.

QuickBooks Online works on the iPad through the Safari browser. (There is no separate iPad app.) Using your Safari browser, you can view accounts; view, add and edit customers, vendors, and employees; create and e-mail invoices; and view banking information, balance sheets, and profit-and-loss (P&L) reports.

Remote access

If you are not excited about the QuickBooks Online's monthly fees or QuickBooks Connect's limited functionality, you can also remotely access your QuickBooks computer using the remote access tools covered in Chapter 10 to run the full QuickBooks enchilada on your Mac or PC from your iPad.

Online Account Management

QuickBooks Online isn't the only web-based billing-and-invoicing application
Online accounting solutions are sprouting up like weeds. Several companies are
releasing iPad apps or taking care to assure the iPad's Safari browser works with the
web service.

One of the more progressive of these applications is FreshBooks (`www.`
`freshbooks.com`), which has several innovative features such as e-mail invoicing
with a "Pay Now" button embedded. FreshBooks looks great on the iPad through
the Safari browser but as of this writing there is no native iPad version.

Another web-based tool is In Dinero (`www.indinero.com`), which has some
excellent business financial analysis and management capabilities.

The iPad Cash Register

It didn't take long for developers to look at the iPad screen and say, "I can make
a cash register out of that." And so they did. Although this software genre is still
developing, there are some early leaders. POSLavu (free) is a full-featured point-of-
sale (POS) system from which you could easily run a retail business or restaurant.

FIGURE 24-6

Processing a credit card payment with Square on the iPad

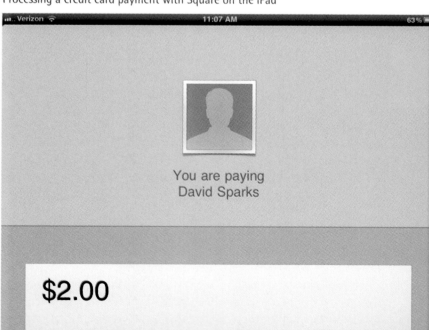

MY BILLING AND FINANCE WORKFLOW

I nearly did not include a workflow section for this chapter. I experimented with all of the tools listed in this chapter and several others that didn't make the cut. The specific tools I use really don't matter because so many of these tools are dependent on your specific financial requirements. I can say, however, that I was most impressed with the emerging class of web-based financial management applications that appear to me more agile than the more ponderous "big" players. My enthusiasm for these new technologies is tempered, however, by the fact these new services require you to store your financial information on Internet-based servers, which certainly comes with risk. Regardless, I think this trend is only going to accelerate and before long, most financial management software will be cloud-based.

The app is free, but the Lavu service (`http://poslavu.com`) requires a monthly fee ranging from $30 to $100 per month.

For a smaller scale POS service, Square (free) is impressive. Set up an account at SquareUp.com (`https://squareup.com`) to have Square mail you a small credit card reader that plugs in the headphone jack of your iPad. Shown in Figure 24-6, Square makes it easy to perform the occasional credit card transactions with customers (or when selling your couch to a friend). There is no fee for the app but Square takes a percentage of each transaction. (2.75 percent at the time of this writing.)

PART

IV

Appendixes

A

The iPad for Specialty Work

Whereas all the previous chapters in this book cover the basics of getting work done on your iPad by task, there are a few professions that have their own unique set of useful apps. This chapter summarizes some of the best specialty apps for academics and teachers, legal and medical professionals, and information technology workers.

Academics and Teachers

There is a rich assortment of apps useful for students and teachers alike at every grade level. Here are a few of my favorites.

Teacher's Assistant Pro

Teacher's Assistant Pro ($5) helps teachers keep track of student actions, behavior, infractions, and achievements. Developed by a teacher, this app lets you enter or import (via a CSV, or comma-separated value, file) a list of students' names, e-mail, and related contact information. You can then track student infractions and accolades from inside the app, recording the date and time of each event along with other event details. Using the students' and other stored contact information, you can send e-mails to parents and administrators.

The app includes filters so you can sort students by class or infraction. The app lets you import and export data for use in other apps. You can also passcode-lock the app so students aren't able to review and "fix" any "errors" in your infraction reporting.

Grammar Up HD

English grammar is not easy. So why not use your iPad to help learn (or teach) the rules of grammar? Grammar Up ($5) is a multiple-choice quiz system for teaching the rules of English grammar. There are more than 1,800 questions in 20 grammar categories. Topics include adjectives, word choice, conditionals, verb tense, and transitions.

In addition to polishing your grammar skills, Grammar Up helps students learn better word selection and vocabulary. You can go at your own pace or use a custom timer to simulate examination time constraints.

When you complete a practice test, Grammar Up provides a summary that shows how long you took, your score, which questions you answered correctly, and where you were wrong. Teachers can e-mail the results to students and parents.

Grammar Up even prepares a bar chart showing your areas of strength and weakness so, during your next session, you know where to, um, Grammar Up.

Star Walk

Star Walk ($5) is an iPad astronomy teacher. Star Walk is also one of those apps you could keep on your iPad for the sole purpose of impressing people.

To use Star Walk, just point your iPad at the sky. Star Walk superimposes the names of the stars, constellations, and satellites you are looking at in real time. If you have an iPad 2, Star Walk uses its camera to calibrate itself and present the night sky with augmented reality, overlaying star and constellation information on the camera's own image of the sky. (With an original iPad, Star Walk shows you a digital representation of the sky without the camera feed.) One of my favorite features is its pointing out the international space station as it flies over.

The time machine capability displays the night sky at any time in the past or future. There is a search mode that puts an arrow on the screen and points to your desired planet. Now you can easily answer the question "Where's Mars?"

MathBoard

I discovered MathBoard ($5) helping my 8-year-old learn her multiplication tables. Using MathBoard, made learning multiplication and division fun for my daughter.

MathBoard gives the student practice tests on a chalkboard-style interface and keeps track of the results. To set up a test, you set a range of numbers and the mathematical operators, and go. You can time the test, or not. Features include random problem generation (up to 250 questions per quiz), addition, subtraction, multiplication, division, squares, cubes and square roots, and intelligent "wrong"-answer generation makes guessing more difficult.

The app also has quick reference tables for addition, subtraction, and multiplication. Teachers can also save student profiles so each student can track his or her progress.

Legal Professionals

As an attorney, how could I write a book about the iPad without including so of my favorite legal related apps? Here goes.

TrialPad

TrialPad ($90) is like a Swiss Army knife for evidence. A challenge for any litigator is quickly finding, displaying, and annotating evidence for the jury. TrialP is a trial presentation app aimed at solving all these problems for attorneys.

As a business attorney, many of my cases involve documents. TrialPad display and annotates documents beautifully with multiple highlighters and pens. It even has a laser point to draw attention to areas of interest in your document. You can two documents next to one another and use the standard iPad conventions (pinch expand, scroll, and tap) to manipulate the document in front of the jury. It is the most fluid manipulation of digital evidence I have ever experienced.

TrialPad also solves the vexing problem of submitting electronic annotations the jury. TrialPad saves your marked-up image or document so you can print it out and enter it in evidence. (Just make sure to bring an AirPrint-compatible printer wi you to court.)

Black's Law Dictionary

Black's Law Dictionary ($55) is the definitive legal dictionary. Every law stude starts the first day of law school with a copy of this dictionary, and every veteran attorney has a much tattered and beat up copy near his desk.

The most recent edition is on the iPad, along with 45,000 terms and alternate spellings or equivalent expressions for more than 5,300 terms. The app also pronounces thousands of hard-to-say legal terms. There are also nearly 3,000 quotations drawn from legal sources through the ages. The dictionary is stored locally on the iPad, so no Internet connection is required to use the app.

For Westlaw subscribers, Black's Law Dictionary links directly to West key numbers. There is something quite remarkable about seeing a dictionary with a century-long pedigree on the iPad.

Research apps

Because every state's laws are different, there is no single research app I can recommend, but I do suggest attorneys and legal professionals search the App Stor for apps that hold the codes and laws important to them. As a California attorney, I've purchased several apps with key portions of California law that I use often.

Court Days Pro

Lawyers have different rules for counting days. Some rules require that you count calendar days and others require that you count court days (just days the courthouse is open.) Inevitably, attorneys and support staff gather around a calendar and debate exactly what day is 15 court days from today. Court Days Pro ($3) takes all the guesswork out of calculating such dates.

Court Days Pro also has rule-based calendar tools so legal professionals can easily calculate dates and deadlines based on a customizable database of court rules and statutes. Once the rules are set up in the app, Court Days Pro performs the calculations using a customizable list of court holidays.

Date results not only appear on the screen but can be added to the iPad's Calendar app. Court Days Pro also can send an e-mail with lists of dates, if you need to get deadlines to your staff.

Medical Professionals

Medical professionals were some of the first to adopt tablet computers in their practice. Therefore, it isn't a surprise that there are several specialty medical apps for the iPad. Here are some of the more popular.

OsiriX HD

OsiriX HD ($30) is a Dicom (Digital Imaging and Communications in Medicine) image viewer for the iPad. OsiriX HD is designed to work with the OsiriX app for Mac OS X, but doesn't require it. This app provides medical professionals an interactive visualization program designed for display and analysis of medical images. You can download and manipulate images directly on your iPad. OsiriX HD can display images from most common imaging types (such as ultrasound, CT, and MRI) in their native standard Dicom format. OsiriX HD can also receive imaging from any Dicom imaging device through a Wi-Fi or 3G network.

When displaying an image, OsiriX can zoom and pan with the standard pinch, expand, and drag gestures. You can swipe among images and easily adjust the contrast and intensity settings for easier viewing. The app also includes measurement tools useful in medical diagnostic work.

AirStrip

AirStrip (free) is a client app for the AirStrip remote patient-monitoring system. The AirStrip service collects data from patient-monitoring equipment. Medical professionals can then log in and keep track of patient data in near real time.

After logging in with your iPad, the AirStrip service streams patient information to your iPad. AirStrip pulls information from hundreds of different types of patient monitors, ECG machines, and other clinical information coming from your facility's electronic medical records system.

With AirStrip, you can monitor your patients' vitals, cardiac waveforms, labs, medications, intakes and outputs, and allergies as quickly as the AirStrip service collects the data and broadcasts it to your iPad.

Heart Pro

Heart Pro ($18) is a fascinating 3D model of the human heart. You can rotate, cut open, and label the components of the heart, all with simple strokes of a finger. Pins are available in any of the standard anatomical views including anterior, posterior, lateral, right lateral, superior, inferior, sagittal, coronal, and transverse views. You can also add your own pins for explaining concepts to patients.

Heart Pro also has an index of heart related vocabulary terms. Tap an entry in the index and the heart rotates to show the indexed term. The app also plays animations showing how the heart works.

This app is also useful for educational purposes. You can even test your knowledge with an interactive quiz. The developer has similar apps for the skeletal, muscular, vascular, urogenital, and digestive systems.

Proloquo2Go

Proloquo2Go ($190) is an augmentative and alternative communication solution for people who have difficulty speaking. The user can navigate through the app using a series of symbols to compose words and ideas. Proloquo2Go then speaks the words using natural-sounding voices (in American, British, and Indian English). This app is useful for working with children and adults with autism, cerebral palsy, Down's syndrome, developmental disabilities, apraxia, ALS, stroke, or traumatic brain injury.

Information Technology Professionals

A lot of IT professionals love their iPads. With its long battery life and ability to turn on instantly, the iPad is well suited to managing a computer network. So it's not surprising there are some exceptional IT management apps.

Prompt

Prompt ($8), is the best SSH client on the iPad. Developed by Panic, a well-regarded Mac developer, Prompt is for system administrators, web designers, and anyone who routinely connects to a server with his iPad.

Prompt stays connected to your servers, even when it is running in the background. Prompt automatically remembers the login credentials for your servers. Log in once and you are set. (You can set a password lock for extra security.) Prompt lets you customize the keyboard with your favorite special characters, and it works with a Bluetooth keyboard. Moreover, Prompt pulls this off with a clean interface and style.

Until Prompt hit the App Store, all SSH apps seemed the same to me. Panic's attention to detail puts Prompt at the top of the list.

FTP on the Go Pro

FTP on the Go Pro ($10) is an iPad FTP client. This app is particularly useful to anyone who works on web pages. FTP on the Go Pro views and edits , CSS, JavaScript, PHP, and ASP files right on your server. (The app also views JPEG, PDF, Word, Excel, and PowerPoint files.) Using FTP On the Go, you can access and modify your website from anywhere.

Use the built-in editor to make changes to a text file and re-upload your changes. The text editor also lets you add custom keyboard codes to speed up typing. There is also a web browser built in so you can see your changes without leaving FTP on the Go.

Analytics HD

Need to see Google Analytics data on your iPad? Analytics HD ($7) displays the data on your iPad with polish. The app connects directly to Google Analytics and shows your Google Analytics data with 55 reports and full-screen charts, including Today and Yesterday. Analytics HD supports multiple logins and multiple accounts, so you can track all your websites with one app. It also has a dashboard report with a quick overview.

Server Admin Remote

Server Admin Remote ($10) monitors Mac OS X Server installations remotely. Using this app, IT professionals can monitor the live status of Mac OS X Server services, start and stop services, and observe the services' logs. Server Admin Remote uses the same interface as the Mac OS X Server Admin tools. It is easier than using SSH or remote terminals, making it the go-to solution for Mac OS X Server IT administrators.

Real Estate Professionals

The iPad is the perfect solution for real estate professionals, who spend so much of their time on the road with dodgy Internet connections. There is no shortage of specialty apps for the real estate industry.

Zillow

Zillow (free) is the iPad app for the popular real estate appraisal website of the same name. All you need is a property address, and Zillow does the rest. The app looks at nearby comparable sales and gives you the approximate property value.

The Zillow app includes a simple interface with overhead photography and photo galleries of listed homes. In addition to approximate values, Zillow also displays homes for sale and homes for rent. You can view more than one home at a time and save a home as a favorite for later viewing.

Realtor.com

Realtor.com (free) is one of the largest websites serving real estate professionals and their clients. Using the free iPad app, you can find homes for sale. In addition to accessing Realtor.com's database, you can save private ratings and notes and share listings with your clients.

When performing a search, you can draw a shape with your finger on the onscreen map to have the Realtor.com app limit its search to just that area. Listed homes include photos, property details, open house information, and price.

Open Home Pro

Use Open Home Pro (free) to manage your open house and real estate listings. The app acts as a database for collecting clients' (and potential clients') information.

Open house visitors can enter their own names and contact information, along with their preferences (such as the number of bedrooms they are looking for). The app saves all the information and lets you export it as a CSV file to import in your address book. You can also e-mail all open house visitors directly from the app, thanking them for visiting or notifying them if there is a price drop.

Construction Professionals

The construction professional can also benefit from mobile technology. There are many iPad apps that are useful in construction.

BuildCalc

BuildCalc ($20) is an advanced construction calculator that computes common masonry, compound miter, stair, baluster, and fencing measurements.

To build a fence, enter your design and the linear feet to have the app compute the required materials. The stair function creates layouts and dimensional drawings for stair components, which can be e-mailed as a PDF file. The app also saves results for later recall.

Drawvis

Drawvis ($15) lets you view building plans and other technical drawings created in the AutoCAD DXF format. In addition to displaying your plans on your iPad, you can attach notes to the drawing.

Drawvis works only in two dimensions, but that is fine for most construction uses. You can transfer plans via iTunes or using a Wi-Fi connection. Using Drawvis, you can carry all your blueprints in your iPad.

I.D. Wood

I.D. Wood ($5) is a clever app that helps you identify different species of wood. The app includes full-screen images and detailed information for nearly 160 types of wood. Detailed information includes species names, origins, descriptions, woodworking properties, hardnesses, and common uses. The app also keeps data on sustainability.

All the data is stored locally on your iPad, so the information is available regardless of having an active Internet connection. The app also performs lumber dimensional conversions and includes reference screens for thickness measuring, pilot holes, nail sizes, specific gravity, and lumber grading tables.

Index

Book Excerpt: Mac at Work

You don't need a Mac to take advantage of what an iPad can do. But a Mac is the better companion PC for your iPad. One reason is that Mac OS X and the iPad's iOS share the same core technology, so the user interface and the core apps both have very similar operations and can more tightly integrate with each other, such as for contacts, calendars, e-mail and documents — if you're using the Mac's Address Book, iCal, Mail, and iWork software, that is. Apple's syncing service iCloud also lets your iPad sync more with a Mac than with a PC.

Whether you're new to a Mac or an old-hand Mac user who wants to use the Mac more for business, my book at *Mac at Work* will do for you what this book does for your iPad business use: Show you what it can do and recommend the best software to do it with.

Mac at Work is available in print, Amazon Kindle, and Apple iBooks formats.

The rest of this appendix is excerpted from *Mac at Work*'s introduction and first chapter:

Why *Mac at Work*?

Because everyone needs an advantage.

A few years ago, I spoke at the American Bar Association's technology conference about how I use my Mac to run circles around other lawyers. This conference happens once a year and is ground zero for cutting-edge legal technology. When I started talking to these Mac lawyers, however, their ugly secret was revealed: although they were using Macs, the only software they had was Word, Excel, and PowerPoint. They were missing out on all the fantastic Mac software. It was like buying a Ferrari, but only driving it in the parking lot.

The Apple Macintosh is a fantastic computer. Not just for its traditional constituents (graphics designers, musicians, and students) but for everyone. Macs are some of the best designed computers available today. The operating system, also created by Apple, integrates seamlessly with the hardware. Everything just works. Moreover, there is a rich ecosystem of software developers for the Mac that have adopted Apple's standard of excellence. Mac software isn't just functional, it is magnificent.

The word is getting out. Macs are showing up in boardrooms, courtrooms, offices, and even enterprise networks. The Mac is a serious business tool. So can you take advantage of this superior hardware and software to up your game at work? Absolutely. I've been using my Mac at work for years.

This book is intended as a resource, not an encyclopedia. You are not going to learn about every Mac application available for each topic covered. Instead you will

A MACINTOSH HISTORY LESSON

Once upon a time, people said that if you wanted a computer, you needed a multimillion dollar budget and a team of engineers. Then two guys named Steve (Steve Jobs and Steve Wozniak) started selling the first personal computer, the Apple 1. It came in a plywood case.

Next, Apple released the Apple II and started a revolution. Computers of that era ran on the command line using obscure textual codes, which was empowering for nerds and baffling to everyone else. In 1984, Apple started another revolution with the Macintosh, the first consumer computer with a graphical user interface. In other words, it gave us the mouse.

Although the Macintosh changed the world, Apple soon fell on hard times and the two Steves left the company. By the early 1990s everyone was predicting Apple's demise.

In 1997, Steve Jobs came back to Apple and kicked off a reboot of the company, including the release of the iMac. The company is now more successful than ever with Macs, iPhones, iPods, and iPads. The Mac's market share is on an upward march. Indeed, the Mac is now entrenched at work.

discover a selected group of applications that work. This important. I have gone down the dark and ugly road of bad software. With this book, you get the benefit of my travels.

You can read this book cover to cover or treat it as a reference. Do you suddenly find yourself looking for paperless solutions and not know where to start Read Chapter 19. Need to figure out e-mail? Jump to Chapter 5. You get the idea.

Whether you've been using a Mac since 1984 or are simply considering switching to a Mac, this book is for you. You'll learn to work more efficiently with superior results than your unfortunate competitors saddled with Windows PCs. This book shows you the way

Mac at Work is available
wherever books are sold.